Praise for *A Sky of Infinite B¹⁻*

"*A Sky of Infinite Blue* is like a beautiful harmonies as she peels back the layers of ship to her beloved husband. Her writing is courageous; she never shies away from telling the truth about her personal struggles and the difficulties of her marriage."

—**Cindy Rasicot, author of *Finding Venerable Mother***

"Poignant and moving. You will be inspired, impressed, and amazed at Kyomi's resilience and devotion to not only the men in her life but to her family and herself."

—**Leslie Johansen Nack, author of multiple award-winning memoir *Fourteen* and novel *The Blue Butterfly***

"*A Sky of Infinite Blue* is a poignant weaving of the difficult and the delightful. Kyomi O'Connor's unfolding life story shows how transformation happens through a mixture of deep love, painful loss, and devotion to faith and community that offers support when life also dismantles you."

—**Gail Warner, author of *Weaving Myself Awake*, therapist, and founder of Pine Manor Retreat Center**

"This memoir grips your heart from the first words of the prologue and doesn't let go. While deeply personal, it shares truths of the human spirit that are so universal, one cannot help but feel a connection to Kyomi's paradoxically unique and yet fundamentally common humanity. She fearlessly and genuinely shares her courage and her pain, inspiring all of us to "turn our scars and wounds into treasures.""

—**Dr. Donna L. Roberts, Fellow of the Royal Arts Society, professor at ERAU, and author of *Psych Pstuff***

"*A Sky of Infinite Blue* reflects Kyomi's spiritual journey starting from her childhood to her own family building bridged between the East and West. Her journey portrays drawing and captivating moments with beautifully woven metaphors and self-reflections. In the end, peace and light were bestowed on her once-wounded soul."

—**Mehmet Yildiz, Editor-in-Chief,**
Illumination Integrated Publications

"Kyomi O'Connor has boldly and bravely written a compelling book. It is full of life, with all its sorrows, joys, moments, thoughts, conflicts, trials, and emotions. Real wisdom lives here, infused with the Buddhist teachings that guide Kyomi. I urge you to read this book and accompany Kyomi on her journey through life. Its richness is guaranteed to inform your own life journey."

—**Michael D. Burg, MD, Consultant, Freelancer, Writer**

"Kyomi O'Connor shares her struggle in finding meaning and purpose that many of us fail to realize. Her story is a modern day telling of Siddhartha's intellectual and spiritual journey to find peace in a selfless life. This may help us all find a little more light and blue sky within the darkness and pressures of modern society."

—**Gregory Daniels MD, PhD, Professor of Medicine**

"This story dramatically begins with the end: the loss of a best friend, lover, and husband. A fascinating page-turner; many lessons can be learned in this tale of passion, friendship, and determination where a bright side to sadness is found. A joy to read and a compelling memoir I didn't want to end."

—**Marian Young, Senior Investigator at**
the National Institutes of Health

"A deeply personal journey filled with moments of intense pain, absolute joy, and, ultimately, a sense of acceptance and peace. Kyomi's efforts to understand and learn from these experiences are influenced by having a foot in two cultures and by the strings that tie her to family of her birth and of her own making. Her compassion for the people in her life is present on every page, even when she struggles to decipher the meaning behind their actions and emotions."

—Lori Shein, editor of Young Adult Nonfiction Books

"A reminder to all of us how life is an ever-unfolding river from which the events of childhood, adulthood, and tragedy can continuously be interpreted, reinterpreted, and altered by new understanding. These can and should be looked at as areas of growth and fodder for our future selves, leading to a sky of infinite blue for all of us."

—Bonnie Szumski, owner of Bow Editorial Services

"An absorbing story. Kyomi explores life through the lens of childhood, teachings, and especially, the flowering of her spirituality. In its fierce quest for meaning, Kyomi's book reveals her amazing, indomitable spirit."

—Sally W. Buffington, author of *A Place Like This:*
Finding Myself in a Cape Cod Cottage

"A love story with many twists and turns. This book will shed light on the tragedy of living a life of feeling 'less' yet ultimately rising above all hardship to ultimately love oneself as much as you love others."

—Laura L. Engel, author of *You'll Forget This Ever Happened*

"*A Sky of Infinite Blue* reads more like a novel than a memoir, never bogging down, a compelling tale of love and loss, rich in wonder, feeling, and surprise. O'Connor will invite you in, serve you tea, and disarm you with her simple warmth, goodwill, and honesty. Your tea, though, may grow cold, forgotten, by the time you turn the final page."

—**Ed Robson, poet, writer, PhD, MFA**

A Sky of Infinite Blue

A Japanese Immigrant's Search for Home and Self

Kyomi O'Connor

SHE WRITES PRESS

Copyright © 2022 Kyomi O'Connor

All rights reserved. No part of this publication may be reproduced, distributed, or transmitted in any form or by any means, including photocopying, recording, digital scanning, or other electronic or mechanical methods, without the prior written permission of the publisher, except in the case of brief quotations embodied in critical reviews and certain other noncommercial uses permitted by copyright law. For permission requests, please address She Writes Press.

Published 2022
Printed in the United States of America
Print ISBN: 978-1-64742-227-1
E-ISBN: 978-1-64742-228-8
Library of Congress Control Number: 2022904053

For information, address:
She Writes Press
1569 Solano Ave #546
Berkeley, CA 94707

She Writes Press is a division of SparkPoint Studio, LLC.

All company and/or product names may be trade names, logos, trademarks, and/or registered trademarks and are the property of their respective owners.

Names and identifying characteristics have been changed to protect the privacy of certain individuals.

To Patrick

Prologue
Patrick's Passing

On the afternoon of July 3, 2016, my husband's condition declined. Breathing had become harder for him; he was occasionally gasping for air. A pulse oximeter on his finger showed that his oxygen saturation was at around 80 percent.

I knew that normal oxygen saturation was above 95 percent—that below 80 percent was severely low and could lead to hypoxia, organ damage, and cellular death.

As I looked at the number on the screen, it dropped even lower. The time was getting near.

That evening I'd been chanting the mantra "*Nomaku Sanmanda Basarada Sendan*" for hours. The mantra is written in Sanskrit, meaning "the true words," and it was the principal chant in the Buddhist teaching Patrick and I had followed since becoming members in 1998. We'd chanted this mantra together countless times.

Patrick loved to listen to the chants—even more so since he'd been ill. I chose this mantra because I felt it had a distinctive melody, reminiscent of a lullaby, that embraced all listeners, regardless of their religious affiliation.

Many practitioners in our spiritual community had felt and

experienced the mysterious liberating and awakening powers of this mantra as we chanted and practiced. Many had been lifted from their ongoing illness, pain, or other difficulties by a combination of sincere practice and the chanting of these words. Now I wished for these sounds to free Patrick from any agony he was experiencing. And, of course, I wanted his spiritual journey to the next realm to be comfortable.

As I chanted, his breathing did in fact become calmer. Each time his oxygen levels decreased, I chanted the mantra more intently and the numbers elevated, stabilizing his condition. I didn't know whether it was because of the mysterious powers of the mantra or because of Patrick's spiritual response.

Either way, I knew it was helping.

Now there were four of us at Patrick's bedside: a hospice nurse, Patrick's caregiver, our good friend Debby, and me.

The hospice nurse had been sent by the hospice company where I'd registered Patrick for home care support. I'd explained to her what Patrick's condition was—he had been fighting stage IV melanoma for over three years—and what medication I'd given him. She'd quietly listened, then said, "Let's watch him carefully and find out how we can help him get through this."

I sensed the strength in her quiet attitude and subdued body language. Her empathy was evident behind her spectacles. I knew I could trust her to guide us through this last part of our journey together.

Patrick's caregiver had come around 7:00 p.m. She was a young, capable Mexican immigrant who'd worked with us for more than six months and become one of the best and most reliable of his caregivers. I was grateful she was there.

Debby, a devout Catholic throughout her life, had been our friend for almost twenty years. For the past year or so she'd helped us with various errands and things I needed as I worked and cared for Patrick, and she'd wanted to be present for Patrick's passing.

All three of them had been listening to my chanting of the mantra.

"I don't know what it is, but it is so good for him . . . and for us," Debby said.

"May I join you?" the hospice nurse asked.

I brought out a couple of chanting books I had and pointed my finger to where she could find the words, and soon we were all chanting together. At first their voices were lower because they didn't know the chant, but with collective energy, our chanting became more powerful.

A few moments later, Patrick's oxygen levels went down to 30 percent. Then the number quickly disappeared from the screen, which meant his life was no longer savable at that point.

Then, as if it were reflex, without thinking about it, we all started chanting the mantra more intently, with our utmost sincerity.

A minute passed.

"Ah! 44 percent!" someone shouted. The number on the screen showed up again at 44 percent, illuminated in red.

"It's a miracle!" someone else shouted.

I knew what the mantra could achieve from my own spiritual experiences throughout my practice. But I also knew that no one, not even the invisible spiritual realm, would be able to change the course of what was happening here.

My husband was dying.

A minute later, Patrick's breathing became much weaker again. I noticed that we were still chanting loudly, and it began to bother me.

"This isn't what I want for him," I whispered to myself in my heart.

I wanted Patrick to leave this world in serene dignity, and I knew that was what Patrick wished for as well. He was responding to the chants of our good wishes. But now, I wanted to stop this intense, loud chanting.

"Sorry," I said quietly, "but I'd like to stop chanting now. I don't want him to make any more efforts for us. I would like him to be in peace."

Everyone stopped chanting and we watched Patrick in silence.

"Let's turn the lights off. And only one person should be in the room," the hospice nurse said a few moments later.

Debby and the caregiver left to the kitchen, and the nurse turned off the light. She stayed in the room but completely faded into the background, giving me space.

As my eyes adjusted to the low light, Patrick's face emerged in the radiant softness of the dim room. He and I were alone in the world.

In our lives there are events of pain and suffering that are impossible to avoid. In Buddhist teaching, we call those events the *Four Sufferings* and recognize them in circumstances of birth and living, aging, illness, and death.

Sufferings are not only caused by physical changes but also by mental, psychological, and spiritual impacts. Throughout our lives, we experience this pain at varying times—birth and rebirths, illnesses, disabilities, and diseases, and through death and the aftermath of other people's deaths.

Patrick and I had survived the difficulties in our marriage that we'd faced over the years, as well as his sudden illness, which had pitched us into constant battles. Now, however, he was dying in front of me, and I was readying myself for another phase of suffering. I wasn't sure I was ready, but I also knew I had no power to stop what was unfolding.

I examined Patrick's face carefully one more time. As the candle was fading away, his life, filled with honesty and humility, was ending along with it. This dying man was showing me solemnity without a word amidst the weight of life and death. Gratitude welled up inside of me. I saw the beautiful, sacred being inside of him.

Patrick had always called me his "bestest friend." He'd been that for me—my best friend and partner—for almost twenty-seven years. I was filled with so much tenderness.

He'd been my *home.*

He'd been my *savior.*

"Thank you, Patrick. I will love you forever," I whispered to his soul.

In this moment, I heard a small, timid voice inside me ask, *Forever?*

The weight of the word hung in the air.

Wait! I'm not ready for being parted forever! Not yet. Wait! Wait for me!

I didn't know what his exiting this world meant for me.

All I knew was that I didn't want it yet.

And yet I knew it was time for him to leave in peace. I had to accept it. I shouldn't cling onto him any longer. I must let go. I must be brave for him.

I'd been a devout Buddhist for years, and now I needed to be a good Buddhist for him. But it was so hard. I was determined to let him die in peace and dignity, yet a little voice inside was still hesitant. I was afraid of losing him.

I was experiencing the two-parted inner voices of surrender—"I should accept and let go"—and attachment—"I don't want it"—at the same time.

But did I have any choice?

No, I had to let go.

I held him tenderly one last time and kissed him on his lips.

A tiny gasp of air, like the littlest sigh, slipped out from deep inside his chest.

The sacredness of his passing touched me so deeply that I couldn't speak; I couldn't even cry.

A moment later I turned to the hospice nurse, who nodded back, her eyes closed.

He was gone.

— 1 —

The Armor

Patrick was pronounced dead at 1:02 a.m. on July 4, 2016.

Independence Day had always been his favorite American holiday. It was also the first holiday we'd spent together twenty-six years earlier. That date had determined our destinies back when we'd been young and filled with hope for our own future and, beyond us, the future of humanity and goodness in the world. Somehow, I felt Patrick had chosen this day for his passing.

He'd dedicated his entire life to saving cancer patients through science. Outside his profession, he'd always devoted himself to helping others in need. He'd lived in every moment with an independent spirit and purpose in life. He'd tried his best in every moment—even while ill, even while dying.

As soon as a nurse pronounced Patrick's death, a couple of men from the mortuary came. They took his body into a cold black vinyl bag, placed it on a gurney, and dashed out.

It was like I was watching a motion picture with no sound. I was present yet didn't exist. With no controller to pause this movie, Patrick was taken far from me. The noise of the black bag zipping shut would linger in my ears for a long time.

—

In the following few days, the hospice company came back and forth, taking Patrick's medical bed, oxygen tanks, IV poles, and other bulky medical devices out of his room. When their business was over, the emptiness of his room symbolized for me what had happened there, but I tried not to think about it. I wanted to just focus on logistics.

Before Patrick's passing, I'd imagined all the emotions I would feel when he was gone. I'd thought it would be like a tsunami washing my existence away. But it wasn't like that at all. Instead, there were no emotions after his passing. I felt like a person without substance, as if I had no capacity to detect or hold anything. I was vacant.

Rather than a tsunami, what I experienced immediately following my husband's death might have been better described as the aftermath of a tsunami. A wooden wreck, an abandoned, broken hulk of an old ship—that was *me*.

Alone in Patrick's empty medical room, now turned back to an office, I imagined myself as a vessel abandoned on the empty sand, body torn asunder by heavy storms and washed ashore. I pictured myself listening to the chirping of the seagulls during the day flying over my head and sitting on me, keeping me company. The bright sun dried me up and I felt thirst, but the soft swoosh of the constant waves washing ashore consoled my spirit. Their gentle sounds offered me comfort. They were the only things that gave me any sense that I was still alive.

Then I came back to myself in the office, alone, and the feeling of peace disappeared.

While I was present for Patrick's cremation and even funeral, I was still absent from myself. If someone asked how I was doing, I didn't know what to say. It was too difficult to grasp any feelings. There was emptiness inside me—a black hole.

I hadn't cried much since losing Patrick because my soul, my mind, my feelings, and my body all felt disconnected. Just my body was moving, like a robot. I did all that I was supposed to do, but that was the only thing that drove me forward: external expectation and necessity.

After Patrick's funeral, I placed a white wooden plaque on top of a small table next to our existing Buddha table at home. In accordance with the Buddhist ritual at his funeral, Patrick's spirit had been transferred and now resided in this wooden plaque, on which his posthumous name was brush-stroked. As I looked at it, I was struck with a sense of newness and unfamiliarity about what I might be facing in the future.

A few days later, while speaking with my sisters and a niece who'd come out from Japan for the funeral, I cried for the first time since the onset of Patrick's illness three years earlier. But the emotions that I could reveal were limited and only at the surface. I had erected thick, protective walls inside of me. Patrick had been the only person in my life to whom I could show many of my emotions, particularly my vulnerability, and now I didn't know how to express those feelings anymore.

I'd been suffering from insomnia since Patrick got ill. I'd kept running for Patrick, and for us, with little sleep for years. Now Patrick was gone, but my entire system and functionality knew only one track—helping him. Without that purpose, I didn't know what to do with my life.

I needed help, but I didn't know how to ask for it.

In the custom and tradition of Buddhist teachings, there are periodic services after someone passes away. Each service is carried out in accordance with a specific ritual and its significance for the deceased. As these services and rituals are performed, families and friends of the deceased also go through grieving, coping with, and accepting the passing of their beloved.

Seven is the most auspicious number in Buddhism. Therefore, every seventh day after a person's passing is regarded as an important step. After the funeral, the first major posthumous service is held on the forty-ninth (seven multiplied by seven) day. Some traditions, like our teaching, also hold a ceremony on the one-hundredth day. Then anniversary services follow in odd years, starting from the first year and then following with the third, seventh, thirteenth, seventeenth, twenty-third, twenty-seventh, and so on.

Immediately after Patrick's passing, I initiated this series of services with bedside chanting with Misa, a fellow practitioner, who had arrived at the last minute before his passing. Many more would follow.

Between Patrick's forty-ninth- and one-hundredth-day memorial services, I flew to Japan. It was late September, and this trip was the first time I'd gone home in more than three and a half years.

During my stay, I planned to permanently transfer Patrick's spirit from the temporary white wooden plaque that the temple had prepared for his funeral to the black ebony one that would serve as his permanent plaque. I'd asked my younger sister, Yoshino, to order it for me in advance of the event.

At Illumination Center in Tokyo, the largest temple in our teaching, I attended a principal Merit Transfer service, meant to console the spirits in the spiritual realm, officiated by Her Holiness.

Through the service, his spirit's residence changed from a transient place (white) to its permanent place (black). Now Patrick's spirit would reside in this temple as an ordained Buddhist, just as he would have wanted.

At the beginning of October, I came back to San Diego and placed Patrick's black tablet next to the Buddha image at my altar table at home. Soon after, I held a one-hundredth-day memorial service for Patrick.

By that time, I'd slowly begun to communicate with people in our local spiritual community again. After over three years of absence from the temple activities, I was going back to the temple regularly and attending leadership meetings and their activities. I'd also received permission to begin re-training myself for serving as a spiritual guide.

I was behaving as if things were back to normal—but I still didn't feel like myself.

In daily Buddhist practice, we offer a glass of water and incense for the Buddhas as we chant in the morning and evening. Water and incense symbolize our sincere offering, devotion to truth, and diligence in practicing and meditating. The glass of water placed on the altar table since the morning is then offered after the evening chanting to console the spirits of the ancestors and extended to all the deceased in the spiritual realm.

When Patrick was alive, we always offered heartfelt devotion to his late parents, my late father, our other ancestors, and anyone who had died in wars, conflicts, disasters, and accidents. We also offered foods and drinks that we knew our parents used to love.

Now this tradition had continued for Patrick. The simple fact of this broke my heart. For drinks, I offered a cup of milk tea every morning, a glass of Guinness or Boddington in some evenings, and

Champagne on holidays and special occasions. For meals, I offered his favorites: bread pudding and various pies that I baked, and candies from a local British shop next to the Shakespeare Pub he loved. At every offering, I talked to Patrick—or I just cried, unable to form any words.

Toward the end of the year, I was still "managing" myself and my life in the way I thought I should. To anyone on the outside, I'm sure it seemed as if I were doing perfectly well. But sometimes after I returned from the temple or a home meeting I'd organized, I would break down crying, overcome with profound loneliness and helplessness.

At the beginning of each year, local practitioners in my following gather at a host home for Annual Training, an organized training that takes place every morning and evening for a total of ten days, held over the course of two weeks.

In late January, almost half a year after Patrick's passing, I decided to host my temple's Annual Training. I hadn't done so for three years, though prior to that Patrick and I had held it in our home for fifteen years in a row.

I managed the training by myself just fine. But after practitioners left, I wept aloud alone for a while in front of my home altar. I couldn't deal with my helplessness. I let tears flow down on my cheeks in streams.

"Patrick, why did you leave me?" I asked his black tablet aloud, half-choked by my emotions. "Why did you? I can't do this anymore . . . I am so . . . *lonely*." The pain was almost unbearable.

My voice echoed in the big Buddha room, but no one heard it. I was all alone. That sharp, cold fact made my heart sink even deeper into my stomach. I wished someone was there to comfort me. But the person had to be Patrick—who else?—and he would never be there to comfort me again. I almost laughed at myself for desiring such nonsense.

No one was there. I was totally alone.

During the two weeks of Annual Training, I began to clearly recognize two polar opposite attitudes and behaviors in whatever I did. My thoughts were split: on the one hand, I felt I should accept Patrick's death; on the other, I felt compelled to deny the fact entirely. These warring feelings were tearing me apart.

The fact that Patrick was dead, his body burnt to the ashes, was not deniable. And yet . . .

"Patrick, would you like me to cook your favorite meatloaf tonight?"

"Patrick, do you want to watch *Endeavor* tonight?"

I asked these questions as if he were still here with me. Then, when I was setting up the foods and drinks for his altar table, I collapsed on the floor, wailing. I couldn't even watch *Endeavor* because the leading actor, Shaun Evans, reminded me of Patrick in his youth—the vulnerable side of him I'd so loved.

With other people, I behaved as if nothing had happened and acted like I always had—being responsible, organizing everything meticulously and in detail. Behaving that way kept me going. But the moment I returned home, I shattered into pieces.

I began to wonder: *Will I be in this state forever? Will I be lost and just swallowing this bitter feeling of lying and going nowhere until I die? How can I accept what is happening in my life?*

But the more eager I became to get on with my "real" life, the more life seemed against me. The more I chased the comfort I'd experienced with Patrick, the farther and farther away from me it seemed to recede. It was as if I was swimming against a strong current, and no matter how hard I swam, the current just kept taking me.

I couldn't understand it. I was desperate to recover my sense of reality, but it seemed like an impossible task.

Life brings various forms of suffering, as one of the Buddhist principles, The Four Sufferings—birth and living, aging, illness, and death—suggests.

One's life consists of many cycles and journeys, each of which may be accompanied by some suffering—physical, psychological, or spiritual. Each cycle will likely involve the lives of many others as well, like loved ones, who are essential and influential in our own life.

Nine months after Patrick's death, I continued to reflect over and over again on what had happened to us during his illness, after his death, and now during this grieving time. I was experiencing my own cycle of suffering. And that suffering came not only from the direct impacts of Patrick's illness and death but also from what life had brought me—unresolved issues from our time together. How was I to restore my lost identity and develop my new life alone now that he was gone? I knew I was on a journey to reclaim my own path of "rebirth," but I hadn't yet taken the first step and I wasn't sure how to do so.

Birth and illness and death, and I was aging myself—I was experiencing The Four Sufferings all at once. They seemed to be gushing out; I felt they were about to swallow me. I feared for my future. I wasn't sure if I would be able to carry out the tasks that lay ahead of me.

Now I realized my own expectation for me to be a good Buddhist practitioner had caused some of the pressure and anxiety I was feeling. Regardless of how I looked from the outside, or how I'd been acting, I hadn't been myself in quite some time. I was struggling, undergoing a series of difficulties every day. I needed to be patient with myself.

But that was easier said than done.

One day after a temple visit, again I fell to pieces when I arrived home. After crying loudly for a while, I picked up one of the quarterly journals my order had published in 2014 and found myself reading Her Holiness's words about her experiences with her own family members' passing.

"When you feel like crying," she said, "allow yourself to cry. Let yourself be."

This struck me so hard. Tears gushed ever harder from my eyes. But these were a different type of tears—tears of catharsis, turning into the joy of awakening. This tiny yet momentous event gave me the courage to begin my journey of reclaiming my path.

Nothing concrete was different, of course. I still didn't know where I was heading. But in this moment, I felt more comforted than I had since Patrick's death. I began to quiet my mind, and to contemplate even harder.

Why did I expect myself to act like a warrior, like nothing happened, like it was my job to get back to normal? Was I being true to myself, or just living lies?

As I pondered this, I got hit by a sudden understanding: *It's my armor.*

Until this point in time, I hadn't had much room to reflect on all that I was doing—but now it was clear to me that I was protecting myself and my raw feelings with armor. During Patrick's illness I'd been afraid but hadn't wanted to be vulnerable—in fact, I couldn't be, because I had to take care of Patrick—so I'd built up armor without even realizing what it was, without having a name for it.

But it all made sense now.

In the "fight-or-flight" circumstances I'd found myself in during Patrick's illness, I'd kept building my armor. Then the fast-moving roller coaster had abruptly come to a halt, and all of a sudden the game had ended: a heartbroken, traumatized warrior had suddenly found herself out of a job.

But the armor wasn't finished. It didn't know it wasn't needed anymore, and it wanted to keep functioning just as it had been. That is how ego and its product, armor, works. So, after Patrick's death, I grabbed for the armor quickly and put it back on. I was so accustomed to wearing it—not just during Patrick's illness but throughout my life—that I felt more at ease with it on. In my armor, I felt my weakness and vulnerability were protected, even if that was a false reality. I felt dependent on it in the way an addict is dependent on drugs: I clung to it.

But my armor was more than just a protective covering; it was also a cage I was afraid to free myself from. Over time, I'd become more and more dissociated from my true reality and built lies upon lies, to the point that I couldn't breathe anymore. I'd lost openness to the real world, for fear that it might hurt me.

And my fear only yielded more fear.

– 2 –
How it Began

My realizations about the armor I'd trapped myself in led me to reflect upon what was happening at this painful time in my life, as well as at other times in the past.

I'd experienced a lot of resistance to seeing my hidden truths. It was like my unresolved emotions and feelings had been trapped in an iceberg all my life. But now I needed to find the courage to break into deeper places and chisel my way into that iceberg—find my truths. How would I begin?

Writing, I knew, would help me.

Throughout my life, writing had held a special place for me. Whenever I'd needed to find clarity and depth, it was the thing I'd always turned to. From experience, I knew that the clearer I saw things, the more solid I would stand, and the freer I would become.

So, nine months after Patrick's passing, I began writing. With much effort, I began to analyze the nature of my armor, and immediately its habitual nature, like an addiction, drew my attention. I also realized that I had been wearing this armor for a very long time. I began to descend into my memories and open pages of my past, little by little. It was like digging into a grave: every shovelful of dirt elicited fear, pain, and sadness. But I needed to be courageous; I pressed on.

Over the course of the next couple of months, I spent many hours writing every day. I wrote about what had happened and how I'd felt in many different periods of my past. As the one-year anniversary of Patrick's death approached, I began to uncover more and more truths. I found myself thinking frequently about my early life in Japan, and about my father, Papa. More than once before then, I'd thought that I'd dealt with my complicated feelings toward him. But now I saw that all the intertwined torments of my adult life were tied back to my childhood—and especially Papa.

One day as I wrote, I saw a small child holding her tiny knees in the darkness, trembling. She came into my vision like a bubble out of muddy water in a pond.

I knew the girl in the darkness was only three and a half years old. She was crying with profound loneliness. She was frightened of the darkness surrounding her.

She was *me*.

I was only a preschooler when I first became aware of my family's abusive patterns and treatment of me.

Before I was born, my parents lived in Papa's parents' home, along with Papa's younger brother and his wife. Papa's family bullied my mother every day.

Mama was a beautiful woman—kind, warm, genuine, intuitive, and extremely sensitive to other people's expectations. She tried to serve others as kindly as possible. But she was also naïve, and more receptive than independent, and her in-laws sometimes treated her meanly, perhaps because they saw her as weak. They deliberately embarrassed her on a regular basis and talked down to her.

Papa's parents, his younger brother, and his wife were all heavily dependent on Papa's salary. But Mama suffered great stress from living with his family, and began to develop anxiety and mild neurosis due to their poor treatment of her.

After my older sister Machiyo was born, Mama struggled even more. She wasn't getting enough sleep, and she was taking care of her new baby, and yet still she prioritized her in-laws before herself.

Eventually, Mama's anxiety began to negatively affect Machiyo. My older sister began to lose weight and wasn't growing well. So Mama finally took action: she asked Papa to separate their household from his family's household, so she could have her own time and control.

Papa agreed. When Machiyo was eight months old, he purchased a new home and the three moved out of his parents' home.

I was born a year later.

After my parents and Machiyo left their home, Grandma began to visit us two or three times a month. Papa's brother and his wife also visited us quite often (of course, I only remember these occasions starting around when I became a preschooler). Whenever they came, they brought us presents.

Machiyo and I looked forward to those treats.

"Grandma, Grandma!" Machiyo would cry happily. "What presents do you have for us today?"

"Thank you, Grandma!" I always came a little behind Machiyo, smiling.

"Here's the present for Maaa chan," Grandma said, using Machiyo's nickname and lavishing her with affection.

Then she'd hold mine out, unsmiling. "Here's yours, Kyomi."

I had no pet name.

The sizes of the two boxes would always be quite different. Invariably, my sister would get something amazing; me, not so much.

On one such occasion, we both got dolls. When my sister opened her box, she shouted with joy, "Wow, it's so pretty . . . I like her dress! Thank you, Grandma!" She jumped up and hugged Grandma.

I leaned over to look at her doll. She wore a beautiful, pink, "princess-like" long dress and a tiara with pink pearls on her gorgeous blond hair. She was the prettiest thing I'd ever seen.

Excited, I opened my box. "Ahh," I cried out. "Thank you, Grandma!" But my doll was nothing like Machiyo's. She was plain and wore a simple blue school uniform.

Before any emotions got into me, I began to act as if I really liked my present, talking to the doll. But I didn't fail to see Machiyo and Grandma having a good time together with the pretty princess doll, and I ached a little inside watching them.

Why wasn't I good enough to deserve a pretty doll too?

It happened like this over and over, and each time the presentation of the gifts was a display of the difference between my sister and me.

It hurt me every time I saw that my gift was lesser than my sister's. I wondered why they did this to me, and I started to wish they wouldn't bring me anything at all. Later, I would understand that this was part of a pattern of abuse, but at the time I was simply a hurt little girl.

Even though I was very young, I understood that it wasn't simply that my extended family didn't like me. They wanted me to *know* that they didn't like me. Also, they wanted to see me hurt. They were making sure to show me that no matter what I did, I wouldn't be any good—would never be equal to my sister.

Every time they visited us, they'd say, "Kyomi is exactly like Mama," and they labeled me "Mama's child" early on. I didn't know what characteristics of mine resembled Mama's. From the way they said it, it was obvious that they didn't think they were positive. They looked down on me and mistreated me, exactly as they'd always done with Mama.

In stark contrast, Papa's family called Machiyo "Papa's child," and she was given every possible privilege and advantage in our family. At just four years old, for example, she began taking traditional Japanese dance lessons, which cost Papa a huge tuition. Twice a year, she got beautiful kimonos and a traditional hairstyle wig for her dance recitals.

At first, I thought I was just too young for the dance lessons. Then I turned five and realized that I simply wasn't going to go to lessons at all. Machiyo, it seemed, was the only girl in our family who deserved such a privilege.

The way I was treated was partly due to Japanese traditions and customs—Machiyo was the eldest child—but it was also because of Papa's family's toxic dynamics.

How did I behave in response to their efforts? Most of the time I behaved as if I hadn't noticed. I knew that must have irritated them; it seemed that they wanted me to cry or sob. But I refused to do so. Sometimes I'd even deliberately act funny, making people laugh, while holding in my tears.

I never confronted their unfair treatment of me, but the repetitive insults affected me deeply. Over time, I began to question what was wrong with me. I began to believe I was less than who I was—that I was unworthy.

Machiyo and I both knew that the unmistakably different way in which Papa's family treated us put me in an awkward position, but she never showed any empathy or interest in protecting me. She just sat on her throne and acted like she was worthy of all the favoritism she received.

As we got older, Machiyo excluded me in other situations too—with the neighborhood kids, for example. We'd usually play some version of hide-and-seek in a group of six or seven. I was the second youngest in the group, but I wasn't the smallest; I was almost as tall as my sister.

Each of us held branches of a tree as our swords. When the seeker found you, you fought back with your sword.

"One . . . two . . . three . . ." the oldest boy in our group began to count one day. He was always the first seeker, which had become our rule. He counted loudly, eyes closed against his arm, leaning on the big fig tree on the back side of the house that we'd often climb on. Next to the tree was a nice wooden swing that Papa had built with thick wooden posts and an iron bar. I loved our big garden with its many fruit-bearing trees and flowering bushes.

I saw a hiding spot near where Machiyo was hiding, and I ran over.

"Hey! Don't you ever come near me!" Machiyo shouted at me when I tried to crouch down a few feet from her. "You are like a monkey! You mimic whatever I do." She pushed me down. "I don't like you at all! You're Monkey!" she shouted, looking down at me. "Go away! Go away, Monkey!"

My heart sank. I didn't mean to spoil her fun. I threw away the big branch I was carrying and went to the dirt ground in front of the fig tree and the swing. I picked up a small twig and began drawing something on the dirt. I didn't feel like playing the game anymore.

"Ninety-eight . . . ninety-nine . . . and . . . one hundred!" the boy finished counting. He glanced at me, then ran toward the front garden, seeking the kids in hiding.

I was often excluded in this way.

—

Papa was a superman in his profession. He was a professor at the local university, where he taught students and led scientific research in the area of light metal. The field had recently acquired spotlights and was quickly evolving in the application of metals like aluminum, lithium, and titanium. Papa had innovated many things and acquired various patents. He'd even procured several critical consulting jobs out of his research, which generated a substantial income outside his university job.

But at home, Papa was not the hero I wished him to be. He treated me differently, just like his parents and family did. Whenever he traveled, he brought back gifts for Mama and Machiyo, but never for me. Later, after my younger sister Yoshino was born, she experienced the same disparity in treatment—always getting the short shrift. At least then I had an ally.

How could an intelligent person like Papa do that to his daughters? I despised how he treated Machiyo as the family favorite and acted like I barely existed. His actions compounded my sense of worthlessness, and my subsequent suffering.

While Yoshino didn't get the kind of treatment Machiyo got, Papa was still affectionate with her in a way he never was with me. He was always harsh and strict with me, finding any reason to scold me.

When Papa scolded me, I never cried, but I trembled inside. I was afraid of Papa—particularly his eyes, like the eyes of a wolf, always piercing me, tearing at me. I began to fear him at an early age.

Yoshino was born when I was five. Even before delivering her, Mama was frequently sick and in and out of bed during the day. So, I'd been helping her in many ways with various chores around the house since I was old enough to do so.

As soon as Yoshino came home from the hospital, I became her mother. Each day when I returned from kindergarten, I spent my time preparing bottles and changing diapers. I often washed dishes for Mama in the kitchen sink by standing on a wooden stool, sleeves up. I was a helper, a maid, a mother, a big sister, and a warrior. Mama and Yoshino relied upon me. That was part of my armor too.

When I was in second grade, my teacher visited our home for a parent-teacher meeting. She was one of the nicer teachers, in her late thirties and a little round. When she smiled, deep dimples on her cheeks made a cheerful and warm impression. Her curly black hair was neatly trimmed just above her shoulders; I always thought it suited her personality.

I peeked into the room through the slightly open door during the meeting. There were my teacher and Mama, both in tears and holding hands and talking about me as they sat next to each other on the sofa. I could see round teardrops falling from my teacher's big eyes.

"How wonderful Kyomi chan is!" she said enthusiastically.

"She is an angel!" Mama proclaimed, and the teacher nodded her agreement.

This scene made a strong impression on me. It showed me that I *could* please others and confirmed for me that being helpful and kind was something others cherished.

But that teacher didn't know what was happening in my life. Sadly, even Mama didn't know. She was just happy to have such a wonderful daughter. They'd never seen me shuddering in the dark corners where I so often hid.

Mama didn't know that I was often unhappy, but she *was* aware all along of how Papa and his family treated me. Mama, of course, was in the same position, and she complained about Papa and his family almost every day. She was sympathetic to my situation because of her own experiences with them.

But at some point I began to realize that her perpetual complaints about them weren't helping me. Instead, they implanted more negativity in me by reminding me of how much my family members disliked me, abused me, and made it so that my own pain and agony had no chance to heal. Mama's daily reminders of my family's cruelty also compounded my doubt and fears regarding my own worthlessness and shame.

"Kyomi chan," Mama said one day, "I've told Papa so many times about your situation."

I was listening to her but I felt like covering my ears with my palms. *Don't tell me this anymore, because I already know!* I wanted to shout.

"I begged him and told him to ask Obah chan"—my grandma—"to be more mindful about treating you and Machiyo equally," she said.

Knowing this made me feel even worse than the original assaults, because it meant that what they were doing was intentional. I really wished Mama hadn't told me about it at all. And I wished she would stop complaining about Papa and his family altogether, at least in front of me. What child could bear such a situation?

Papa and his family slighted me or criticized me occasionally. But Mama's complaints about them were an everyday event, and ultimately they were much more damaging. She was so hurt herself that she couldn't protect me wisely. Though it wasn't her intention, she made me the victim of her struggles, and in doing so made my own struggles that much worse.

I had no choice but to turn to armor for my survival. As soon as I wore it, I felt warm and protected. Inside the armor, I was able to perform and act like the perfect, bright, cheerful girl everyone wanted me to be.

I tried hard to become a better, stronger, and more cheerful and likable person. Teachers and my friends' mothers always complimented me. Mama was so proud of me. But the dweller inside the armor was lonely, miserable, and frightened. Every morning on the way to school, I had to stop walking a few times to take deep breaths and quell the anxiety rising inside me. I'd put my little left hand extended on the neighbor's outside fence and my right hand on my chest, gasping for air and trying to calm my nerves. I felt like throwing up. I experienced chronic nausea. But I didn't tell anyone, not even Mama.

At such a young age, I experienced profound emptiness. I couldn't find any meaning in life. I was envious of other kids. I watched them giggling and jumping around in happiness and wondered why I couldn't be that way. In my own life it seemed as if I was endlessly struggling not to get hurt by anything or anybody.

Creativity was one of my escapes from my real life. As a child I took lots of lessons—ballet, piano, singing, painting, and calligraphy—but I had few distinct things that I really liked. I wasn't a typical girl who liked playing with dolls. I preferred assembling complicated plastic models by putting pieces together into various shapes. Doing this gave me a strong sense of achievement.

Later, in my adolescence, I started writing poems and essays. As I wrote, I could shape my thoughts. I began to see myself more deeply and clearly. Self-expression allowed me to breathe more easily. It provided me with necessary hope that there was a better future out there for me.

—

As I grew older, another problem started to affect our family—Papa's infidelity.

Since I was six or seven years old, Mama had been complaining to me about Papa's other women. In fact, he'd had many affairs throughout their marriage.

Papa had lots of younger admirers due to his line of work at the university. Most of his affairs were short-lived and not serious enough to affect the daily functions of our family life, but they still cast shadows over our emotional well-being. Listening to Mama's complaints became our duty as Mama's daughters, and she seemingly had no concern about how profoundly her disclosing his affairs might affect us.

When Papa was an associate professor and I was almost ten, one of his affairs became a significant threat—to Mama, and to us. The woman who he'd become involved with was his secretary. She was capable and strong, and seemingly wanted to be Papa's wife. Mama was frequently anxious, depressed, and even hysterical about this particular affair because it was so much more serious than all the rest had ever been before. Our family life became a wreck.

This became one of a few times that Mama hired private investigators to shed light on Papa's affairs. Then she was weak and confused enough in her judgment to show Machiyo and me the many photos and reports of Papa and the woman, on their trips or in hotels. It was no secret between Mama and her daughters how much sadness and agony her marriage brought to her. She moaned in front of me and asked me what she should do almost every day. Mama set no boundaries between parents and children and I always had to prioritize her problems over my own.

This all contributed to my developing a distrust of men, and a fear of as-yet-unknown sexual activities. My sense that our family life was broken also made me believe that I would never marry anyone, or have children. I thought that any child I had would become a victim like I was.

Mama was totally devoted to Papa, and totally dependent on him—especially financially.

That's why Papa's having affairs wasn't simply a matter of his physical needs—it was much deeper. Papa couldn't let Mama go but he longed for a stronger person, someone to be his equal. Meanwhile, the entire family suffered from their dysfunction.

I lost my childhood to this sad entrapment. My armor was both the thing that allowed me to achieve much in the way of friends and good grades and praise and the symbol of my failures. Inside my protective shell, I was completely alone.

— 3 —
Life Sentencing

I can see now how my armor's boundaries were defined by Japanese culture, customs, and traditions, as well as the situations I witnessed and the value system imposed on me by my family.

Papa was in many ways a kind, progressive, modern, and intelligent individual. But due to prevailing traditions, he acted as he was expected to as the eldest son of his family. When it came to decisions regarding extended family affairs, including his parents, he obeyed his parents and prioritized them over us. But within our core family, he insisted on being the sole decision-maker. He never allowed us to talk back to him; we were required to always show him the utmost respect.

My sisters always had the good sense to obey the rules dictated by custom and tradition. They were quiet and obedient, and could wrap up their emotions in fluffy pink paper and put them away as if nothing bothered them.

Not me. I was a seeker of truth and a warrior when it came to expressing my beliefs. Even from a very young age, five or six years old, I didn't bend to authority. And I didn't like nonsense. Though I was traumatized by Papa and his extended family, I still had a sense of myself and what was right in my heart—and my eyes were sharp enough to see that Papa was insecure and indecisive. When he imposed his supposedly untouchable authority on us, I sometimes reacted strongly out of a sense of injustice. I was different from my sisters.

I had respect for Papa too, of course. But if I felt something was wrong, sometimes I questioned why. In response, he'd scold me sharply in front of my sisters—something he never did to them.

One weekend, Papa was in and out of the garage, working on his car. That was one of his hobbies; he'd often spend hours on his car during the weekend. My sisters and I were outside in the garden, wanting to be close to him. Today, he'd promised that all of us could take turns sitting inside his car while he was working on the outside.

Of course, Machiyo got the opportunity first, and she spent quite a long time in there. Papa was smiling, explaining something to her very patiently. I thought I would be next.

Instead, Papa picked up Yoshino. "The littlest is next," he said.

"It should be me," I said.

"No," he said, "Yocchan is the littlest. You are next." He always called Yoshino "Yocchan," a name he used with affection.

When Yoshino finally came out of the car, I thought it would be my turn at last.

"Papa has already finished the car," he said. "Let's go inside the house."

"No, it's my turn!" I cried. "I should get a turn too."

"Didn't you hear what Papa said?" His thick eyebrows drew together irritably.

"But you told me I would be next!" I protested. I was upset. This wasn't the first time he'd done this to me.

"What kind of words are you using? Are they proper for talking to Papa?" he asked, his eyes growing sharp.

I was frightened, and I felt myself shaking, but still I stood there looking back at him.

"Never talk to your father in the way you just did!" he snapped.

I knew I was right. He always treated me differently from my sisters. *Why?* I wept inside over this injustice, but I didn't say anything more.

Now I think that perhaps Papa was afraid of *me* in some way. I always had my eyes fixed on the truth, and he felt threatened by that. When I spoke up, I sometimes became more than his daughter; I became his rival.

When I was almost sixteen, we found out that Papa and another young woman had had a baby together.

We'd known that Papa had been having an affair with her for about a year. She was in her twenties, a daughter of the owner of the printing company that subcontracted with his university. Mama was destroyed by this news, but still refused to leave Papa; she asked Machiyo and me to stand by to support her.

Several months later, after I turned sixteen, I had a big argument with Papa.

It started as a discussion about possible university choices for the following year. Machiyo was already studying at a private dental school at this point and was gone from home. Papa had always wanted me to attend one of the national medical schools. He'd originally wanted to become a medical doctor himself, but because there were no scholarships or student loans at all in Japan at the time and he needed to financially support not only himself but also his parents' retirement living and his two siblings' education, he'd pursued applied science and engineering instead of taking more years for a costly medical education. Now he wanted me to do what he hadn't been able to do. He'd sent me to the most prestigious high school in the region—the same school he had attended decades earlier—and he hoped I could now attend one of the national medical schools, almost all of which ranked much higher than private ones, yet required less tuition.

I'd known Papa's wish since I was little, but what I wanted was to pursue a career in journalism. Since the fifth or sixth grade, I'd had a burning desire to be an advocate—to help people with no or little voice to be heard.

It was after dinner, and we were in the living room watching TV together. Papa was sitting nearest to the TV, with the rest of us scattered around him.

"Papa," I began, "I'm thinking about where I'd like to go for university." I felt nervous, but determined.

"What about it?" he said. "You're going to medical school, aren't you?"

Though he framed it as a question, he of course was not really asking.

"I'd like to go to Waseda University for political science or anthropology," I said.

As soon as I mentioned Waseda, Papa began to shake his leg irritably. Waseda was one of the most prestigious private schools in Japan, but it didn't have a medical school.

"Waseda is an excellent school, but you don't know what you're going to end up with," he said sharply. His leg shook faster.

I was getting into a risky spot. Tension was in the air. Mama turned off the TV, then Yoshino, Papa's wisest daughter, stood up and escaped upstairs.

"I'd like to pursue journalism in the future, not medicine," I said, lifting my chin. I felt a little relieved to have finally said this out loud. It was the very first time I'd told anyone about my decision.

Papa turned his body toward me. Now his hand on his thigh became a fist. "NO! I don't think so," he said. They were short words, but the weight he put into them made each one feel like a heavy boulder.

"I've always been worried about you, your way of thinking . . . too pure to survive!" Papa shook his head.

I felt he was rejecting my entire existence.

"Listen to me," he continued, "life is NOT like that! If you go into journalism, you're going to end up being killed!" He was red, trembling with emotion. His voice became a weapon—sharp and impactful, as if he wanted to cut me. I knew he'd been worried about my genuine, rather naive heart feeling against injustice in society. But I couldn't help reacting to his words.

"If you reject what I think is worth pursuing in my life, you are rejecting me, and MY LIFE!" I shouted. Feeling desperate, I punctuated my point by saying, "I shouldn't even have been born!"

It didn't really matter which universities or what subjects I was pursuing. I was reacting to Papa—his years of rejection and of stamping me as "unworthy." I'd never cried in front of Papa in my life. But now I felt like breaking down into tears.

He hit the table with his fist. "You idiot!" He was now in a total rage, quivering with anger. His face was red, and his eyes were too sharp to leave any room for empathy. I knew those eyes; they were dangerous. I suddenly felt I shouldn't have provoked him.

"Life is NOT black and white! You are looking at ONLY white, but you're wrong. In reality, it's gray. Life is *gray*, Kyomi!" he asserted forcefully.

An instant after his explosion, he seemed a little more withdrawn. I thought he was partially talking about himself and his own life, not me or life in general. I sensed sorrow in him.

I could have stopped our conversation there, but I didn't. Instead I shouted, "If I have to live in the gray world as you have, I prefer not living at all! Don't you know that you've tormented your own wife and your children for so long because of your gray world?"

As I said that, I saw myself entering into an infinite wilderness from which I might never find a way back. I knew I should stop there, but I couldn't help but delivering my next words—for Mama's sake. She was standing there next to me, listening and already crying from the emotional impact. I felt the pressure from her: I must deliver.

"Do you think you can be happy with that baby at the expense of *our* unhappiness?" I went further. "That's a LIE! You can't be happy living in such a lie!"

Even as I heard the words coming out of my mouth, regret began to blossom inside me.

I wanted Papa to understand how lonely I'd been, how hurt and terrified. I wanted to make sure he felt guilty for what he'd done to our family, and to me. I wanted him to suffer just as we'd all suffered.

Because he had to know what he'd done to me, didn't he? What he'd done to all of us? What I'd endured for all these years? I tried to believe that Papa had known my value and strength since I was little, and that was why he'd always been so strict with me. But was this true?

I loved Papa. Nonetheless, what was done was done. I'd delivered the words. I'd pronounced a life sentence; I'd thrown him too far away from me to reach him any longer.

I looked at Papa. He looked so small—back hunched, sitting there so quietly.

I lost myself in total blankness.

I left the room. That was the only thing I could do.

—

From this point onward, Papa must have felt somehow relieved that he wouldn't have to hide his affair and the baby, because the situation became "officially" recognized after our argument.

In fact, a couple of months later, Papa told Mama that the woman's family had threatened to bring a case against him and the university, and he had to stay with her for a while in order to prevent her from going through with it.

This could have simply been an excuse to leave Mama, but we believed Papa's story. He was in one of the highest positions in his university. Any legal issue could have damaged his career and reputation.

After moving out, Papa only visited us on occasion. What started as days and weeks became years, and then he finally stopped coming back home altogether. He continued to pay the mortgage and give us a monthly allowance, however.

Mama never stopped crying.

It wasn't my fault, but I blamed myself, and my shame deepened. Was the life sentencing Papa's? Or mine?

— 4 —

The Abandonment

After the big argument with Papa, I once again hid deep inside my armor. With the additional guilt and shame layered onto my existing feelings of unworthiness, my inner world became even more desolate.

I had been planning to take entrance examinations for university soon, but now I'd lost my zeal for academics. I felt disconnected from the rest of the world. I skipped the exams and entered a preparatory school for the next year.

At school, I was exposed to a much different environment from my home environment, which had been a prison for me—the umbilical cord to my shame. Over the course of a couple of months, I noticed a small yet substantial change in me.

As a preparatory student, I had to study and memorize—but I also had the opportunity to dig more deeply into my interests: writing poetry and essays, and reading lots of books across different genres— the classics, modernism, philosophy, the arts, the humanities, and science. I traveled to the Kyoto and Nara regions by myself, and wrote pages and pages. I felt more fulfilled, and had a sense of happiness and independence that I'd never had before.

Of course, when I returned home each evening, I was dragged back to our reality: I'd sit and listen to Mama's never-ending complaints about Papa, his woman, and his new baby.

Mama had always been my primary concern—someone I'd looked after. She'd molded me to be her ally and companion. Now I knew that this dynamic had actually cost me more than the slights from Papa and his family. It was my empathy and compassion for Mama that had imprisoned me and tied me up in the darkness for so many years. I needed to separate myself from her somehow.

I felt like the once-neglected and abused cat beginning to eat for herself, cleaning and mending her coat. I was aligning my body and spirit a little differently, for the better. I was learning that engaging in things I really liked doing had the power to heal my soul and spirit.

I felt like stepping away from all the rotten roots inside me and building an independent life for myself. I knew I would need to leave home soon.

In late spring, when I was still eighteen, I ran into Hiro on a commuter train. We'd gone to the same high school, but he was two years my senior, so we'd lost touch after he graduated. But he'd played bass in a rock band in high school, and I'd always had a crush on him, though I'd never told him that. I still felt a rush of exhilaration when I remembered what he'd been like back then, and the sounds of his bass in the storms of rock music his band played.

Now Hiro was a second-year student, studying economics and seeking to earn his MBA in the near future. Though he was a university student, he was already financially independent, making his own money by tutoring students and playing bass in a professional band.

Soon after reconnecting, Hiro and I began to date.

One afternoon at a local coffee shop, he and I were talking about the Women's Liberation Movement (WLM), which had recently erupted from a leftist activist group in Japan. The movement empha-sized the liberation of women from the male-dominated system tra-ditionally followed in our country.

"How about abortion? Do you believe in that?" Hiro asked. He was radical yet practical in many ways. The WLM stood for the legal-ization of birth control pills and for women's rights. In Japan, birth control pills wouldn't be legalized until 1999.

"Yes," I said, "but more important is the proper preventive mea-sure: birth control. That way, we can protect women from being vic-timized by their sexuality." I was an advocate for anyone who was a victim in our society.

Whatever Hiro and I talked about, my attention was always on him. His thick throat and high cheekbones. His hoarse, deep voice and thick lips. I felt warm whenever I looked at him. I played our first kiss from the week before over and over in my mind. The thought alone made me boil inside. His soft, long, curly hair somehow made him look more exotic and masculine.

I was deeply attracted to this intelligent man—to his independent spirit and his body, too, though I didn't know yet what it meant to be physical in that way.

We were so compatible. Hiro was an artist, but a person of many opinions. We discussed diverse subjects: politics, civil movements, anthropology, science, art, and culture. He sharply criticized the Vietnam War, saying that the US and our government had been engaged in it for far too long. Our conversations reminded me of my own sense of justice and philosophy.

Hiro was my boyfriend, but he represented something more than that for me: he was my comrade in the pursuit of a more liberal world. He was also a symbol of my hope to one day become a journalist and writer. He often expressed his support and encouraged me to achieve my goals.

The challenge that faced me still was to try to close the space between my two worlds—the one in which I hid behind my armor, and the one where I allowed my true self to shine through—and merge them into one. The experience of pursuing my writing more seriously had vanquished many of my fears already. I was sure it was one important key to succeeding in integrating my two worlds together.

Someday, I would have to bring these two realities together into one and free myself from the past—but I wasn't sure how to yet. For the time being, Hiro was my only ally, and I was beginning to fall in love.

In the autumn, Mama's uncle, now in his eighties, brought a proposal to our family.

Mama's uncle was the original successor of his father's (my mom's grandfather) extremely successful dental clinics. Now he wanted to pay for one of Mama's daughters to become a dentist. He said he would pay for all of her tuition, her cost of living, and even the cost to open her own practice. There was only one condition: she must use his family name, Takahashi (my mom's mother's maiden name), for her dental office.

Papa was thrilled.

Machiyo was already a dental student and was costing Papa lots of money. Yoshino was only in junior high school but would eventually need to go to school as well. That left me as the only candidate who could accept our great-uncle's proposal.

I wasn't thinking about dental school as a real possibility for many reasons: Hiro, university, journalism, and my new, independent life. Considering a path in dentistry felt impossible.

There was part of me, however, that was still haunted by deep regret. I felt an urge to ease or mend Papa's feelings—to please him.

I would later understand that I was being reactive. I was living as if I were a battered child, swinging between two split attitudes: rebelliousness and desperately seeking his approval. I lacked confidence and self-compassion.

Eventually, to buy time, I took all the exams for both dental school and my original choice of university.

At the end of February, I passed all the entrance exams I'd taken.

By this point, I felt the pressure to fulfill my great uncle's proposal, and yet I also wanted to carry on with Waseda and pursue journalism.

One night in March, Papa brought me a white envelope. As I grabbed it I could tell that it contained a lot of money.

"Here's the money, Kyomi. However you want to use it is up to you," Papa said with a subtle smile on his face.

The meaning of the smile wasn't clear to me.

"What do you mean by *however I want to use it*?" I asked.

"I'm sure you've decided to go to dental school," he said. "But I know you've long wanted Waseda. So you can use this money either to pay the tuition for Waseda, or go to Europe or somewhere for traveling. As I did for Onei chan"—big sister—"I am giving you the money for your tuition."

Now I understood. He wanted to prove that he, as my father, hadn't failed to pay for my tuition. It was a point of pride for him.

"Thank you, Papa," I said, and took the money.

Ultimately, I agreed to go to dental school—paid for by my great-uncle—*and* I enrolled as a student at Waseda, using Papa's money. It wasn't unusual to enroll dually in order to hold choices of universities before making a final decision. But I knew I would have to give up on Waseda sooner.

As predicted, within a month or so of beginning to attend classes there, I stopped going to Waseda.

I was a coward. I felt as if I'd betrayed myself and taken the easier path. What was the most hurtful to me was that I'd given up on my dream to become a journalist without even putting up a fight. The loss wasn't only about my choice of career—I felt like I was compromising my life.

I'd begun to punish myself because of my self-betrayal. As Papa had said in our argument before, my mind became fixated on only a rigid, "white" way; I judged myself harshly, which caused me even more pain.

"I'm leaving Waseda," I told Hiro a few days later. "It's stupid to hang on to it . . . it's impractical."

"Why do you say that?" he asked, surprised. "If you're serious about what you've wanted, you can still continue. What's good about becoming a dentist? Do you even like it?"

I felt like I was being criticized. My stomach clenched.

"If you really want to be a journalist," he went on, "you can quit the dental school, then live with me. We can do that together. You go to Waseda instead of dental school, and study journalism, just like you've wanted."

I felt like crying. I didn't know how serious he was about us living together, but I desperately wanted to take his words as the sign of love I'd been longing for.

Hiro's proposal offered a glimpse of possible independence from the life I'd suffered through up to this point. Though he didn't say so, I thought he might even want to marry me.

I loved him, and now I began to imagine a possible life together with him.

Then other thoughts came to my mind and began to haunt me: *You shouldn't trust him.*

In Japan, no scholarships, fellowships, or student loans were available at the time. And as a woman, I faced an uphill battle. Employment opportunities and salaries weren't equal between men and women; women had to work much harder for fewer opportunities.

And I had no idea, of course, what living with Hiro might bring. We'd been dating for over a year, but I wasn't truly confident about the stability of our relationship. Plus, I'd been traumatized by Papa's constant extramarital affairs and was filled with fears generated by Mama's agonizing and perpetual complaints.

How could I be optimistic about stepping into a new phase of our relationship and trusting in our love when I had no model for what healthy love could look like?

By the time I was almost twenty, Hiro and I had grown quite close and I was beginning to think about introducing a physical element into our relationship. I decided that if I had the chance soon, I would step into this new unknown. I wanted to encourage myself to move past the traumas of my parents' broken relationship and accept a more natural progression of my relationship with Hiro.

Then Machiyo called me.

"Ah, Kyom chan, I've heard an interesting story about Hiro," she said. "Remember my old friend, Sanae? She went to your high school . . ."

"Yes, I remember her." I remembered specifically that she'd played electric piano in his rock band.

"I have to tell you . . ." She seasoned her voice with a hint of criticism.

"What? What is it??" I tensed; something important was coming.

"Sanae said she had sex with him back then."

I took a moment to take that in. High school was more than four years ago. That didn't matter, did it?

And then Machiyo interrupted my thoughts.

"And . . . she said . . . even now."

No! I couldn't believe it. I saw my world collapsing in slow motion. A skyscraper exploded inside my mind, falling down to the ground and leaving a heap of rubble. I could even hear the noise.

"Kyom chan, that's not all . . . she said not only her but also other women are sleeping with him . . . ongoingly!" Machiyo sounded triumphant.

I sat, miserable, in total silence.

Then I thanked her in short words and hung up.

It was unbearable. I couldn't breathe. My anxiety and uncertainty about Hiro seemed to have just been confirmed.

I'd just begun to trust someone for the first time in my life. With Hiro, my thick armor had become a little thinner. Though I wasn't totally confident about him as a possible partner, he was still the symbol of my hope to build my own independent life.

Now, the dream was over. I was heartbroken.

It wasn't long before I told Hiro that we had to end our relationship. I didn't even ask whether the story was true; I didn't need to ask. Any explanation or excuses would only have made me even more miserable. I was afraid to be hurt, so instead of trying to work things out I simply slipped into my armor once again.

Now, looking back, I know I could have asked Hiro to tell me his side of the story, and share my desires with him—but I didn't know exactly what love meant back then. I knew relationship-building was based on mutual potential, trust, love, compassion, and growth. But I was too damaged to engage in that way. I couldn't even muster the voice to tell Hiro that I loved him.

Though it was I who ended the relationship, I was the one who got wounded more deeply by our split. My family was broken. Papa had started another family and had all but left us. Mama was depressed, still complaining about her situation every day. My hope for the future had been obliterated. The last thing I was still hanging on to, Hiro, had now betrayed me. I didn't know who or how I could trust anyone anymore.

As long as the armor had prevented me from getting hurt, it seemed like a benefit. But now I saw that it wasn't serving me. I hated what Hiro had done to me, but most of all I hated myself—my armor, my pretention and lies that kept it seeming as if nothing bothered me. Now, my upset and all the shame, regret, and unworthiness in me seemed to surge inside of me. I felt out of control.

Over the next couple of years, I used a couple of men in different ways. They wanted to possess me, but I would never let them do so. I would let them develop feelings for me, and then, disgusted, I would end the relationship to punish them.

I'd never really wanted men—except for Hiro—but now my ambivalence grew into a strong distrust and disgust toward them. I felt I'd been ruined by Papa and jaded by Mama. I was truly sick and broken.

When I was in my fourth year (out of six) of dental school, we started more clinical studies and lab work. From the next year until my graduation, I would start to see actual patients, not mannikins, in the university hospital.

I began attending the weekly radiology reading. A few faculty members from different departments attended the meetings frequently, including a handsome assistant professor, Seiji, who happened to be one of Machiyo's former classmates at dental school.

We met at a gathering after a reading one day.

"Hello," he said shyly, not fixing his eyes on me. His eyes were so big, yet they were almost hiding behind his long eyelashes. I got a very positive impression of him from his modest and rather quiet attitude. He often joked and laughed with other faculty members while we were eating, but I sensed some sadness in him.

It was a sadness I could relate to.

I'd continued to wear my ever-thickening and ever-hardening armor, pretending everything was normal. But inside I was still suffocating from the sense of having abandoned myself, compromised my value. I'd begun to think that one day I might even take my own life.

Soon, Seiji became my boyfriend—but I never let him come completely into my world. I cared about him, but I didn't have any capacity to truly love anyone. I'd been living at the edge of my two worlds, staring into the abyss, for too long.

One day at the end of November, Mama came to visit me and drop off my monthly allowance at my apartment in Yokohama. I'd told her in advance that I would be between two classes. She arrived a little late, and with one of her friends, which I wasn't anticipating.

Mama came in while her friend stood outside the door, waiting for us to finish.

"Here is the money for you, Kyomi," Mama said.

I noticed that her voice sounded a little distant, detached, but I didn't have time to address that.

"Oh, thank you, Mama," I said, reaching for it. I checked the clock. "I'll have to leave here soon, it's almost time for my next class."

But it was clear Mama wanted to stay longer.

"How is school? I haven't seen much of you lately . . . what's going on?" she asked me.

I didn't have the time to tell her anything, and I certainly I didn't want to go *there* with her . . .

"Mama, sorry, I really don't have time to talk. I have to go!" I grabbed a couple of textbooks and my handbag and edged toward the door.

Mama was right in her accusation, of course; I hadn't been going to see her. I was depressed, totally out of balance, and in this state it was difficult for me to accommodate her. I'd been avoiding her as much as possible. Now, as she kept talking, I grew irritated.

"I came here all the way from Chiba," she complained. "It took over one hour to get here. But you have no time to serve a cup of tea to your own mother?" She was quivering with anger now.

For my part, I felt that she was pressuring me, just as she'd always had, to attend to her at the sacrifice of meeting my own needs. I felt like breaking into a helpless cry. I stood there, unmoving.

"I will tell Papa about this!" she cried, eyes filling with tears, and then walked outside.

When I came out, she was complaining about me to her friend and sobbing.

Her friend stood tall at the door, staring at me with a harsh look.

"Kyomi san, didn't you see how your mother made effort to get here?" she demanded. "You're so rude to leave her in this state."

Mama's friend's words landed very hard, like bullets, in my vulnerable heart. But I had no room to deal with this emotional wreck.

Please, please leave me alone. I felt like breaking down, but the armor stopped me. *No, not here—never in front of them.*

I apologized for my misbehavior, but then I walked away, even as Mama shouted at me. I was at the edge. They had no idea what was going on with me, my life.

I was late to class, but it didn't matter. I couldn't fix my life. I felt deserted.

After Mama's visit, I sank into an even deeper depression.

Two nights later, Mama called me.

"I spoke with Papa about you, what happened in your apartment when I went there," she said.

My heart sank. *Oh no. Not now.*

"When I told him everything, he said I should regard you as no longer my daughter but a dead person," she said, almost proudly.

Her words stabbed into me like a sharp knife. I was mortally wounded, bleeding to death.

I sat there in silence. I couldn't find the words to respond to this. How could she attack her own daughter in this way? My breath came fast and shallow.

Then she took a breath and repeated again the same exact words, as if to nail into me what Papa had said.

Papa's words cut me. In saying this to Mama, he was drawing a line not just between her and me but also between him and me—denying me, and reiterating for me how broken and irreparable our relationship really was.

After I hung up the phone, I felt the glass castle I'd been living in shatter to pieces and collapse to the ground. I couldn't hold all the dark emotions in anymore, and finally everything exploded in the infinite space. It was like an explosion of the dark, compressed black hole inside me. I had no weight left to hold myself together.

All of these years, I'd seen my role as being Mama's protector; now I saw clearly that she'd been manipulating me into acting on her behalf for many years, and she was too pitiful and timid to stand up for her own daughter with integrity and conviction.

This betrayal by Mama was the final straw. I could no longer bear my life. *What was the point of my existence?*

There didn't seem to be one.

I was ready to be done with my life, and destroy these two dual worlds—armor included—altogether.

I was ready to die.

I didn't sleep that night. By the following morning, I'd become nothing more than a braindead body. The only thing driving me that next morning was my desire to kill myself.

I wrote a resignation letter to the dental school and posted it. Then I hurried to CVS to purchase a box of razor blades. I cleaned my apartment meticulously. I looked through my drawers to collect any writings that I wouldn't want anyone to read, shoving them into a trash bag, and threw the trash into the chute.

Finally, I left a short note on the kitchen table, where a razor blade had been waiting for me for the last several hours. I filled the bathtub with water and got ready. I put on my swimsuit and submerged myself in the tub.

I placed the blade on my wrist and held it there for a while.

Do it, I urged myself.

But I was frozen . . . I couldn't move my hand.

Red blood stained my skin from pressing the blade tightly against my wrist. My eyes were glued to the spot. But I couldn't do more.

Just do it!

But I couldn't.

My eyes and right hand were frozen on my wrist for what seemed like forever.

Tears ran down my face, but I felt nothing as I stared at my wrist.

The knuckles of my fingers were fixed tight and frozen like a rock. They couldn't be released to open my hand.

Finally, I dropped the blade onto the bathroom floor outside the tub and slowly came out of the tub, my whole body trembling.

I had failed.

— 5 —

The Cocoon

A few hours after exiting the bathtub, depleted, I pushed myself to gather up enough energy to stuff a few of my most essential items into a bag. I felt as if something were chasing me; now I felt a deep need to run—escape from this life.

But where should I go?

In the blink of an eye, Nara came to mind.

There were many reasons why I would think of Nara for my escape— foremost of which was that had always been one of my favorite places. It was also where I'd begun writing in a more conscious way back when I was teenage. There, writing had become a healing force in my life. I'd learned that writing curved my thoughts into concrete shapes and helped me find the best part of me. It helped me not to get drawn too far into the deep end, but rather to lift myself up.

I thought there must always be millions of microdroplets of moisture in the atmosphere in Nara, because in the evening there, as the sun set, the air was thick and expansive, making the size of the sun gigantic, the color brilliant orange edged in blazing vermillion. The sky in Coquelicot became even brighter where it met the dark silhouettes of the mountains.

In Nara, I could hear the voices of the people who'd gone there before me. There was something visceral, and healing, about its rural, earthly setting.

I needed that now.

I felt like a zombie just out of the grave, but I knew somehow that escaping to Nara would bring me back to life.

I thought about my attempt. Why couldn't I cut my wrist? I remembered how I'd felt that someone, or something, had stopped me—something that felt like a clean, awakening light reaching through the heavy clouds enveloping me.

The sense of intervention made me feel hopeful that somehow, despite how broken I felt, there was a deep and enduring light inside of me. Now I needed to stand up and live so I could find it.

Soon, I might be able to begin to rebuild something else—something other than the armor I'd enclosed myself in. I wasn't sure I had the energy to do it, but I did sense that I could hold onto hope, if for nothing else than for that little girl still trembling in the darkness. I wanted to save her.

I began to remember the hope I'd felt during preparatory school, when I was writing and when I felt more fully alive.

I left my apartment knowing I wouldn't be coming back. I took a bullet train to Kyoto, then a local train to Nara. I brought my hope with me all the way to Nara, imagining the ways the serene setting might help me to heal. I was a refugee seeking asylum from my life, and Nara would be my safe landing place.

"Kyom chan, Kyom chan . . ."

I recognized the voice. But it seemed to be occurring in my dream. *Who is that?*

A knock at the door.

Somebody's knocking.

For a minute or two, I was still listening to the voice in my dream, trying to figure it out. And then I woke up and realized that someone was actually there, at my hotel.

"Kyom chan, Kyom chan . . ."

I looked at the clock on the night chest, showing 2:05 a.m.

I got out of bed and walked to the door. "Who is it?" I asked.

"It's me, Machiyo," my sister called from behind the door. "And Seiji too."

Oh, no.

In this moment, my sister and boyfriend represented my darkness. They were part of what I'd escaped from, part of the past from which I needed to heal. And now they were beckoning me back into my armor again. My body tensed.

But how did they find me?

Then I realized: my friend Yukari. I'd called her earlier that night. She had some deep wounds of her own, and I thought she might be able to understand my pain.

I was a fool. I thought she was one of the few I could trust. I didn't expect her to betray me in this way, sending the very people I least wanted to see to come to retrieve me.

At the moment of my realization, the little hope I'd had that I might be able to start over in Nara was snuffed out. No matter what I wished, I would be taken back to where other people imagined I belonged. I would have to don my armor again. I would have to live as a prisoner for the rest of my life.

I felt like throwing up. A helpless, desperate cry resounded deep inside of me. I knew nobody would understand my odd behavior, this extreme reaction to their intrusion into my life and future.

I had to open the door.

I reached for the handle and let them in.

"Ah, Kyom chan," they both said with a mixture of relief and annoyance when they stepped inside the room. Then Machiyo explained that she and Seiji had driven all night to "rescue" me. Papa had gone to my apartment and found my note on the kitchen table. He'd then contacted Machiyo, who must have connected somehow with Yukari, who had eventually disclosed my location.

"Papa was worried about you," Machiyo said sharply.

Papa must have felt dreadful; he must have known that Mama would deliver his words—"Kyomi is dead"—to me. Had he imagined what that might lead to? And now here he was trying to save me from the very thing his words had precipitated.

Deflated, I submitted to Machiyo and Seiji. I obediently packed my things and went with them back to school—back to my bleak reality.

Meanwhile, I continued to hemorrhage from the deep wounds inside me, with no hope of healing.

A year and a half later, just before my graduation from dental school, Seiji told me, "I will leave you alone if I haven't been good enough for you."

He cast his big, beautiful eyes slightly downward and couldn't even fix them on mine. I saw his eyes holding back tears in his thick long lashes.

"But if you'd like to continue in our relationship, I'd like you to live with me," he said.

I was moved by this sweet and sincere offer. He'd been kind, generous, and faithful to me. What else could I ask for? I wasn't sure about my feelings for him, but he was a good man, and I desperately wanted to be one of the *normal* people.

Since Nara, I'd been pretending and perfecting my armor, acting like a normal person. But I knew I wasn't. I was a wreck. Was this how I could save myself? Committing to Seiji?

"Yes," I said. "Let's live together."

Two years later, Seiji and I got married.

Seiji continued to teach as an assistant professor. I was a graduate student in one of the basic science departments at a different dental school. Besides our main work, we both worked in a part-time clinical practice.

We earned good salaries and enjoyed a good life—lots of vacations and travel. We spent our time consuming. We liked to go shopping, to the movies, and out to eat. We looked happy. From the outside, everything seemed smooth.

But I harbored this idea that Seiji saw himself as my watchdog. I knew he cared about me, but I also felt sure that he didn't trust me; he worried about me. And yet he never once asked me why I'd been so broken in Nara. Though he knew I'd been suicidal during that time, we never talked about it. Perhaps he was afraid to ask, but my feeling was that he wanted to keep me away from it to control me.

Did Seiji imagine I'd healed? I suppose he thought he'd mended me, now that I was dependent on him. So, although I appreciated him, I also hated our relationship. I was still living the life of a prisoner, entrapped and hating my life.

And the armor I wore was only getting more impenetrable.

Nine months after our marriage, I was still making efforts to pretend to be an ordinary and happy person, but in reality I hated the person I had become. I felt I was unworthy, no matter what I accomplished. I was filled with emptiness and held unresolved, smoldering darkness within me. The person I wanted to become would keep receding farther and farther away if I continued traveling this road.

I'd become a ghost. Who was I?

A little over a year into our marriage, Seiji got promoted to an associate professor position at a different dental school—this one in Sapporo on Hokkaido, hundreds of miles north from where we lived.

"The appointment will start in a couple of months. I'd like you to come with me. Will you be able to do so?" he asked me with a little hesitation.

"No, I don't think so," I said straightforwardly.

"If you can quit graduate school, we can go together," he said hopefully. "You can enroll at this school and continue your studies there."

"How would I be able to continue the research I'm doing in a different school and department, and with people who've never done the research that we've been doing here?" I demanded.

It was a reasonable question. I'd just received a prestigious post-doctoral fellowship through the ministry of education and science. But really, this was just an excuse. The truth was, the project I was working on didn't matter that much to me. I just didn't want to go with Seiji.

I didn't want to make my life's misery even worse and more inescapable by relocating to the middle of nowhere. I already felt trapped.

Though he was distraught about my refusal to go with him, Seiji relocated by himself, and after that we began living our lives totally separate from one another. He visited me once a month, but I only visited him once in Sapporo.

It soon became clear to me that I didn't love him. After all these years of dwelling in my armor, I'd become too broken to love anyone.

I needed to fix myself before I could hope to be happy with someone else.

I'd been married a year and a half when I moved from the center of Tokyo to the suburbs in Ichikawa, near my family.

By the early spring, I was in despair about my life. I still remembered the little hope I'd felt in Nara. I sensed there must be a better place than inside this dysfunctional armor.

Out of desperation, I began to read spiritual and religious books. I also took some classes and workshops in spirituality. During my earlier spiritual pursuits, I'd begun a yoga practice, which I still continued. I also attended a self-awareness group called *i*WD *(it's* a Wonderful Day!).

After each course I took with *i*WD, I would feel something inspirational, transformative, and joyous, but it never lasted; soon, the darkness and fear returned, as if they were tides. Every spiritual pursuit I attempted felt superficial, rootless.

Now I can see that I had so much unresolved sediment and lies in my heart at the time that the effect of pouring a little clean water over them did very little. I was like a pond full of garbage; I needed to be dredged fully before I could be restored.

I needed to heal myself, but instead I just kept tormenting myself.

Almost one year after Seiji left for Sapporo, I received a letter of invitation and acceptance from the US to become a researcher at the National Institute of Dental Research—part of the National Institutes of Health in Bethesda, Maryland—for my post-doctoral training.

A couple of weeks later, my friend, one of the attendees of the *i*WD seminar, showed me a beautiful diamond ring she'd recently purchased. I was intrigued by it because I could see a special light—the distinct, symmetrical shape of an eight-pointed star—perfectly reflected within the diamond. The light was so clear, translucent, and beautiful that I felt it was spiritual and sacred. I wanted something like it for myself. I asked my friend where she'd gotten it, and a few days later, I went to the jewelry shop and chose a ring for myself.

"Would you like spiritual counseling by a spiritual reader?" the woman who sold me the ring offered. "She is a very close friend of our shop owner, and she's excellent."

I'd never had a spiritual reading before; I was curious. I nodded. "Sure."

I walked upstairs, navigating by the dim light that came from the top of the stairs. As I climbed, I thought about what I should ask about for the reading.

At the landing, I smelled burning oil. A lamp glimmered on top of a tiny round table with burgundy velvet draped over it. The wooden door on the right was slightly open, as if inviting me to enter.

"Please come on in," the voice inside bade me.

I entered into a small, dark space. Only a tea candle in the right corner was giving off light. I tried to adjust my eyes. Gradually, I saw that a long, velvety curtain, the bottom of which trailed across the carpet, was separating me from the rest of the room. I hesitated.

"Please come in," the woman repeated from behind the curtain.

I walked through the curtain and took a seat in front of her.

She appeared to be in her mid-fifties, wore metal-framed glasses, and had short hair and an ordinary face. She was wearing a sweater in unappealing, dark colors.

I was surprised; I'd expected her to be eccentric and glamorous, though I wasn't sure why.

"What do you want to know?" she asked.

I told her about the ongoing separation from my husband and the research opportunity in the US, which would keep me away from Japan for at least two years.

She looked into a crystal ball the size of a small grapefruit that sat in front of her.

She asked a few more questions and looked again into the crystal ball, gently touching it with both hands and moaning a few words intermittently. I waited.

Finally, she raised her eyes slowly.

"You should divorce your husband before your departure to America. You and your husband have two distinct paths. You have your own, and he has his own."

She was clear and solemn, her eyes fixed on me.

I felt as if something inside of me had been dislodged.

The reader's advice shocked me, but it was also a wake-up call—and somehow, it felt right. I thought this advice to redirect my life was sacred; it was clear to me that it had come from somewhere deep. I felt clear about what I should do. I would have to face the reality of my broken marriage before my trip.

A month later, I called Seiji and told him I wanted a divorce. At the end of December, we signed the papers. Our marriage was over.

I was at the Tokyo Narita Airport, about to leave for the US. Many people from various departments and my family members came to bid me farewell, but Seiji wasn't there.

Time was ticking. I felt my tears trying to well up in my eyes, but I blinked them back. I didn't want to show any emotion.

I felt very sorry for how I'd comported myself over the last few years, and sorry for living in lies.

As soon as I stepped through into the security area, tears began to stream down my cheeks. I walked toward the gate without stopping. All my friends and family were gone. My life as I knew it had been wiped out. All my body's energy depleted, and my spirit occupied the emptiest place I'd ever known.

I was leaving the country I'd lived in all my life.

I won't ever live here again. I knew it in my heart.

As I flew high into the sky, I shed my armor, the protection I'd used for so long against my desperate loneliness, sadness, and vulnerability. I didn't want or need to cling to it any longer; it was part of the past I was leaving behind. I didn't know what might evolve from this empty shell—everything was unknown. But what I wished for was simply to live, to laugh, and to have a fresh start.

It was February 1990.

As I lost everything, I opened the door to a new life.

— 6 —
A New Life

I arrived in the US from Japan with just a couple of suitcases, ready to start anew. Everything I came across in my new home was foreign. My only previous experience in the US was a short trip to Chicago to present my research a few years earlier. Now was different: I wanted and needed to learn everything I could about living here in the States for good.

In Japan, I'd felt as dry as the desert. Now, I felt like a sponge. I wanted to absorb everything I might see, smell, hear, feel, and contemplate through all my senses, and transform them into nutrients for my soul and spirit.

I arrived at Washington's Dulles International Airport around one o'clock on February 3, 1990. My new supervisor, Nancy, a molecular biologist at the National Institute of Dental Research (NIDR, presently NIDCR), greeted me at the gate.

"Hey Kyo-om!" she shouted, waving at me with a big smile.

I didn't correct her. "Hello, Nancy," I said, smiling back. "Thank you for coming to pick me up." I was happy yet a little nervous to see her, finally, in person.

Nancy had a likable smile, a thin face, a prominent chin, and big blue eyes with long eyelashes that sparkled with kindness and curiosity. She put me immediately at ease.

After exchanging a few words, she was already leading me to the parking garage—walking slightly in front of me, talking quickly, her beautiful, long, blond hair bouncing rhythmically with every step. I found she wasn't bossy at all, just friendly. I already liked her.

Nancy drove us directly to a leasing office in an apartment building in Bethesda. We'd arranged in advance for a furnished apartment just a twenty-minute walk from the NIH for me to live in.

I signed the lease and got a key for my apartment, and that was it—in only ten minutes, I had my new place! I was amazed; in Japan, it would have taken a formal meeting that would've lasted at least one hour.

It was a studio, but roomy. At a glance, I saw the daily essentials were all equipped: a bed with two nightstands, a small desk and chair, a large chest of drawers, a big TV. In the separate kitchenette were a refrigerator, a microwave, an oven, and even a pot and some plates in the cabinets.

I was so happy; warmth rose in me and spread through my whole body. I was about to begin a novice's life in Bethesda.

As if sensing my emotions, Nancy hugged me.

The next morning, I poured myself a bowlful of Kellogg's Raisin Bran from a huge box (it seemed more than double the size of the ones I got in Japan), put in slices of banana and milk from a gigantic jar, and ate my first breakfast in Bethesda.

Nancy had told me to meet her at the lab at nine. Just to be safe, I left my apartment a little after eight o'clock.

I walked to the edge of the NIH campus, which was also huge. There were countless buildings, offices, and laboratories, all covered with orange-brown bricks and spread on hilly slopes of green grass. They were divided and connected through nicely S-shaped white concrete pathways. The smell of freshly cut grass filled my nostrils, then seeped into my chest.

I was amazed by the sizes of the buildings, the width of the roads—the scale of this country in general.

Within this huge campus, every building had a number on its façade denoting its address within the NIH. After some searching, I finally found Building 30, which would be my workplace for the next two years. It was a small building compared to the others I'd seen so far on the campus, particularly compared to the one behind our building—Building 10, the largest hospital in the world.

I took an elevator upstairs. The second floor's walls were all painted in pink and trimmed with light blue and ivory. It was Nancy's molecular biology laboratory and my new workplace.

I opened the heavy, pink metal door.

"Hey, Kyo-om! How are you doing?" Nancy met me with a big smile and a hug, then cheerfully introduced me to everyone in our department and many other people in the building, including the cleaning lady, Hyacinth. She was African American and wore white sneakers and a light blue polyester one-piece dress with a white collar and an apron—all part of her uniform. Hyacinth laughed a lot. Her easygoing optimism quickly made her my favorite person in Nancy's lab.

Later that morning, Nancy introduced me to her boss, Jim, the head of the NIDR.

Jim was big like an elephant, with thinning gray hair and a thick beard all around his jaw and neck. He wore glasses with very thick lenses, which made his big eyes seem to float, tiny, in the lenses. His presence and laugh were big and impressive. When Nancy told me his parents were from Italy, I immediately imagined the movie *The Godfather* and realized again how much I was being exposed to here in the States that hadn't been a part of my reality in Japan.

I was astonished when everyone in the building called Jim by his first name, without any title or prefix. *Don't they care about hierarchy?* I wondered, bewildered. I was still getting used to how things worked here in the States, so much more casual than back home.

The second surprise was that Jim, the head of the NIDR, basically spoke the same way Hyacinth did. In Japan, there are many ways to express junior and senior statuses conversationally. When Jim spoke about himself as "I," in the first person, I was almost knocked over. Everyone in this country referred to themselves that way—as "I." For people who know English as their only language, this is not revelatory, but in Japan we have many ways to refer to "I" that express differences not only in gender but also in hierarchy—levels of education, social status, age or seniority, and more. Speaking in Japanese comes with many layers of nuance, and if you speak too casually to someone who is senior to you, you're out of line—and maybe even out of a job.

My own experience of this adherence to hierarchy and formality in Japan was in part what had caused some of the serious conflicts and difficulties between who I was, who I wanted to be, and who I'd always felt I needed to be. So these experiences at work on the first day of my new job were incredibly eye-opening. They made me think more critically about the influences that a language brings—on cultures and on individuals—and deepened my appreciation for the commonality and humanity in all of us.

Within a couple of weeks, I got situated in my new environment—got used to the people around me and the system and how people seemed to work. But still, everything in each day was a learning experience.

I had to use English for all communication, and I often got stuck trying to express what I needed to say. Other times I kept quiet due to my lack of familiarity with the proper culture, customs, and social contexts; I didn't want to offend anyone.

At work, I learned everything by watching, following others, and reading articles. There was so much to learn and absorb. I kept my "dictionary" nearby, filled with new findings and surprises, and I was exhausted at the end of each day. But all the challenges were good for me. I enjoyed these myriad learning opportunities and managing my life as a "visiting" scientist from Japan. Living in the US had already affected me in a positive and constructive way, and I felt as if this experience had arrived to become my tutor in the world.

— 7 —
Falling in Love

My plan from the beginning was to stay in my furnished apartment near the NIH for just a couple of months, and then to find an apartment or a house to share with Americans so I could learn a "real" version of America through my senses and experiences.

After I felt a bit more settled in at work, I obtained a list of about thirty places for possible rentals from the Fogarty International Center—the place I'd gotten my fellowship from, and which supported the international researchers at the NIH—and started making calls. I thought it wouldn't take too long for me to find a place I would like.

I visited one or two homes every day after work for a couple of weeks, and by the first week in March, I'd seen twenty-two places for possible rent—none of them appealing. I kept going out on cold, windy, snowy evenings, only to find disappointment.

Around this time, I also signed up for a yoga class. I was eager to keep my feet on solid ground with something I knew well, and since I'd been practicing for years, it seemed like a perfect choice.

After class one evening, I mentioned to one of my yogi friends, Michi—a visiting scholar for a short program in psychology who was an assistant professor in one of the female-only colleges in

Japan—that I had plans to go see one of the last few options on the housing list. She offered to drive me, and I gratefully accepted.

As we approached the house, I saw a young, fit man in a white running shirt and red gym shorts through the front window. He seemed to be busy tidying up the house.

This was my first sight of Patrick; even before we spoke, I was somehow already intrigued by him. I felt his existence, as if this man already knew me and was speaking directly to my soul. I could tell he knew I was there. It was as if we were watching each other and talking directly before I even walked into the house. I was moved; whatever was happening here, it was spiritual and profound.

Michi, oblivious to the emotions taking hold of me, got out of her car before me and walked toward the house. She was acting like my big sister, as if protecting me was her responsibility. I let her lead, and did my best to catch up with her.

The house was large, with two big, beautiful oak trees in front. The one on the right, standing much taller than the other, penetrated through the wooden deck. The slate steppingstones, flanked by blooming pansies and crocuses, led us through the beautiful moist green grass to the front door. It seemed that the owners of this house cared about their garden, which gave me a positive impression.

Now Michi was knocking on the door.

Someone—I couldn't see who, but perhaps it was the young man?—opened the door without delay and Michi wedged herself into a narrow space between the edge of the door on the right side of her body and the doorframe on the left, blocking me from view.

"Hi, how are you?" Michi said.

"How do you do?" a man's voice answered. "May I help you?"

Michi kept the door halfway open so only she was visible to the man. Was she blocking me intentionally? I was puzzled.

"I've been looking for a house to share," she said. "Actually, I have an appointment today. The owner of this house has planned to show me a possible room for rent."

"The owners of the house aren't here at the moment, but they asked me to show you the room." The man's voice was gentle. "Are you KI-O-MI?" he asked, delivering his words with emphasis.

"Oh, no, *I* am not Kyomi, but she is here with me . . ."

And with that, Michi finally swung the door open and pulled me out from behind her.

I stepped forward and shyly introduced myself. "Hello, my name is Kyomi. Nice meeting you." I looked at him, extending my hand.

A brightness flashed across his face. "Wow . . . you are Kyomi! Nice to meet you. I'm Patrick." He shook my hand.

I felt a little bad for Michi, because Patrick was suddenly smiling widely and his voice was bouncing faster and more cheerfully than it had a few seconds before, when he hadn't seen me yet.

"Please, come on in!" He waved us inside.

Patrick's distinct British accent and conscientious politeness pleased me a lot. His neatly trimmed, short mustache balanced well with his strong jawline. His curly, soft brown hair was trimmed horizontally in front of his ears, but the rest came down comfortably, touching his forehead and long, thick neck. Cute.

He was about six feet tall and very fit, with a broad chest under his running shirt. It was obvious that he worked out regularly. He gave me the impression that he was very tidy and well-disciplined, and I appreciated his kind, detail-oriented approach to showing me the house.

The available room was upstairs. The room was charming, filled with gentle sunlight. The homeowners had recently painted the walls in a sweet, light French vanilla color. Through one of the windows, I could see the branches of one of the big oak trees, which were almost within reach of the window, swinging with the wind and catching the light peacefully.

Patrick showed us around and even took us to see his room in the basement. I liked the openness of the house—I found it inviting and uplifting.

Almost immediately after the tour, I made up my mind to rent the room. I called the owners, Paul and Elli, to let them know that I'd like to move in at the end of March.

The following week, I visited the house to meet Paul and Elli in person and sign the contract.

They were a nice, kind, and easy-going couple. Paul was an American MD working at the NIH's downtown Washington DC location. He was skinny, with moderately balding blond hair and a thick, ginger-colored beard and mustache. He talked fast and joked a lot (I didn't get many of his jokes). Elli was from Finland, had completed a master's course in the States, and was working with special needs children at an elementary school. She spoke even faster than Paul and with a Swedish accent—her words sounded to me like darting birds. She had a blond bob, and her eyes changed color—from dark brown to hazel to light blue—depending on what she was looking at. When she spoke, I stared at her eyes with curiosity. I'd never seen someone's eye color change like that; in Japan, everyone's eyes were either dark brown or black.

For this visit, Patrick had baked dessert: peach cream cheese strudel.

"I baked this for you," he said.

I couldn't help but blush.

I was so grateful for his hospitality, and I meant to taste a piece. But I was so nervous all night that I never even took a bite.

After I moved in, Patrick was always kind to me and tried to have more conversations with me than any of our other house mates did. We got to know each other very quickly.

"I have six brothers and three sisters," he told me early on.

My eyes widened. "So many!"

He laughed. "I know, it's a typical Irish family. We even have twins, Sean and Adam."

"It must have been tough for your mom to raise so many kids," I said, shaking my head. "How many years' difference between the youngest and the eldest?"

"Hmm . . . let me see . . . at least fifteen years, I guess. Andy is the eldest, and Brenda and me . . ." he said slowly, still calculating the age difference.

I pictured a younger version of Patrick helping his siblings in his household, and the thought made me smile.

We were fairly close in age, but I learned during one of these conversations that he was three years younger than me.

He often invited his friends to the house—mostly international post-doc fellows or American lab technicians—and while they were there, he always took care of their needs and joked a lot, trying to make them feel at home. I thought he was born to be in this kind of service.

Though Patrick was younger than Paul, he was much more mature and practical than our landlord. Paul was smart and talkative, and once the conversation became a little controversial he tended to become sharp with criticism. Patrick, in contrast, was gentle; he could always mediate such conversations, even if he didn't like what Paul was saying.

As I observed Patrick more, I noticed that efficiency defined his life. As soon as he got up at 7:00 a.m., he turned *Good Morning America* on and got in the shower. He ate breakfast and left the house before seven thirty every morning. I could always predict what time he would leave his work, go to the gym, come back home, eat, watch TV, etc. He went to the grocery store, cleaned his room, and did laundry and ironing on specific days of the week. While ironing, he always put on Fox Sports or listened to CNN World news or C-span on the radio. I'd never seen anyone so organized in my life.

One Wednesday evening, Patrick was ironing in the basement while watching the football game on his TV. The dryer was still tumbling another load of clothes.

I knocked and came in. "Excuse me, Patrick. I'm wondering if I can do my laundry after you."

"Sure, Kyomi," he said. "I've already finished with the washer—it's all yours."

"Thank you. Oh, by the way . . . I've just bought spray starch for ironing. Do you want to try it?"

"Sure! I'll try it."

I handed over the bottle and he tried it immediately.

"Oh, this is fantastic!" he enthused. "I really like it. I just used it for my shirt collars and it worked very well—thank you!"

"I'll leave the bottle here so you can use it any time," I offered, my cheeks growing warm. It felt good to do something for him—even something as small as a little spray starch.

I wanted to know him better.

—

In our home, Patrick took the initiative on everything from domestic issues to interactions and entertainment with friends. Though it was Paul and Elli's house, Patrick was in many ways the leader, mediator, and organizer of the household.

He also tried to help me in many small ways to adjust to the life-style in this country. He guided me to effectively use the Fogarty International Center, helped me prepare for my driver's license test, and guided me through the steps to get health insurance.

I soon grasped that Patrick must have acquired his sense of lead-ership early in his childhood; that he had served a similar role in his own family. I also learned that behind his easy-going attitude, he was a very serious, earnest, and disciplined person. I quickly developed both empathy and admiration for the person he was showing himself to be.

Because of his sense of responsibility and his fun-loving lifestyle, Patrick often hosted parties and had people over to watch American and English football games over drinks, not only during weekends but also on some weekdays. During the games, he and his friends would wear their favorite teams' uniforms. For Patrick it was always red for Manchester United. They would go crazy as they watched, shouting and singing their country's name and dancing and jumping around with excitement.

Paul and Elli were enthusiastic participants at these parties. I attended as well, though for me it was more out of a sense of obligation and friendship as a housemate. Not that I didn't enjoy socializing, but watching sports and drinking beer weren't my favorite things to do. I missed the quiet time I'd enjoyed while living alone—listening to classical music or jazz, or reading books.

One day in mid-April, Paul, Elli, Patrick, and I went to a sushi restau-rant in Bethesda. As I poured soy sauce from a small container, a drop spilled onto the counter. I wiped it up with tissue paper, then folded the paper neatly and quietly placed it underneath the container for future use.

I looked up to see Patrick watching me.

He smiled. "You're the first person I've ever seen do that before," he said. "I love it."

"Oh," I whispered as I met his gaze and returned his smile. I was gratified that he appreciated this small example of my mindfulness and consideration toward others.

We kept looking at each other for a while, communicating our quiet admiration to each other through our eyes. Now that he'd acknowledged such a subtle quality in me, I suddenly saw that we shared this mindfulness as a common value.

I loved America's vastness, wilderness, boldness, diversity, and generosity. But the sensibilities in this country were quite different from those in Japan, and I was still accustoming myself to them. I now held a new appreciation for my home country—and that night at the sushi restaurant, I missed Japan.

I wasn't quite fluent in speaking English at this point, and sometimes I couldn't express as much as I wanted. So it sometimes felt that nobody in the US truly knew who I was or what my thoughts were. In Japan, there is an appreciation for just being in silence—sharing quiet moments to get to know each other. But in the States, individuality is emphasized everywhere. It seemed to me that my quiet, delicate, more subtle way of being was often swallowed up by all the noise. But Patrick appeared to understand that there was more to me.

That's why although that exchange over the spilled soy sauce was just a tiny moment, it meant everything to me. In Patrick, I felt as if I'd found my first real friend and ally in this country.

—

Toward the end of May, two and a half months into my living at the house, Elli finished with school and left with Paul for a summer vacation in Finland for one and a half months. Patrick and I were left in the house alone, just the two of us.

I gradually realized how little Patrick paid attention to eating and to food. He made a sandwich every evening to bring it the next day for work, but it was always simple and mechanically assembled: just a couple of slices of bread and ham, a slice of tomato, cucumber, and dash of mayonnaise, all purchased from a large local grocer, Super Giants.

To me, that sandwich represented Patrick's humble lifestyle. Something about the simple fare made me feel more tender and affectionate toward him. I wanted to share "my kind" of sandwiches with him, and hopefully enrich his life.

So, one day, I drove to one of the best local bakeries in Bethesda and purchased some homemade bread, and the next morning I made two sandwiches: one for me and the other for Patrick. I shredded the oregano chicken I'd roasted the night before, thinly sliced some celery, and mixed in mayonnaise, zest of orange, salt, pepper, and a dash of curry powder. I sliced the fresh pumpernickel bread I'd bought, spread four pieces with butter and mayonnaise, and assembled both sandwiches with plenty of the chicken salad and green lettuce. Then I cut them in half, wrapped them in napkins, and put them in Ziploc bags.

When Patrick came into the kitchen to pick up his sandwich from the refrigerator that he'd prepared the night before, I held out a lunch bag containing the sandwich, along with bags of red grapes and baby carrots.

"Here's a sandwich for you," I said. "I hope you like it."

Puzzled, he peeked into the bag. "Oh, wow! For me? Wow, Kyomi... you're so kind, thank you!"

"You're very welcome," I said cheerfully. "It didn't take any time . . .
I was making one for myself anyway."

"Thank you, Kyomi! I really appreciate it." He looked so happy. "I
wish I could stay and talk more, but I have to dash out for a meeting."
His face fell a little.

"No problem!" I said. "We'll see each other tonight."

I was in a good mood all day.

That evening, as soon as Patrick walked through the door in his gym
clothes, he came straight to me in the living room.

"Thank you so much for the beautiful sandwich! It was so tasty.
I've never had a sandwich like that before."

"Oh, I'm glad you liked it," I said, beaming.

"No, I *loved* it!" he said. "I went shopping today; I'd love to cook
something for you tonight as a thank you."

From that day on, we ate dinner together whenever possible, and
I continued to make sandwiches for both of us every day—usually
something using leftovers from whatever I'd cooked the night before
for dinner. It was a labor of love; I enjoyed doing it.

But soon it became more than sandwiches for both of us.

Before I came to the States, I'd sent for a compact stereo system and
a currency converter from Japan. I liked listening to classical music
or jazz, like Bill Evans and Keith Jarret, on my stereo. Patrick, in contrast, loved UB40, Phil Collins, Sade, and reggae music. He did enjoy
jazz, but classical music had never been in his genre. Soon we began
to exchange lots of our favorite things with one another.

We began sharing most parts of our lives with one another. I'd
already loved cooking and decorating the house with fresh flowers,
but now doing those things became an expression of my love and

care for Patrick. I cooked almost every day and evening, even if just something simple, and shared every meal with him. He, meanwhile, offered me generous support and showed me things he'd learned. Whenever I needed something, Patrick had good ideas for where I could find it. When I purchased something, he was always willing to help me carry it in.

We had a strong synergy, and we could both see it. Something deep and meaningful was growing between us.

One night in mid-June, as I set the table, Patrick lit a tea candle on our plain IKEA dining table. He dimmed the overhead light in the dining area, and we sat at the table. He said grace softly before we began our meal.

The light flickering from the candle created a cozier and more intimate environment than we'd ever experienced together before. We ate quietly, appreciating this world of silence. Inside, though, my heart kept pulsating faster and faster, and I found it difficult to rein in my expanding emotions.

I chewed rather mechanically, trying not to look up because I knew I was blushing and I could sense that his eyes were fixed on me.

Then Patrick extended his hand across the table and gently placed it over mine.

My body reacted with a subtle movement, like a small, frightened rabbit. My heart leapt. It was the first time he'd ever held my hand.

"I've been hoping you'd like to go somewhere for dinner with me," he said gently.

I stopped my inner clock for a second, took his words into my deeper place, and consulted with my inner judge: *Should I allow myself to open to the possibilities between us?*

My inner voice said, *Yes!*

A second later, I said it aloud: "Yes."

Patrick grinned.

I felt my heart begin to pump fresh blood throughout my body, and emotions that had stagnated for years began to flow once again. I hadn't had this invigorating feeling for many years—perhaps since Hiro.

That weekend, Patrick took me out on our first date. We went to Alexandria, Virginia—a beautiful port town situated alongside the Potomac River, rich in history.

Patrick was romantic and escorted me in a gentlemanly manner everywhere we went. His voice held warmth, care, and love when he spoke. In the evening, we had a wonderful Cajun dinner, a first for me. It was a stew of smoky sausage, onion, vegetables, and rock shrimp with garlic and distinct spicy seasonings. The restaurant was decorated in a rustic, warm, old-fashioned, French-influenced style. From the draperies to napkins, all the raw, vivid colors of the decor made the atmosphere even warmer and more inviting. I liked how lively the place was, but it was a little noisy.

Luckily, Patrick felt the same way.

"Let's go outside," he said as soon as he paid the bill.

I nodded in agreement and we headed for the door.

"It's nice to be out . . . just the two of us," he said sweetly as we walked toward the river. He curled his arm gently around my waist. The sensation made my heart beat even faster than it already was. I felt a melting sensation in my heart.

I feel like kissing him, I thought.

Then the mixture of the spicy, rich foods and the drinks from dinner caught up with me. "I'm sorry, Patrick," I said, "but I feel sick

. . ." I darted behind one of the nearby buildings and threw up. My head was spinning.

"I'm sorry . . . I'm sorry . . ." I kept apologizing. I was so embarrassed; I felt I'd ruined the evening.

Patrick drove us back home, with me apologizing all along the way. My brain just wouldn't stop spinning; when we arrived home, I went straight to my bathroom and threw up again.

Our first night out was over. I'd ruined our first date, an experience I'd hoped would be one of the best, most memorable days of my life.

Patrick would laugh about this occasion for years to come.

Patrick and I wanted to be together all the time. We often ate lunch together at work, and as soon as we came home we acted like a pair of lovebirds that had been separated for a long time. We were like "adult teenagers." We held hands all the time. I felt the connection between us when our hands were clasped, as if my blood were circulating not only within my body but also in Patrick's. Our hands felt like the chargers of our interconnected energy, augmenting our mutual vitality and happiness.

At the end of June, an iWD workshop took me to New York for a weekend.

I'd previously attended a dozen of their classes and/or workshops in Japan, but since my move to the States I'd been only infrequently in touch with them.

I'd signed up to attend this workshop before moving into the house with Patrick. Now, I wasn't sure if I wanted to attend: iWD no longer figured as importantly in my life, and I would miss Patrick. But when

I learned that several friends who I'd known in Japan would be there, I decided to attend.

I enjoyed the reunion with my friends from the olden days at the workshop, and experienced some good awakening moments over the weekend. I was reminded how I'd been in Japan and how I was here in the States, and I felt a renewed gratitude for my new life. I felt I'd begun to heal, find myself, and build the life I really wanted.

But I also couldn't stop thinking about Patrick. As I thought how important he'd already become in my life, the ripples from the epicenter of my heart grew larger and larger, and I couldn't stop the waves. The workshop became less meaningful to me. Two days without seeing Patrick felt like forever.

We had made a plan for him to pick me up at the end of the weekend. As soon as the workshop was over, I rushed to where we'd agreed to meet.

I saw him waiting outside the entrance, bathed in sunlight. The light was everywhere on him; his long eyelashes and eyebrows, bleached by the sun, shone as if nymphs were dancing around them. His blue eyes were much bluer than usual, clear and sacred.

I ran to him and we held each other tight. Then I kissed him on his lips.

As our lips touched, the world exploded into an infinite universe, and I knew.

I was in *love*.

– 8 –
Becoming Us

A few days after the iWD workshop, Patrick organized a big gathering at the Mall in Washington DC for the Fourth of July with his sister, Brenda, her husband, James, and their three-month-old baby, Katie. It would be our first Independence Day together.

Patrick and I drove to the Mall at eight o'clock in the morning. We situated ourselves on the West Lawn of the US Capitol, with the Washington Monument and Reflecting Pool to our left, and covered the ground around us with blankets to reserve the space for our friends.

This was a place I'd only known from the movies back in Japan. Though the concert would be held around eight o'clock at night, hundreds of people were already here—moving around, carrying chairs and coolers, and even setting up gazebos.

While Brenda and Katie staked out our spot, Patrick, James, and I carried loads from the car—foldable chairs, a beach umbrella, large coolers, ice bags, food, and drinks.

A few hours later, Paul and Elli showed up with a large portable BBQ grill and their own cooler. Several groups of our coworkers and other friends arrived one by one with their dishes, desserts, and packs of beer and other drinks. Everyone was wearing red, white, and blue.

As more and more people gathered, the sense of excitement in the atmosphere grew. Near us, a group of kids tossed a football and a Frisbee back and forth. I saw kids and adults hula-hooping, and a stand where kids were getting their faces painted. A middle-aged man in a clown costume was shaping animals out of colorful balloons in yellow, orange, red, blue, and white. Each time the clown made cracking sounds by twisting the balloons into fun shapes, the kids jumped, giggled, laughed, and shouted with unstoppable joy.

We were all gathered together to do the same thing: barbecue, eat, drink, laugh, chat, and enjoy the day. *We are just one of the many*, I thought to myself. Somehow, everyone at the Mall felt like part of our extended family that day, and I marveled at the diversity I saw.

Paul and Elli had just returned from their vacation in Finland the evening before, and this was the first time they'd seen Patrick and me together. We'd left home before they got up that day.

"Patrick, did I miss something? You both seem . . . I mean . . . *closer* . . ." Paul asked, his facial muscles pulled tight.

Patrick just smiled.

"What exactly happened while we were gone?" Paul was now half-laughing, seemingly in ridicule.

Elli opened her eyes wide in surprise, then pulled the corner of Paul's T-shirt for him to stop.

Patrick took my hand in his. "Yes, we're together, Paul."

Paul clearly wanted to say more, but Elli took him elsewhere.

Paul kept talking about our newly developing relationship for the rest of the day. He seemed almost upset by it.

I wondered why.

As it got darker, we all felt the anticipation of something special—the concert, followed by fireworks!

I'd seen fireworks almost every summer in Japan, but this was my first time seeing Fourth of July fireworks. I imagined it would be spectacular, and I'd brought my camera; I was looking forward to capturing some impressive shots.

Now the orchestra started. Light pop music led us to a more uplifted mood. The music brought us not only the enjoyment of music but also the sense of *us*—in unity, connectivity, and commonality.

When "America the Beautiful" and "God Bless America" were sung, many of us stood up, sang along, and held each other. I didn't yet know the lyrics, but I hummed along and interjected a word here or there. Then came Dvorak's "New World," followed by Tchaikovsky's 1812 overture. Toward the end of the piece, spectacular fireworks erupted as if the earth behind the Washington Monument had just cracked open. Hundreds of dazzling colorful sparkling fireworks lit up the sky and white smoke began to accumulate over the Potomac River, creeping toward us, filling our nostrils with the smell of gunpowder.

In the darkness, expansive warmth bloomed in my chest and tears fell on my cheeks. It was a profound, beautiful feeling. Patrick and I looked at each other at the same moment, pulled each other close, and kissed one another on the lips.

I felt in that moment that everyone at the Mall was collectively reaching something bigger than any one of us: humanity and love. Being there reminded me of my aching desire since my childhood to know what my life was meant to be. The tears came, and I let myself cry, which surprised me; usually I didn't like to cry in front of anyone. But since I'd moved to the States, I'd noticed I'd begun to allow myself to feel whatever I was feeling—and it was liberating. How long had I prohibited myself from feeling my emotions? Now I was coming alive, and I felt overwhelmed with hope.

As Patrick and I walked back to his car later that night, I promised to myself quietly yet firmly that I would do whatever it took to build up my own self, become a person I could count on. Then I would try to use that truer version of myself to do something good for humanity.

I knew that I'd already begun to restore myself; with the help of Patrick's love and care, the tight knots inside me were beginning to loosen up. With growing hope, I squeezed Patrick's hand softly. He responded with a gentle yet firm squeeze back.

Several days later, Patrick told me about a dream he'd had months earlier, before we met.

"I knew you were going to come to look for a room a week before you called Paul for that appointment," he told me. "I dreamt that an Asian woman came here looking for a room to rent, and I immediately knew in the dream she would one day become my wife—that she was my destiny."

I wasn't surprised when he disclosed this dream because of how I'd intuited that Patrick felt he already knew me when I arrived that first evening. Now his reaction made more sense to me.

"I'll never forget the first day we met," he went on. "Including what you were wearing—a light-weight blue jean shirt and pants and Fatimah's hand around your neck."

"As you know, the word 'Fatimah' comes from the name of a sister of Muhammad, founder of Islam and a prophet of God," I said. "I know it's very important to us. I believe Fatimah has brought us together in this present life."

"We must have shared past lives," Patrick said, nodding. "As long as you wear this necklace, I will always find you. I want you to carry it always, even to the next life."

I promised I would.

—

That July, I began to contemplate many things about my past. Before coming to the States, I'd been hiding inside my armor. My existence had been like the desert, devoid of love for so long.

But ever since Patrick had come into my life, his love and support had been like a spring of glacial water, nurturing me with essential nutrition. In our daily life, he was always protecting me, looking after me. His love and support were unconditional, and were helping me both heal my wounds and grow and transform further.

I thought about my ex-husband, Seiji, and how he'd taken advantage of the fact that I dwelled in my protective armor. I hated that Seiji and his ego used the damage and scars I'd held to keep me trapped in our relationship. I'd thought it was love at the time, but I now understood that it was more like possession.

Now, because of Patrick, I began to fully trust and respect someone for the first time in my life. I also felt encouraged that I might become a person who I could trust—a person who could love someone else with true conviction.

That summer we built our relationship together, one day at a time.

Since I'd first met Patrick in March, he'd treated me like his princess, and I'd treated him as my king.

The problem with this dynamic was that I wasn't always honest with him. Though I wanted to, I sometimes couldn't express my honest feelings, which sometimes left important issues unresolved.

This dishonesty wasn't only because of my language barrier but also due to my conditioning. I was usually able to get at the heart of any problem internally, but my upbringing had discouraged me from directly expressing true feelings in communications with others. Those unresolved issues would pile up, along with their associated emotions and fears, and when I finally got up the courage to try to express myself honestly, it usually resulted in my sobbing, releasing all those pent-up feelings.

The first time I experienced a crying episode like this with Patrick was in late July, right after his thirtieth birthday. We were still living in Paul and Elli's house and Patrick had organized his own birthday party there, hosting two sets of Agatha Christie's "murder mystery nights" over fabulous dinners.

The party was seamless, impressive, and fantastic—far beyond what anyone had imagined. After everyone left, there was nobody but us left to clean the post-party mess. Paul and Elli had already gone to bed upstairs. I felt sorry for Patrick, who'd hosted his own thirtieth birthday party and done all the work by himself.

I helped him tidy the rooms, clean dishes, and begin the dishwasher.

All of a sudden, Patrick got emotional, talking about the people who'd just left. It was unusual for Patrick to complain about his friends, but tonight he unleashed his feelings. "I am the only one who ever organizes a party," he fumed. "No one offered to do anything to help." His shoulders slumped.

"But you had a wonderful time," I said, hoping to cheer him up. "And it was perfect. Nobody could've done it as wonderfully as you did." I wanted him to focus on how amazing the party had been.

"The Fourth of July picnic on the Mall was the same," he continued, undeterred. "I organized everything for that."

As his words sank in, I realized that maybe he was also disappointed with *me*, though he hadn't named me. Had I contributed anything in these events he'd organized, besides helping to clean up? Maybe Patrick felt that something was missing in our relationship because of my lack of initiative.

Patrick always treated me as if I were something special, precious, and fragile. Now, I realized that playing the role of a special "ornament" meant that I wasn't pulling my weight. He seemed to be happy with me, but now I imagined his feelings were leaking out about me, not just about his friends, and I felt some pressure to act more proactively.

As I analyzed this scenario in more detail, however, I realized I was already under too much pressure to handle—the pressure to entertain so many people all the time. I didn't really like the constant parties Patrick organized. I appreciated all he'd done for me, but I would have preferred to spend my time differently—more quietly, and without alcohol involved.

Of course I hadn't told Patrick even once in the past that I needed more quiet in my life. He didn't even know what my preferences were, because I never asserted them.

As I was contemplating all this, my unsaid feelings burst out of their cage and all of a sudden I broke down crying. The pressure I'd been holding inside my chest for some time needed to be released.

"What's wrong? What's wrong?" he asked, lost.

I took a deep breath. It was time to be honest.

"I've appreciated all that you've done for me . . . introducing a lot of people, places, parties, and so on . . . whatever you've tried to share with me," I said slowly. "Please do not take this in the wrong way, but I haven't always felt like my feet were on the ground. I don't think all the things you've introduced to me are always my favorite things to do."

I watched as his jaw dropped in disbelief.

"For example, I don't even drink." Finally, I was able to say the *truth*.

I saw a vacant gray hole, a sadness, growing at the center of Patrick's face.

"I thought you enjoyed that stuff. Honestly, I've done everything for you." He hunched over a little as he said this.

I felt sorry for him, and regretful, but I knew that I had to come clean. "Yes. I've appreciated your efforts, but most of the time I've just felt I need to follow. The pressure has been always on my shoulders."

I spelled out what I'd truly wanted to share with him.

Patrick was frozen with shock for a number of minutes. To me, it felt like forever. I didn't want to lose him. Was this moment of honesty going to destroy our relationship?

Finally, he said, "I am sorry for how you've been feeling. I didn't know that at all. But it won't happen like that anymore. I promise I will make efforts to make you feel better."

This was my first experience of the power of honesty, and of feeling wholly accepted for who I was. It was an incredible feeling.

From that night onward, Patrick listened. We participated in fewer big group activities, and when Patrick did invite people over, he offered me other options, encouraging me to do my own thing if I wasn't in the mood for socializing. He also never again insisted that I drink any alcohol.

Without saying a word about it, Patrick took all these actions with decisive commitment. As he did, I began to feel even more supported and encouraged by him than I had before. We both started to become more compassionate toward one another. And as we began to spend and appreciate more time apart, we cherished our shared moments even more and our relationship deepened.

In this way, we began to build common ground—little by little, step by step. As I was building my own self up, Patrick was doing the same, which led us to become stronger and better as a couple. We were becoming *us*.

— 9 —

Married Life

One late morning in early October, Patrick and I went to a nearby park for a picnic lunch. The sun was kind, and the morning dew sparkled. As we got situated on the blanket, Patrick suddenly said, "What do you think about moving out of Paul and Elli's house soon?"

This was something we'd been talking about for a while. I nodded. "Yes, I think it's time."

"They're not going to be happy about it," Patrick said.

It had been seven months since Patrick and I had first met. Since his birthday at the end of July, Patrick and I had grown more and more serious. Before, Paul and Elli had been somewhat been dependent on Patrick. Now they had to accept us as "the couple" tenants, which they were clearly struggling with.

"Yes," I said. "It will be difficult for them."

Patrick shrugged. "They need to be responsible for their own lives."

"I know," I said, nodding again.

"They need to sort out their own problems," he reiterated. "We need to be out of their issues."

The closer Patrick and I became, the more evident the friction between Paul and Elli had become. Loud verbal fights. Arguments over small, tedious things at the dinner table where they leaned toward us, making us judge who was right.

"A lot of things to think about," I said carefully. I agreed with Patrick that we should remove ourselves from our current living situation.

But moving out meant something else I wasn't sure I was ready for: commitment. This decision would affect my future, his future, and *our* future. Was I ready for it?

After Patrick and I returned home from our picnic, Patrick left to check on an experiment at work. I lay on the bed, legs stretched out, and contemplated—drifted into a hidden corner of my mind.

My past. It was the biggest of all my concerns. Relationship building with Patrick hadn't been linear or straightforward because of my baggage. I still remembered the sense of darkness I'd felt not so long ago. How could I be sure that I'd finished with all these things and was now ready for Patrick? That I wouldn't make the same mistakes I'd made in the past? I still kept my old wedding album—it was the symbol of my failed marriage, and my past guilt and shame. I never opened it, but I knew it was there. I still had a sense of self-imposed punishment for what I'd done to my first husband.

Since leaving Japan, I'd lived my life looking forward. I'd built my new world from scratch. Patrick had been my strength throughout this process; his unconditional love and support had been the source of my restoration and become the foundation of further transformation. But I couldn't pretend that my past never happened.

I thought about fear. What was I afraid of?

Since childhood, I'd been afraid that someone might hurt me, insult me, or intimidate me. Papa and his family's direct insults and

Mama's repetitive imprinting had made me fear my unworthiness and shame—no matter how well I behaved, no matter how thick my armor was. Then I'd begun to fear that I'd be trapped in my armor for the rest of my life. In this way, I'd allowed myself to be controlled and enslaved by the past and my ego.

When we experience a hurtful event, it plants the impact of the event inside us. Once it's repeated, our memory of that past painful event can become a seed or mother of another fear, multiplying the original event into "repetitive impacts." Then we start to fear the next thing, and the next, and so on. In this way, fear proliferates, poisoning our mind.

To overcome my fears, I knew I needed to trust myself and this ongoing process. If I focused on the past and allowed my ego to unnecessarily punish me at this point of my life, I would destroy my chance to build a new life with Patrick.

I hoped that someday I might fully heal from the wounds of my past, but even if I didn't, that was okay with me. I could still commit to living in the present, rather than the past.

Patrick was right: we should move out of Paul and Elli's house, and start our life together for just the two of us.

It really was time.

A few days after our picnic at Rock Creek Park, Paul and Elli went to Paul's parents' house for dinner, so Patrick and I had the house to ourselves.

As we finished dinner, I took Patrick's hand in mine. "Let's move out of this house and start our own life," I told him.

His face brightened with happiness. He stood up and hugged me tight, as if he couldn't stop his overflowing happiness; then we looked into each other's eyes, kissed on the lips, and embraced again, the only sound in the room our heartbeats.

This was how it should be. Just the two of us.

We needed to give Paul and Elli one month's notice.

Patrick didn't waste much time. The very night they came back from dinner, he sat them down.

"Kyomi and I have been thinking about this for a while . . . finding our own place. We haven't decided where to move yet, but we'd like to let you know that we might be moving out sometime in mid-November."

Though they might have anticipated or feared this, they both appeared to be totally shocked.

"That's good . . . congratulations!" they said one after the other. But they were unsuccessful in hiding their sadness. Their eyes were watery, and they had trouble making eye contact with us.

Tearful myself, I told them, "Thank you for your love, kind care and support since we moved here. This has been our home. Both of you have offered whatever is available in your genuine hearts from the beginning of our lives in the States, and our relationship."

They were blinking back tears.

"We're still going to be in the neighborhood," Patrick said. "Let's continue to grow our friendship."

Several weeks later, we moved to a two-bedroom condo just a few miles north off I-495 and Rockville pike—our first sweet home.

Valentine's Day the following year marked the one-year anniversary since my arrival to the States. Patrick and I had been living in our condo since autumn. Our relationship had become more secure and steady during that time.

That evening, Patrick decorated the dining table with two-dozen long-stemmed red roses in a glass vase, and even cooked a special meal: poached salmon with fresh dill and caper cream sauce. He laid the table beautifully, and put soft music on in the background. The lights were turned low and long, dipped candles were lit on the table.

"How beautiful," I noted. I sensed something was coming.

Patrick led me to the living room, and we started to dance.

"Will you marry me?" he asked me softly.

I looked at his eyes, radiating profound love and solid conviction about our future.

"Yes." I looked down, blushing. Patrick raised my chin and we kissed each other. A few tears fell from my eyes. We didn't need to speak or ask anything more; we just embraced.

We already knew, when we'd decided to move out of Paul and Elli's house, that we were going to build and nurture our lives together, no matter what circumstances might occur. Since we'd met, there had been no looking back.

"This last year has been the happiest time of my life," Patrick told me. "I've felt as if I were born in the wrong family since I was a child."

I looked up and gazed into his eyes. "So did I."

"Though I have brothers and sisters, I've often felt I was a stranger to them all; I've been lonely in my life in both England and the States."

I knew that feeling, because I'd lived all my life like that too. What Patrick and I needed was each other, *us*, for the rest of our lives. I thought of us, and how I was in our relationship. In our short time together, I'd been able to create a life that I actually liked. I could sense that I was being myself and building something that mattered to me. Now I began to feel more able to envision our future together.

In April 1991, after Patrick and I got engaged, Patrick showed me some information he'd received about applying for a green card. Both of us had already been granted J-1 visas for our stays in the States, which guaranteed our stays from the initial two years to up to five years—until the end of 1993 and 1995, respectively. Now Patrick wanted to apply for a lottery to become a legal permanent resident in the United States.

The US government grants some foreign, mainly professional people their legal permanent immigration status through lotteries each year. A much higher number of people from England receive green cards through this process compared to those from Japan—but after we both applied, I, not Patrick, was the one who received a card.

I completed all the paperwork to process a legal immigration and finally received a green card alone in the beginning of 1992. (Around that time, Patrick's visa status was elevated to H-1, the dual-intent professional visa, which we knew would later allow him to apply for a green card by himself, supported by the NIH. Accordingly, we didn't have to hurry to get married just so he could get his green card.)

In this miraculous way, even before our marriage, I became a legal alien, a green card holder in my new country. This wonderful turnout made me feel that someone or something invisible yet powerful must have helped me yet again.

On April 24, 1993, twenty-six months after getting engaged, Patrick and I finally got married. His brother-in-law, James, who had been a minister of the Dutch Reformed Church, married us at his church in New Jersey.

Our close friends—Nancy, Elli, Emilie, and their spouses; and George and his fiancée, Mary; and Patrick's sister Brenda and her daughter, Katie—all attended our intimate celebration. Patrick's dad, his older brother, Andy, and two of his younger siblings, John and Shauna, also joined our wedding from England.

As for my family—I never expected that they'd come for my

wedding. Practically speaking, it was taking place in America, where they'd never visited before. And this would be my second marriage. I knew that my sisters had their own lives to focus on, juggling their lives with their young kids, all under the age of seven.

But beyond these logistical questions, I knew our family dynamics must be playing a role as well. When I'd left Japan three years earlier after my "abrupt" divorce from Seiji, my family must have felt very strange about my departure to the US—perhaps even abandoned.

So now, even though they said they were happy for me, I suspected that my decision to marry Patrick and stay in the US confirmed for them their sense of abandonment by me. I thought about this constantly. I knew my sisters wanted me to share the responsibility of looking after Mama. Did they want me back in Japan?

I felt guilty, but I wasn't going back. I needed to stick with my wish to forge this life with Patrick in the United States. I'd spent my whole past life pleasing and serving the people around me, and it had almost destroyed me. Now, I'd committed to mending my scars, healing from them, and creating my own path. I wouldn't change my course of action. I'd found my life here with Patrick. I was not yet ready to talk to my family about these truths, but one day soon, I would.

— 10 —
Changes

Right after our marriage in the spring of 1993, I felt I was standing on more solid ground. My feet were planted in my shared life with Patrick. We were happy. We solidified our friendships with many friends and colleagues.

In this "normal" life, however, I'd begun to recognize a little anxiety growing inside of me about my career. I hadn't told anyone yet, but I'd begun to reevaluate research as my permanent path.

Within a short period of time, I had experienced many important life events: my initial adjustment to living in the US; meeting Patrick; moving; obtaining a green card; getting engaged and married. Now, for the first time in years, I had time and space to think more seriously about what I could do in my work life that would better fulfill my inner world. The thought of changing what I was doing started to feel like a call from my being.

Our jobs, of course, were our source of income, the anchor of our lives, and the basis for all the connections we'd built together in our lives here in the States. Because of this, I worried that perhaps it would be too difficult for me to even bring up the subject of this degree of change with Patrick.

I decided to wait for a while.

In early April 1994, before our one-year anniversary, Patrick and I purchased a new home in Germantown, twenty-five miles north of Bethesda. We both were still working at the NIH, but with a longer commute every day.

We also were committed to enjoying our lives. Patrick often went fishing at local lakes like Little Seneca Lake or Clopper Lake. In a long chest wader, his favorite angler's fishing cap, and a khaki vest with lots of pockets and a pincushion with a few of his favorite flies on his chest, he'd set out in a good mood and come home happy—though never with any fish, because he was practicing "catch and release." Sometimes I joined him and watched him in his quiet satisfaction.

My passion was home decorating with hand-sewed draperies and crafts and fresh flower arrangements. I also continued my monthly camera club gatherings and went out sometimes with Patrick or other times alone to take photos. Our life seemed to be smooth sailing.

In mid-May, one late morning, I was home alone and sitting in bed reading Stephen Covey's *The Seven Habits of Highly Effective People* when I came across a passage that sharply penetrated my heart:

"In your mind's eye, see yourself going to the funeral of a loved one. Picture yourself driving to the funeral parlor, or chapel . . . As you walk down to the front of the room and look inside the casket, you suddenly come face to face with yourself. This is your funeral, three years from today."

When I read the paragraph, tears welled up in my eyes. "Begin with The End in Mind." I knew exactly what part of my life this specific message referred to. Even though I'd known I wanted to change careers, I'd prioritized other things, delaying facing what I'd wanted. Now it was time to face my calling.

—

In the following days, I began to contemplate what it would take to make the change I was considering. I needed to reevaluate things and play out possible scenarios.

I loved research, which was about finding truth in the invisible world. Doing basic research was like finding a key and then using it to open a new door. But there were aspects of my job that I didn't like. My work at the lab was very competitive, and it required me to work weekends. I was also as far removed as I could be from directly serving patients. It had become difficult for me to focus on my goals; I felt very out of balance when it came to what I wanted to do and what I actually did in my daily work.

When I was in Japan, I had always worked part time as a dentist in a clinic, working with underserved communities, in addition to doing research. I'd found the work particularly fulfilling. In the States, I didn't have a dental license, so I'd never had the opportunity to practice since my move.

Looking back, my failure to become a journalist had been a traumatic event in my early adulthood. Entering dental school had meant closing off the possibility to become a journalist. In addition, the argument I'd had with Papa over my career path had precipitated a lot of negativity in me that distorted my future and limited my possibilities for a career choice.

Back then, becoming a dentist had felt materialistic somehow. But here in the States, my confidence in myself had grown. I'd become more practical and resilient. My trust for Patrick and in other people had grown. I'd been becoming a "naked" version of myself, someone who didn't need to be hiding behind armor. Focusing on practicality and sensibility every day was sculpting me into a truer version of myself who felt ready to do what she wanted with her own life. And suddenly, I was seeing dentistry in a new light.

I was no longer looking to seek something from the outside. Instead, I was looking to build and grow opportunities from the inside out. I believed in my own agency.

I wanted to contribute and provide something more tangible in the world. I wanted to offer treatment and care to patients and to provide more realistic merits and tangible benefits to improve people's lives than I was able to do as a researcher. The time had come to seek a way to realize my wishes.

One night over dinner, I talked to Patrick for the first time about everything I'd been thinking about.

"Are you going to quit the NIDR?" he asked. "What's going to happen with your career?" He sounded a bit offended, or at the very least annoyed. He didn't seem to understand how important this career move was to me.

Patrick was an excellent principal investigator and leading cancer biologist. He was popular in his scientific community, and had been invited to be a speaker or a panelist for many international meetings. Science was part of who Patrick was—his motivation and life. Was it this that blinded him to why I would want to leave research in favor of working as a clinician?

"What's going to happen to your tuition?" he asked. "You are still paying back the special fellowship you'd been awarded by the Japanese government."

He reminded me of other difficulties, too.

"Our income will be cut in half. We've recently purchased a new home. We won't be able to pay our mortgage and bills." He presented all the cons and fears associated with my idea.

I knew him to be somewhat conservative, sensible, and careful, but I was still troubled by how strongly he opposed my idea. I understood that considering our new mortgage and other expenses, taking out a student loan, and living on half of our income could be a big hurdle—perhaps even risky.

But I was determined. I would figure it out. And I would convince Patrick.

Patrick and I continued to talk. At first, he avoided it—kept saying, "No time to talk," or "You need to be practical." His reactions were not encouraging.

It was clear to me that he harbored a lot of fear about this potential change. As I reflected, I realized what he was truly worried about was what such domestic and practical burdens might do to our relationship. *He doesn't want to test our love,* I thought. *He's afraid this could ruin our relationship.*

Once I came to see that he was trying to save our relationship from possible negative changes and challenges, I was able to cultivate a more mindful understanding and compassion regarding the obstacles as he saw them, which in turn presented me with ideas for how to avoid the challenges he was afraid to face.

On a Sunday at the beginning of June, I invited Patrick to eat breakfast with me at the table by the window in our kitchen. I'd brewed tea, added milk, and placed two cups on the table with a plate of just-baked scones with butter and old-fashioned English orange marmalade.

When Patrick entered the room, his face was slightly stiff, as if he was protecting himself. He seemed to know that I had a proposal for him.

We sat next to each other overlooking the woods enriched in shades of green through sheer curtains beyond our wooden deck, and over tea, I began to talk. I emphasized that this change would build something positive in our life—that it would be an investment in our future.

Patrick reacted positively to the word "investment"; he turned his body slightly toward me, and suddenly seemed more open—more willing to listen.

"Research alone isn't my career," I said. "I can't imagine myself engaged in routine work like pipetting, collecting, analyzing data, and writing papers for the rest of my life. My true strength is being around people, helping them out of pain and into living better lives."

He was listening carefully as he chewed a bite of his scone.

"Every time I treat patients, I feel I get rewarded, much more so than what I provide."

I knew Patrick had a big heart and liked to help people in need as well. His face softened as I explained my motivations.

I added a few more ideas I'd been thinking of. "I need to think about not only myself but also our future together. I want to treat this country as *home*. I want to be more serious about how I'm living my life and how I can contribute to society in this country."

Patrick looked a little brighter now, as if some knots in his mind were loosening up.

I now explained my proposal to seek a career in pediatric dentistry. In this way, I told him, I would combine my desire to help children in need with my strength in science and dentistry.

This time he was asking me more questions, and I was able to share more with him about possible future faculty positions, and licensure processing, and other logistics. He stopped eating and just listened.

I told him that I'd like to target the residency program in pediatric dentistry at the University of Maryland, School of Dentistry. Since we were residents of Maryland, it would reduce my tuition and other expenses.

Now Patrick seemed to acknowledge all that I'd researched and better understood my plan. Better yet, he began to accept it.

"But how will we find the financial resources?" he asked.

"We can apply for a student loan, but we'll need some money for living to compensate for the loss of my salary . . . As a last resort, I can ask my father to lend us some money."

I said this even though I wasn't sure if it was possible. I hadn't spoken to my father in years, and I was surprised this option had even sprung into my mind. Asking him for help would be a major shift in terms of how I'd felt about him in the past. Papa had been the major cause of my distrust of people and the trauma in my childhood. I'd transformed so much since I came to the States; did I really want to reopen a door to my past?

But in starting to seek what I'd always wanted in my life, it seemed that I'd become strong enough to enter into the painful field of my earlier memories. I felt that I'd begun to accept and embrace the events of my past; I felt ready to weed out the bad and restore goodness. Everything that was unfolding seemed to present new opportunities to heal.

At the end of July that year, I was invited for a formal, in-person interview for the Pediatric Dentistry program at the University of Maryland.

The night I returned home from the interview, I called Mama in Japan and explained what was going on with me. Since Papa had left her for his other family, she'd been receiving monthly financial support. I worried that my request to borrow money from him might affect her financially.

She assured me that it was okay to ask him. "Since Papa is the only one who can help with finances, you'd better talk to him directly," she said.

"Yeah," I said slowly. "I know . . . I just wonder how he may feel about this after all the silence we've had for years . . . Mama, would you be willing to talk to him about this?"

"I can't promise he'll say yes, but I'll try," she said. "I'll start the conversation. But in any case, you'd better come and talk to him directly."

"Yes, you're right," I agreed. "I'll plan a trip to come see him as soon as possible."

Two days later Mama called me and told me, "Papa is willing to meet with you to talk about it."

At the end of August, Patrick and I made a trip to Japan. This was Patrick's second trip to visit my family; we'd gone once right after our wedding. My family had been very welcoming toward him, but we hadn't seen Papa; he and I had still been estranged at the time. After leaving Mama and us, he'd moved to a large condo where he lived with the other woman and their daughter, and after that he wasn't invited to any family gatherings. I felt sorry for him, but I couldn't change my family's minds. I wasn't sure back then if I was even really ready to see him myself.

Now, at Papa's home I started to feel some real compassion toward Papa. I also wasn't afraid of him any longer; rather, I felt sympathy for him. Feeling all my overflowing emotions for Papa, Mama, and my sisters, I realized the extent to which my time in the States had healed me. I felt very grateful for this opportunity to see Papa, my family, and to share all of this with Patrick.

Patrick tried to lighten the atmosphere from the beginning of our visit with Papa. He made cute jokes in his simple Japanese just after our arrival, and we all laughed. The small exchange led us to more comfortable time together.

We made small talk about our house, our work, Patrick's love of fishing. Papa was smiling the whole time as he listened.

We ordered dinner from a local restaurant, and Papa continued to smile a lot throughout the meal. As we chatted, my thoughts drifted to the past. The last time I'd seen Papa was at my first wedding, seven years earlier. I remembered how nervous he'd been back then, likely bogged down by all the pressures inside of him—all the lies, guilt, and shame he'd held in his life. I'd felt sorry for him. Now, here with Patrick, he looked happier and more relaxed than he ever had with Seiji. Perhaps it was because he could see how much I'd changed—how much more content I was.

After dinner, I brewed fresh green tea and cut up a musk melon for everyone. As I sat back down Papa said, "Mama told me there's something you want to talk to me about."

"Yes," I said. "I'd like to become a dentist in the States, and hopefully obtain a faculty position later." I began to explain about the two-year program I was interested in.

"I heard a little from Mama, but it's good to know exactly what you want to do," Papa said, nodding.

I'd been waiting for this moment all night. I was a bit nervous, but finally, I asked, "Can you help us for two years? I promise we will pay you back."

"Well . . . wonderful, Kyomi," Papa said.

I stared at him. His face was kind and smiling, at peace. I was more than relieved. In our culture in Japan, praise or even positive acknowledgment from parents to children is very unusual. We don't express love openly, either verbally or by physically embracing. But here was Papa, praising me.

"I'm impressed with what you've become, planned, and are about to execute," he said, beaming.

"We will pay you back," I said again, making sure this was clear.

"When Mama's uncle's plan to pay your tuition fell through, you took responsibility for your own tuition for four years. That helped me tremendously back then. So now I will help you, Kyomi, for two years."

I was elated. I translated what he'd said to Patrick and they both looked happy, smiling to each other.

I'd had to take out a student loan in dental school after the plan from Mama's uncle didn't work out. I'd known back then that Papa had many financial burdens, but I'd never realized he'd appreciated my decision to take care of my own finances in that way. It had taken these many years for Papa and me to talk frankly, but now I finally felt we were seeing eye to eye.

I took Papa's act of kindness that night as a token of his love and respect for me. He hadn't been able to show me that for a long time— perhaps ever, really. I was grateful for the support, love, and tenderness, and also that I'd become a person who could receive those offerings with an open heart. I looked forward to continuing to develop this newfound relationship with Papa.

The following spring, I got an official acceptance letter to the residency program at the Department of Pediatric Dentistry. At the end of May 1995, I resigned from NIH.

Nancy, William, Cindy, and my other colleagues held a farewell party for me. Lots of people came to wish me well. Tears rolled down my cheeks as we said our goodbyes, and Nancy, Julie, Cindy, and Terry teared up too. Hyacinth was there as well, and she hugged me goodbye.

Though nobody at NIH knew the depths of the abyss from which I had risen, they'd all helped me find my way in this new world. With their consistent love, kindness, and support, I'd been able to come so far.

Now it was time to spread my wings.

I started my residency program in Baltimore on July 1, and with it began to commute over ninety miles each way from my home every day—leaving at 5:00 a.m. and not coming home until after 7:00 p.m.

Patrick was incredibly supportive during this time. Every night, he made dinner for us both and then tidied up the kitchen and washed the dishes while I studied for the next day. We knew this would be our lifestyle for next two years, and he was patient, never showing discontent or complaining.

I had to study a lot, but it was worth it when, during my first year of residency, I passed both of the National Board I and II Exams. I'd heard lots of stories about how difficult these exams were for international students, and now I understood. I was a licensed dentist in Japan, but I'd had to re-learn everything—in a language I was still learning.

In the clinic, I loved to see my pediatric patients. Because of the location of the school—in inner city Baltimore—the majority of our patients were black and on the lower end of the socioeconomic spectrum. I had a great sense of mission in providing care for those in need. I felt the treatments could honestly be a life-changing experience for some of the children who came to the clinic. I held a strong yet gentle sense of "empowerment" in my mind, and I loved seeing my young patients leave the clinic feeling a little braver and more confident despite feeling a little uncomfortable numbness inside their cheeks. Every day I worked at the clinic, I became more convinced that I was born to serve others. I was in the right place.

Toward the end of my program, I got appointed to a faculty position as an assistant professor. It was a joint position with the Departments of Oral and Craniofacial Pathology and Pediatric Dentistry. I began to receive a salary from both departments just before my graduation.

Patrick came to my graduation ceremony. He looked at me in my black graduation robe with its blue lines and said, "You've made it. I am very proud of you, Kyomi."

"*We've* made it!" I said. "Without you, we couldn't have done it."

He kissed me and hugged me tight, overflowing with joy. I hadn't been aware of how special this moment would be until now, looking at Patrick's face full of such happiness.

I was grateful for Patrick and to my new country for helping me transform the scared little girl I'd been—for coaxing her not only to finally come out of the dark basement but also to hold her torch high with a sense of mission. I realized that day how much our relationship had changed over the last two years; the way Patrick looked at me now was different than he had before. He now regarded me with respect, and our relationship would be forever altered for the better.

I was no longer his Japanese princess; I'd become his partner.

— 11 —
A Mission

In August, after I graduated from my residency program at the dental school, we received our very last monthly support check from Papa. To thank him, we called him and left a message that I'd just completed the Maryland Dental Board Exams and begun to work as a joint assistant professor.

A few days later, Papa called back. He was struggling with his speech, severely stuttering. We had him on speaker, but when we both noticed his struggling I quickly switched the mode to normal and pressed the receiver against my ear. Patrick was watching, brow furrowed with worry.

"What's wrong?" I asked. "What's happening with your speech?" A chill ran down my back, and my muscles tightened.

"W . . . well . . . I . . . I've got ca-ca-cancer. It's b-b-bad. The-they say it's all over m-m-my body . . ." Papa struggled to express even these simple words.

"What?" I said dully. "I . . . how?" I couldn't believe what he'd just said. My mind quickly tried to dissociate from this reality as if it were a bad dream.

Though Patrick couldn't understand us, he sensed what was

happening, and he leaned over and hugged my shoulders tight. I felt as if I'd lost my balance.

Papa explained that he'd begun losing words during a graduate class he was teaching. He thought that he might have had a minor stroke. But when he went to the hospital to get checked out and they took CT scans—starting with his brain, then his lungs, and then his abdominal region—they found the cancer.

I could hear his deep breath at the other end of the line.

"The ca-ca-cancer has mmm . . . metastasized in mmm . . . multiple organs," he said.

"Oh no! Can they do something to stop or cure it?" I brought myself back to reality, but was still struggling to put my thoughts together.

"No," he said. "Nothing. They caca-can't do anything. I . . . h-h-have only a . . . a . . . a few months to live."

A few months! My heart dropped into my stomach. It wasn't beating anymore; it was shrinking itself into a hard knot.

"No! It can't be!" I was in shock. My father was dying? No. He couldn't! He couldn't die so soon!

After many years of almost no communication, I'd just begun to get to know Papa better, and rebuild a relationship with him. Patrick and I had been planning to invite him to visit us in the US. Papa had never seen us in the States—our house, and how we lived here. There was so much I wanted to share with him . . . What would be left for us now?

I was so grateful for Papa's help over the previous two years and couldn't thank him enough for his support for me and for us. I hoped that his calling me now was a sign that we truly had mended the issues from our past.

How could I make up for all the lost years when he had so little time left? We'd been slowly rebuilding harmony within our broken family. But now it felt like that was all crumbling into dust.

Papa continued on: "I . . . I don't c-c-care about my life. I . . . I don't mind d-d-dying a-a-alone. If I have to go to hell, I don't m-mind it. B-b-but I have one thing I . . . I need to complete. Otherwise, I c-c-cannot die in peace."

"What is it? What do you want?" I felt a tightness in my throat as I asked him this.

"K-K-Kyomi, I . . . I need to ask you a favor. I've already t-t-tried to speak to your sisters, b-b-but they didn't want to hear anything from m-me. They got so . . . ahh . . . upset and hung up on me. They w-w-wouldn't talk to me."

"What is it? What did you try to tell them?" I implored him. Patrick continued to watch me carefully, trying to grasp the situation as it evolved despite his limited understanding of Japanese.

Then Papa began his story.

After our big argument when I was sixteen, he said, he had lived with the woman and their baby daughter for thirteen years. Their relationship had ended with the woman's marriage to another man—someone with whom she'd been having an affair for over ten years.

Upon her marriage, Papa's daughter got re-registered from being under Papa's custody to her mother's new husband. After, Papa had begun living alone. Lonely, he'd begun to ask Mama to consider reconciling with him. But Mama hadn't wanted Papa to come back home. In fact, she'd said she wanted a divorce.

A few years later, about a year before his diagnosis, Papa's sister-in-law had begun matchmaking for him. Papa had met a woman and decided to marry her. The woman's older brother pushed them to hold a wedding ceremony as soon as possible. They'd gotten married a couple of weeks ago. But in fact he hadn't yet divorced Mama, so he hadn't been able to submit his marriage registration to the new woman yet. And then all of a sudden, he'd been diagnosed with terminal cancer, and now the woman's brother was threatening Papa, telling him he'd better submit the marriage papers. He needed Mama to grant him a divorce, officially.

Now I understood why my sisters were so upset. I felt a pressure inside my chest.

"I . . . I didn't mean to d-d-deceive anyone; I just needed a . . . a little more time," Papa pressed on. "B-b-but now I have n-n-no time left. I d-d-don't care about m-my life anymore. B-b-but I c-c-can't betray this woman who's just m-m-married me. Now I . . . I am responsible for her."

He was clearly desperate.

"P-p-please help me, K-Kyomi," he begged. "I won't be able to d-d-die until I s-s-settle this issue."

I was flooded with warring emotions. He sounded like he was determined to complete his last task with this woman. But was it fair to Mama? What might be possible in this "retrospective" fix? Were there any laws to help this situation?

Whatever the case was, he was my father, and he was dying. I had to try to help him in any way I could.

"Okay, I understand, Papa," I told him. "I will try my best to talk to my sisters. It will be very difficult, but I'll try. Also, I will come back to Japan to visit you with Patrick as soon as possible. I'll let you know when I have firm dates arranged."

"Th-th-thank you, K-Kyomi," Papa said. "I owe you." He sounded as if he'd finally released the rock weighing upon his heart.

As soon as I hung up the phone, all the pressure that I'd held inside of me during the conversation was released at once. I cried into Patrick's chest as he embraced me gently.

"Papa will die soon," I said.

Patrick just nodded; he'd already sensed what was happening. I started to share the content of our conversation—about Papa's terminal cancer, and then the situation with his new wife.

"Though I said to Papa that I would try my best to talk to my sisters, it won't be easy . . ."

I shared my concerns with Patrick about my sisters and Mama. I could now picture my sisters' anger toward Papa and the newly developed story in his recent "marriage" with this unknown woman. My sisters and Mama were still angry with Papa about our past; accepting this new marriage would be unacceptable for them.

My sisters' concerns would be about Mama, and about the money and security she should receive after his death. Mama had been financially dependent on Papa for her entire adult life. If she lost his pension, social security, and inheritance, we as daughters would have to take care of her financially. This would be a big challenge for all of us.

Then again, after Papa had lived alone all those years, he'd approached Mama on a few occasions for reconciliation, but Mama had insisted that she'd wanted to divorce him. Then Papa and Mama had sold our original home and split the money. After the transaction was done, Papa had said clearly, "That's it. No more for Mama."

But even after that split, he'd still given Mama monthly financial support, and they'd left the matter of their divorce undecided. Maybe they feared more drama—more pain.

I did think it would be unfair for Mama to lose everything after all her years of agony married to Papa. But she was the one who had asked for a divorce. So if Papa decided to leave any money he might have for someone else, that was up to him. He was dying. Were we really going to spend his last days fighting against this woman? It shouldn't be that way.

I would have to work around my family to settle this challenge.

I shared my determination with Patrick to support Papa's dying wishes. I would be there to support my family's communications with Papa. I wanted to help our family access their courage, learn to see their past wounds in the light of love and kindness, and find a grounded, harmonious solution to this situation without any regret or resentment.

"I need to repay his kindness," I told Patrick.

"Yes, it's the right thing to do," Patrick said, and he kissed me to express his full support in my decision. Then he suggested that I begin the process by calling my sisters in Japan. He also said that we should visit Papa as soon as possible.

We began to look at our schedules and organize a trip to Japan.

I felt awful for my long period of absence from our family. I didn't know exactly when that absence had begun, but I suspected that it had started in my earlier childhood. I was physically present in every aspect of our family life back then, but in order to protect myself, I'd been mentally absent. I'd always needed to disconnect.

Then, after my dreadful argument with Papa, I'd gone on a downward spiral. I'd married, then divorced Seiji, and then I'd fled for the States. My family hadn't known what had troubled me at all; I was sure that in their eyes, I was the most irresponsible and crazy person in the world. And when I married Patrick and got a green card, they must have confirmed their hidden sense that I'd abandoned the whole family.

And now here I was, the one who was supposed to piece us all back together. I knew the challenge I faced.

Patrick and I decided to visit Japan in the first week of September.

Once our plans were set, I called Machiyo.

"Ahh . . . Kyom chan! Did you hear anything from Papa?" she said immediately, as if she'd been expecting me to call for a while.

"Yes," I said.

"I can't believe that old man!" she launched in. "He stuttered so badly that I couldn't hear anything!"

I didn't want to interrupt her, so I just listened quietly.

"Did you hear that stupid story? Unbelievable! Papa must've gone crazy . . . he's just awful!" Machiyo had built up powerful resentment toward him; she hastily continued, "After all he's done to Mama, and to us, how could he have made yet another mess? He got married to *a new woman*! Unbelievable! He's asking Mama for a divorce!"

She wasn't done yet.

"And now he's telling us lies, saying he'll die soon. To tell you the truth, I don't care what happens to him. Even if he dies tomorrow, he deserves it!"

After all that she said, Machiyo no doubt believed that I would agree with her.

"But do you think Papa can still redeem himself?" I asked gently. "After all of his decisions and actions, do you think there's a chance to make things right?"

Silence. It grew even longer. I waited for Machiyo's reaction, but none came.

"Papa is dying, Sis," I said.

"Oh, no!" she exploded. "Are you taking Papa's side? You must be kidding! What about Mama? After two decades of infidelity, how do you think she'll feel?"

My stomach grew tight.

Now she started to criticize me: "You've been in America; you don't know anything! You don't even care about Mama, and what we're going through every day!"

"I know . . . and I'm very sorry," I said. "But I remember that Papa tried to reconcile with Mama, and Mama said no. And she did receive half the money when they sold the house five years ago . . ."

"Kyom chan! Are you serious? After all these years of living in despair while Papa was doing whatever he wanted . . . how do you think Mama feels?"

Machiyo's voice was now cloudy with emotion. I could tell that she was crying in silence. I felt that she didn't want to talk to me anymore. I knew that in her mind, I wasn't on her side.

"It's unacceptable," she said. "Giving away even a single penny to someone like this woman, who has just appeared in his life, should never happen! Unless Mama signs divorce papers, the money will be only for Mama anyway. Just ignore Papa! Mama deserves all the pension and social security Papa has accumulated during their marriage."

I felt like Machiyo saw me as an outsider when it came to our family affairs and didn't want me to voice my opinion. But I continued anyway.

"But Papa said no more money for Mama after they sold the house five years ago," I pointed out. "And at this point he and Mama have been separated for almost the same amount of time as they were married. It should be up to Papa to decide."

"No way, Kyom chan! You are out of this situation. You've escaped from all the family affairs and responsibilities for many years now. You don't know anything about the family. Papa left Mama by force! Did Mama have a choice? Did she want this to have happened? Mama didn't want to be alone all these years. Even if Mama *has* been separated from Papa for the past twenty years, she shouldn't give up a cent for this woman who believes she's married to Papa! And for only a few weeks! Think about how much hardship Mama's gone through. Papa must be crazy! Anyway, no more talk! No more talk about this!"

With that, the air between us on either side of line became like a solid boulder. Machiyo was a mass of unyielding emotions.

I understood my sister's point of view. But I had promised Papa. I would keep trying.

I called Yoshino the following day—with no better luck than I'd found with Machiyo. My younger sister was always respectful of anything that came from our older sister. She also expressed much anger against Papa and deep concern about Mama. It seemed that all the resentment they had felt toward Papa over the years had formed an unbreakable bond between them.

I told my sisters that I would keep discussing the matter together with them when I got to Japan. But I knew their hardness was not only toward Papa but also toward me, for my many years of absence in our family affairs.

I'd chosen to take this mission on. But it looked as if the road to accomplish my goal would be more difficult to navigate than I had initially thought.

— 12 —

Papa's Passing

Patrick and I arrived at the Tokyo Narita International airport in Japan one late afternoon in September. As the large exit door opened, Yoshino and her husband Hisashi came into sight.

"Patrick san! Kyom chan!" They greeted us with big smiles from behind a metal rail divider.

"Welcome back, Patrick san! You must be so tired." Hisashi immediately grabbed our cart and began to push it forward for us.

"Oh, thank you, Hisashi san! *Hisashi buri desu ne!*" Patrick said. This was a pun and jokey version of a Japanese greeting phrase he'd learned and created from the past two visits in Japan. It meant, "Mr. Hisashi! Long time, no see!" Patrick cleverly used the Japanese word "hisashi buri," meaning "after long-time absence," to make a play on Hisashi's name.

Hisashi grinned. He loved to speak with Patrick. During our last two visits, they'd become buddies, joking and talk about anything over eating and drinking. Hisashi enjoyed taking Patrick sightseeing and was always willing to give us a ride to wherever we needed to go.

As we walked to the parking building, Yoshino began to whisper in my ear about the situation with Machiyo and Mama. She said Mama didn't know anything about Papa's recent news.

"I've discussed this with *O nei chan*"—"the older sis," meaning Machiyo—"since our telephone conversations, but she has deep-rooted anger toward Papa," Yoshino said.

From the way Yoshino spoke, it seemed as if she'd separated herself from Machiyo's point of view. I was encouraged to see that she was feeling more open about Papa's situation than she had before.

We all piled into Hisashi's car and he sped straight to the hospital, where Papa had been hospitalized for the last ten days. Yoshimi had prepared some snacks and drinks for us from home.

"*Arigato gozai masu!*" Patrick thanked Yoshino as he opened his favorite kind of bottled tea, Oolong tea, and began to drink it happily.

When we arrived at the hospital, Yoshino and Hisashi didn't want to come in with us to see Papa. As we got closer, their faces became stiffer, and I could feel the tension rising.

"We just wanted to help you both get here, that's all," Yoshino said.

Since I'd seen her mixed feelings back at the airport, I knew this sudden change in her attitude must have come from her respect for Hisashi, who was very serious and had given the cold shoulder to Papa regularly in the past.

"Please call us whenever you're *finished* with Papa," Yoshino said rather mechanically.

"Thank you," I said. "Since we're so tired from the long flight, we won't be staying too long—only one hour or so."

"We'll see you then," Hisashi said.

Patrick and I waved at them as they drove away.

We took an elevator to the second floor. As I walked down the hallway to find Papa's room, the shiny floor reflected the fluorescent lights above us from the ceiling. The smell of disinfectant reminded me of how little I liked hospitals in Japan.

My muscles were tightening up, but I didn't know if it was a reaction to the smells and general atmosphere of the hospital or my fear of seeing Papa, who was now dying. I was deeply aware of how quiet it was.

Papa's room was getting closer. I stopped walking, took a couple of long, deep breaths, and then placed my palms on my cheeks, moving my facial muscles up and down to loosen them up.

Patrick put his hands gently on my shoulders. "It's going to be okay, Kyomi."

Papa's room door was open. We could see from the hall that he was dozing in the bed. I felt a sense of relief that I wouldn't have to face him right away when we walked in.

The room was fairly large, with three beds, but Papa was the only patient inside. We walked over to him and stayed there for a moment, watching him sleep.

Just two years had passed since I'd last seen Papa. As I examined him now in bed, I saw that he'd lost weight and his thin skin was showing every vein underneath it. His beautiful gray hair had become thinner at the top and even whiter and shinier. His skin color, by contrast, seemed darker. When I saw a PICC (peripherally inserted central catheter) line on the right below his collarbone, I gulped, my throat suddenly caught. Through this PICC line, he would be receiving medications, particularly morphine for his pain.

Just then, Papa woke up. "Ah, Kyomi! ... Wha ... what time is it? I-I-I've been waiting for you, b-b-but I must have fallen asleep."

Patrick and I greeted Papa softly. Though I acted as normal as possible, the emotions that had been building up inside me were now about to gush out; I was quivering inside.

"We've just arrived. How are you feeling, Papa?" I asked, tears filling my eyes.

Papa said he'd been better, and his speech had become better, too. Patrick and I hugged him and thanked him again for all his support for the past two years. Now tears started to fall from my eyes.

Patrick held my shoulder and said gently, "No need to interpret for me, just enjoy your conversations with Papa."

My husband was always so thoughtful; with his egoless attitude, he faded into the background as Papa and I talked about the program I'd just graduated from. I showed Papa my faculty member badge from the university where I worked. I also told him how I'd passed all the state dental board exams. Then, I'd become a pediatric dentist in the United States.

"Wonderful! You've become a p-p-person of importance in America!" Papa said with his watery eyes. "Now I don't have to worry about you any longer. I am v-v-very proud of you. What you've done in A-America isn't easy. You did something g-g-great that even P-Papa c-c-couldn't do by himself," he said proudly.

Though Papa had been a full professor for decades in the engineering department in one of the universities near Tokyo, he was so happy to see me become an assistant professor in the United States. I felt a rush of gratitude toward him. In effect, he'd supported me to change not just my career but my entire life.

Again I promised that we would pay him back.

"No." He shook his head. "Not necessary. No need to p-p-pay me back. But when M-Mama needs something small, you can support her."

Papa now changed the subject to what he really wanted to talk about. He once again shared the story about his recent wedding and the woman he'd married. Her name was Yaeko.

While he was talking, I stared at the wedding band on his skinny left ring finger. The sandblasted platinum, along with glossy shiny rims, was sparkling light. When I'd seen him two years before, he'd been wearing a thick 18K yellow gold band, his wedding band with Mama that I'd known for so long. I remembered that Papa and Mama's wedding bands had lost their original sparkling, glossy shines and looked dull from many years of wears and scratches, as if they'd been sandblasted.

Papa's voice was bright and happy as he told me, "She's been a C-C-Christian since she was in high school. She's j-just retired from Salvation Army International, where she worked for th-th-thirty years. She's n-never been m-married."

Papa acted a little like a young man who'd fallen in love for the first time with a woman he was proud of. He clearly cared for Yaeko. He repeated all the same wishes he'd expressed in our previous conversations, but I still wanted to make sure this was what he wanted—to divorce Mama for this woman.

The situation that he'd so far created was nothing illegal, because he'd had only a private wedding ceremony without any official public registry. If he reconsidered, he could still change everything by dealing privately with this new woman and her brother.

"Are you sure this is what you want?" I asked him directly.

"Y-Yes," he said firmly. "I am very sure. I want this n-new p-p-path with Yaeko until I die. I n-need to make sure Yaeko will be s-s-secure after my d-death." He glanced over at Patrick, then looked at me again. "You are a good couple," he said.

I felt like crying. I was finally developing a good relationship with Papa, and soon he would be gone.

Papa started to doze off again. He needed to sleep.

"We'll be back tomorrow," I said gently, and patted his hand.

Patrick and I left his room, and I called Yoshino to ask her to pick us up.

Patrick and I stood outside the hospital, holding hands and waiting for Yoshino and Hisashi. I thought over my conversation with Papa, and his decision. It was time to fully engage in my mission: I needed to get my sisters to come together with me and accept this hard decision.

I squeezed Patrick's hand, looking up at his face. He leaned down and gently kissed me.

I thought about Mama. She was kind, genuine, compassionate, and sensitive. From what I could tell, she still loved Papa, but her feelings had been hurt too much and for far too long for the rift to be mended. Her relationship with Papa had completely lost its momentum; it would never again correct its course.

But even if my sisters succeeded in keeping Papa from divorcing Mama, keeping Mama on her throne as his wife forever after his death, what good would come of it? Would Mama be happy to accept his pension against his will? I couldn't believe she would. I felt very sure Mama would make a concession for Papa on his deathbed.

From the hospital, we headed to Machiyo's home. Since she was the eldest, we all needed to gather at her home to respect her leadership and responsibility in our family.

When we arrived, Machiyo, Yoshino, and their husbands were eager to know how Papa was doing and how he'd explained his own situation. I told them what I'd seen, and what Papa had said. I answered all of their questions, but I didn't express my opinion. Instead, I waited for them to speak.

I explained to them that yes, Papa had terminal cancer. Yes, he would die in several months. I also explained that he'd held an actual wedding ceremony with Yaeko, at which point Machiyo stuck out her lips in disapproval. I'd seen her do this countless times.

"How could he hold a wedding like that, deceiving Yaeko and everyone else?" Yoshino asked.

"Yes, legally speaking, he's still married to Mama," Machiyo said. "Holding a wedding ceremony means nothing."

I tried to show understanding for what my family thought about the situation. Machiyo confirmed that they hadn't spoken to Mama about this, so she didn't know anything about the situation yet. I expressed Papa's wishes again. He would die soon, and before then he wanted to legally re-marry this woman; in order for him to do that, he and Mama would need to divorce.

My sisters were trying to protect Mama, but I wasn't sure if they were even representing Mama's true wishes.

"Let's try to look through the facts and the sequenc of events," I suggested.

"Kyom chan! Even though you say 'the facts,' these are all choices only Papa made, without any participation or agreement with Mama." Machiyo's eyes narrowed; she was on the defensive.

I reminded my sisters of the sad story of Papa and Mama. Even though the situation wasn't fair to Mama, to be sure, things had evolved to the point where neither of them had wanted to be together for a long time now. Though Papa had been free to come home for over ten years, they'd chosen to live apart. They were no longer a couple, and had not been for years. Eventually, perhaps subconsciously sensing his own death was looming, Papa had taken this final opportunity to be happy. *These* were the facts.

In order to release all the agony, anger, sadness, and resentment we'd built inside of us for so many years, we all needed to let go.

Doing so wouldn't be just for Papa but also for Mama and for all of us. I encouraged my sisters to accept the difficulties and see something beyond what we were facing here. I asked them to rise above the difficult emotions of the past and think about what might be achievable for us now—to stand for a better future.

Initially, Machiyo and Yoshino both frequently interrupted as I spoke, but over time they became quieter and quieter and the gaps in between their words became longer.

"If we block Papa from fulfilling his will, we will have to accept the consequences," I said. "And that may include suffering from never-ending legal issues with this new wife, Yaeko."

They became silent.

"But most of all, it would haunt us, because this is what Papa wants," I added.

Just as the Buddhist principal *"Cause and Effect"* describes, whatever actions we take become the seeds and causes of subsequent outcomes. We needed to follow the principle, "Begin with the end in mind," and keep positive and achievable options in mind, starting now.

"I know it will be difficult," I said, "but instead of pushing away the pain we've experienced, we need to embrace all the difficulties we've undergone. Otherwise, they will come back to us even more intensely, and we'll all continue to live in agony."

Machiyo and Yoshino sat in silence. Their husbands stared at their hands, which were clasped before them on the table. I began to remind my sisters of their innocent love for Papa in their childhood, before things turned bad. I urged them to open their hearts to him.

My sisters began to reminisce about how they used to play with

Papa and how they learned from him as girls—how they had openly loved him.

"Papa always helped me with my homework," Yoshino said.

"Papa used to comb Yoshino's tangled hair with camelia oil for hours and hours," Machiyo recalled.

I saw an opening and took it. "It might be difficult, but try to see what is most truthful to your hearts without looking at and focusing on only your scars . . ."

Now I saw tears in my sisters' eyes. My brothers-in-law were also wiping their noses. They were reminded of how much they'd loved Papa before things got so entangled and complicated. Their anger long gone, stillness became clarity.

"Thank you, Kyom chan," Machiyo finally said. "Yes, let's meet with Papa."

The following afternoon, Yoshino dropped us again in front of the hospital. Patrick and I gave her an approximate time for our pickup and then walked down the same hallway, but this time my heart was much lighter.

When Patrick and I looked inside the room, Papa smiled and waved, totally alert.

"Hello, Papa! You look nice today," Patrick said cheerfully.

At this, Papa's face brightened and looked even happier.

"We spoke with Machiyo and Yoshino last night and they will come see you for lunch tomorrow," I said.

"Oh, yes?" Papa said, and he leaned forward to eagerly hear a little more detail.

I summarized our conversation for him, focusing on Machiyo and Yoshino's concern for Mama.

"How about we all go to a restaurant for lunch, then catch up more?" I asked.

"Yeah, yeah, . . . th-th-that's a g-g-g-great idea!" With the excitement, he seemed to be stuttering more.

Papa picked up the room phone and called the nurses' station. He requested permission from the hospital to go out for lunch the next day.

A few minutes later, a nurse in a white uniform entered the room.

"Hello, Yamakoshi san, I've just talked with the doctor. He said no problem for your outing tomorrow. Who will be going with you?" She was looking at us as she asked.

"Th-this is Kyomi, my second d-daughter, and her husband, P-P-Patrick," Papa told her. "I have t-two m-more daughters. We all are going to lunch t-t-together." Papa smiled with contentment.

"Wow, that's wonderful! You must have a very nice family!" the nurse said, also smiling at us. She nodded with courtesy, then left.

We chatted for a while longer before Papa asked us to accompany him to the hospital veranda for his smoke. He'd been a smoker for decades, and at this point in his illness, his doctors had given him permission to continue to smoke.

On the hospital veranda, as the smoke trailed out of his mouth, Papa looked so happy and relaxed.

"I have no pain," he said, smiling in the bright, warm sun. His beautiful gray hair shone in the light. A sense of happiness penetrated all of us, like the warmth of the sun. I wished this precious time with Papa would never end.

"Thank you, K-K-Kyomi," Papa said.

"You're welcome, Papa . . . no problem at all." I looked at the time. "We are going to leave soon. Do you want to go back to your room?"

"N-No, I'll stay here to w-w-watch you both walking d-down the street," he said happily.

Patrick and I hugged Papa, said goodbye to him, and left him on the veranda, still smoking.

When Patrick and I walked out of the hospital, holding each other's hands, we looked up at the veranda on the corner of the third floor on our way out and there was Papa, still smoking, comfortably smiling and waving at us. We waved back at him with our hands still clasped together. I started to cry and Patrick squeezed my hand gently yet firmly. When I looked back again, I couldn't see Papa through my tears. But I knew he was still there, smiling and waving at us.

We walked down to the next corner and turned onto another street. After we turned, I pressed my face into Patrick's chest and cried for a while. I didn't want it end. These were the happiest moments I'd ever had with Papa.

The next day, Machiyo, Yoshino, Patrick, and I met Papa at the hospital. As soon as they saw Papa in the bed, Machiyo and Yoshino trotted toward him. They cried beside his bed, and in that moment they became Papa's daughters again. Patrick and I stood near the foot of Papa's bed, and faded into the background, watching them talking to Papa.

I was very happy that my sisters were able to express their kind, honest feelings toward Papa. I felt as if I were their mother, warmly appreciating who my daughters had become. This was one of the best days Papa and my sisters had shared in many years. Their hearts were open and the door to harmony was unlocked.

After Patrick and I returned home to the US, Machiyo and Yoshino continued to visit Papa regularly. They also talked to Mama about Papa's cancer, his short life expectancy, and the divorce that Papa had been asking for. Mama cried and accepted everything he'd asked for. She didn't show any discontent or ask for any conditions. She was determined to follow Papa's wishes and honor him before his death.

In October, when I visited Papa again, he was still at the hospital, getting weaker. My sisters and I decided to make an arrangement for Mama to meet Papa in a private setting.

Mama accompanied us to the hospital room a few days later, carrying a large bamboo lunch basket full of Papa's favorite foods, a dozen different items she'd prepared in small amounts and various colors and arranged beautifully: sweetened egg omelet, charred egg-plant with ginger sauce, shrimp and chicken custard in broth, shrimp tempura, slices of seasonal fruits—Papa's favorites, persimmon and Asian pear—and more. When she unwrapped the scarf from the basket and showed the contents to Papa, he swallowed a deep breath and cried quietly for a while, then thanked her for her love, kindness, and perseverance. He even apologized for their divorce.

"No," Mama said. "You were a wonderful husband and a great father. You've been the Number One for us. I've been so lucky and happy because of you."

Papa broke down in tears, overwhelmed with emotion. My sisters and I decided to leave them alone for a while.

This would be the last time Papa and Mama ever talked. Profound love and gratitude were evident in that conversation, even after all that had happened between them. Mama must have received what she'd been longing for so long from this hospital visit, because after that, Mama would never speak ill or complain about Papa ever again.

—

In mid-November, my sisters left a message with Patrick to let us know that Papa's last minutes were approaching. When Patrick received the call, I was in the operating room with a patient. It was too late to cancel on that day's patients, so Patrick and I decided we would leave the next day.

On the flight, whenever I sensed Papa was at a critical stage, I made international calls from the airplane and spoke with him, letting him know that Patrick and I would be there soon. I asked him to wait for us.

Though Papa was weak, I could hear his breathing and knew he was making his best effort to wait for me. Later, my sisters told me that each time I called, they held the receiver to Papa's ear and they could tell he was listening to my voice through the receiver. His final decision in this life was to be intubated, they said, because he hoped he would be able to last until I arrived.

When Patrick and I arrived at the airport, Hisashi was waiting for us. Wasting no time, he sped over to the hospital. We walked fast down the same corridor I'd walked down so many times before and into Papa's room.

Papa was in the middle of the room, hooked up to countless wires and intubated for the ventilator.

"Ah, Kyom chan!" My sisters came fast toward us, crying. Their eyes were red and swollen, and they looked exhausted.

"Papa got the flu and his breathing became extremely difficult while he was waiting for you," Machiyo said.

But now we'd finally arrived! I was so grateful that he'd held on for me.

"Kutoon, kutoon, kutoon . . ." The ventilator was making mechanical, rhythmical sounds.

I thanked my sisters and my cousin, Yoriko, for their tireless support of Papa and of us. Then I sat next to Papa, holding his hands.

Patrick searched for something deep inside his carry-on bag and then pulled out his brand-new shaver. He gently began shaving the beard that had grown on Papa's face over the last several days. Though my sisters had helped Papa every day, they'd been busy taking care of so many other things that Papa's beard had become a low priority.

After Patrick was done, I said, "Papa, you look so very handsome." I couldn't hold back my tears.

"Thank you, Patrick san," Machiyo and Yoshino said simultaneously.

Papa had always been so handsome and stylish in his life. What Patrick had offered Papa through this small action was to revere his life and dignity. Now Papa could courageously face his destiny—his journey to the spiritual realm—with his head held high.

I was so grateful for Papa, for Patrick, and for my sisters, that we could all be here to embrace these beautiful moments together.

During the night, many of us gathered to say farewell—my sisters, Yoriko, Yoriko's mother (Mama's elder sister), and Papa's brother and his wife. I hadn't seen them for many years. My father's new wife, Yaeko, hadn't been there all night. My sisters told me they hadn't seen her for days.

Just after 8:00 p.m., Yoriko abruptly stood up, approached me, grabbed my shoulder, and pulled me out of Papa's room. She led me fast to the equipment room at the end of the hallway.

I was surprised by her actions, which were almost violent.

"What's going on, Yoriko san?" I asked her. "What do you want?"

"Kyom chan . . . please listen to me," she said, her face stiff and serious. "This is very important . . . I don't want you to misunderstand this, but it is important."

I waited for her to go on.

"Before Papa dies, I have to tell you something important. Something that your father asked me to tell you."

"What is it, Yoriko san? What does Papa want me to know?"

"Well . . . it's the Buddhist teaching I follow. Your father became a member and wanted to pursue the teaching more deeply."

I didn't know this; I figured it was Yoriko who must have introduced this idea to him.

"But when he realized he would have no time to do so, he said that he would like for you to pursue it in his place."

What? Had I heard that correctly? Papa wanted me to pursue this Buddhist teaching on his behalf after his death? I had knowledge about some Buddhist denominations, but I'd never heard of this one before. And I had trouble imagining Papa asking me for something like this. Either he'd been touched especially by this teaching, he'd been deeply concerned about me, or both.

Yoriko went on talking, but I was still digesting the impact of the news she'd just delivered, so I stopped her; I wanted to think about this by myself—what, exactly, it meant.

"Let's get back to the room," I said quickly, and began the walk back without waiting for her response.

Yoriko had a reputation in our family for being erratic. I wanted to avoid any hassles and gossiping, and wanted to get back to the room before people began to speculate.

When we entered the room, everyone stared at us strangely. As I'd predicted, Yoriko's odd behavior had clearly set off some alarm bells.

Papa's brother and his wife in particular couldn't hide their surprise. Later, each of them approached me and whispered in my ear, asking what had happened with Yoriko.

"Oh, nothing," I said. "It wasn't really important."

—

As the hour grew late, one by one, people left Papa's room. Patrick went home with Hisashi. Finally, only my sisters, Yoriko, and I continued to stay in his room.

A little after 2:00 a.m., I was the only one wide awake and still watching Papa peacefully. Suddenly, I saw a bright orange ball of light come straight up out of his abdomen, without any noise or weight. The light ball hovered in the air for a few seconds, as if Papa were staring at me, and then it flew out through the window and vanished into the dark for eternity.

I knew what had happened and what Papa had wanted me to know. He was gone. I was at peace.

A few minutes later, everyone woke up.

"Papa is gone . . . it happened a couple of minutes ago." I told them.

"What? How do you know?" Machiyo asked.

I explained to them what I'd seen in the final moment of Papa's passing. Machiyo looked down, gazing at her hand. She seemed disappointed that I was the only one to see Papa's last moment ascending to the next realm. Perhaps as the eldest daughter of our family, she wished it had been her.

At the moment of witnessing his solemn passing, I felt Papa was sending his everlasting love, hope, and wishes to all of us—me, my sisters, and our families. I knew our family's story had been complicated. Papa had made poor choices in the past. But we had transcended that, and managed to settle into much straighter and better situations. Things that had negatively impacted all of us as family members had been miraculously lifted. The dark clouds of doubt, jealousy, hatred, resentment, and segregation had been cleared away.

We now found ourselves in unity and harmony as a whole family, able to express our love for each other.

I knew it was Papa who had made this new peace possible. I sent my silent thanks into the universe for this last, precious gift.

— 13 —

Go West

Patrick and I remained in Japan for Papa's funeral. One night a few days before our return to the States, Machiyo, Yoshino, and I spoke, trying to tie up some loose ends pertaining to Papa.

"By the way, what happened that night that Yoriko san pulled you out of Papa's room?" Yoshino asked.

"Oh, yeah . . . she was strange, wasn't she?" Machiyo made a face.

"What happened?" Yoshino asked again.

This was the first time they'd asked me about that incident. I shared what had happened.

"What . . . ?" they both uttered. After that, they couldn't find another word.

"I know . . . it was strange, but I've already decided to honor his wish and pursue it," I said carefully.

"What? No, no way, you shouldn't!" Both my sisters hailed objections at me. They felt suspicious about Yoriko's message; they thought she was making it up. When she was nineteen, Yoriko had quit university and run away with a classmate. Since then, both her mother and my parents had constantly been involved in sorting out Yoriko's and/or her partner's legal and financial problems. My sisters didn't trust her.

In my mind, however, Yoriko was simply a messenger—no more, no less. Papa's wishes were what I should be focusing on. I didn't know why he wanted me to pursue this path, but I was ready to try.

Furthermore, ever since I'd felt interrupted in my suicide attempt by someone or something when I was in my twenties, I'd had a sense of being led to encounter something sacred. I didn't know if this was it. But I needed to find out.

"With Yoriko's help, I'm going to become a member of this teaching," I told my sisters firmly.

They burst into emotional reactions.

"No! No! I'll have to go with you to stop Yoriko from brainwashing you!" Yoshino shouted.

I was undeterred. "That's fine," I told her, "you can go with me."

We ended the discussion there that night.

The following day, I called Yoriko and made arrangements to visit her house two days before my return to the States.

Yoshino drove me there on the agreed-upon day, determined to stop me from becoming a member.

Once we arrived her house, I asked Yoriko straightforwardly, "How can I become a member of the teaching that Papa asked me to pursue?"

She opened her eyes wide. "Well, the teaching is based on the Shakyamuni Buddha's last teaching, the Great Nirvana sutra . . ." She began to explain various aspects of the teaching. "I introduced the teaching to Papa as soon as he became ill. As you know, Papa had been praying for all these years . . ."

She talked for five minutes without pause; I imagined this could go on perhaps another hour.

"Yoriko san," I broke in, "thank you for your kind explanation.

But it's not necessary to know all the details. I've already decided to honor Papa's wishes. So, how can I become a member?"

"Aw, okay. Are you sure you don't want to know more about it before you say yes?" she asked me.

I understood her desire to give me more information, but I already knew what I wanted. The choice had already been made.

"I will figure it out later," I said. "For now, since I'm leaving Japan in two days, I wanted to know if there are any temples I can visit before my departure. I'd like to experience it at least once before I return to the States."

Yoriko had all the paperwork there at her house for membership enrollment. I signed my papers right there and then.

"Can I sign up too?" Yoshino suddenly asked.

"Of course," Yoriko said, though she was clearly confused by my sister's change of heart.

I didn't blame her; I was surprised too!

In a matter of thirty minutes, my sister and I both became members of the teaching. Yoriko was blown away.

She said we'd go to visit the temple near her home the next day.

When we got in the car, I looked at Yoshino. "I thought you weren't interested!" I said.

She smiled. "I was moved by your determination," she said. "If you are going to walk this path, I want to follow you."

The following day, Yoriko took Yoshino and me to a temple in Chiba city, and I attended the service called "Merit Transfer" for the first time in my life. The service was to console all the spirits in the spiritual realm and bring compassion and wisdom to those who now offered such prayers. It was a timely event; it gave us a chance to console one another and reflect on Papa's passing.

I'd known about Buddhism from our customs around funerals in Japan, books, lectures, and some retreats at Zen temples that I'd attended when I was in twenties. But this was very different from anything I'd experienced previously.

As we chanted together with other practitioners, the collective energy of chanting was so powerful that it gave me goose bumps. My ears and skin vibrated; my heart and spirit felt invigorated, particularly when we chanted the mantra "Achala's Benevolence and Liberation," though I'd never heard of it before. With its distinct, beautiful melody, I felt as if an arrow had hit deep inside my heart, and now blood had begun to circulate through it for the first time in my life. I cried quietly, with a sense of deep comfort and acceptance; I felt I'd finally found a home.

The service and its ritual was televised live at the Grand Holy Temple in Tokyo. The head of the Buddhist community and the head priest of the Head temple gathered our prayers and officiated the rituals. As I listened to her voice during the ritual, it penetrated deep into my soul and spirit, and again tears fell down my cheeks. I felt a great sense of healing.

In that moment, I knew that this teaching had powers to embrace us all "as we are," regardless of our differences, shortcomings, ego-driven pretentions, delusions, and imperfections. That day, I knew my decision to pursue this path was the right one.

Immediately after Patrick and I returned home to Maryland, I began to read the book written by the founder of my new teaching and started to chant in the mornings and evenings. As I did, the sense that I'd had from the first experience at the service—something invigorating—came back to me. The teaching's contents were so pure and profound.

Since my childhood, I'd had true feelings but learned to hide them from others' eyes. But in this teaching, everything seemed defenseless, open—totally vulnerable and yet full of strength. I thought the flow of the teaching ran like a pure stream of water, with no obstructions, hesitations, or pretentions. As I soaked myself in the pure water, I felt embraced. I felt that this path would allow me to be more honest with myself.

I shed tears every time I read my teaching's publications; it was as if they'd cleansed my heart on a much deeper level than I'd ever experienced. I sensed that this path would be an infinite source of awakening wisdom and loving kindness and compassion for me. It was something profound and essential that I could trust.

Yoshino later told me that she shared her own feelings and experience with Mama and Machiyo after our visit to the temple, and eventually both of them also became members. From Papa having shared his dying wish, all of our family became members of the Buddhist teaching that would change my life.

Just before I left Japan, I told my sisters, "I don't need anything from Papa's inheritance. Whatever is available for me, I'd like Mama to have."

In the days following his funeral, my sisters and Papa's closest colleague, an associate professor in Papa's department, took on the time-consuming tasks of sorting his papers, photos, and other belongings. They also began to look into Papa's life insurance and possible inheritance distributions. Of course, this meant communicating with his new wife, Yaeko, who'd shown her true colors in Papa's final days.

Machiyo and Yoshino sometimes cried to me on the phone, their voices trembling with emotion, telling me things like, "Yaeko san asked us to put away all Papa's clothes into trash bags. Though they'd been worn until recently, she didn't want to even touch them. How can she do that? These are her late husband's items, aren't they?"

My sisters also wanted things that Papa had created with his own hands. But Yaeko simply saw them as old trash that she wanted to get rid of, and threw them away before my sisters could salvage them. Furthermore, as soon as his funeral was over, she began to renovate Papa's home to totally erase his presence. Though it was too late to change things, my sisters couldn't bear that she would receive his home and all the money that Papa had left behind.

I felt sorry for Mama through all of this, but I refused to take on the emotions my sisters carried. These were Papa's final decisions, and we couldn't change that.

Finally, through my sisters' painstaking efforts and tears, we reached a settlement with Yaeko. Unfortunately, the laws in Japan did not protect a long-term wife like Mama; they were more favorable for Yaeko. Mama couldn't ask for anything else but what she had already received five years earlier. Following the law, we as his three daughters and our half-sister and Yaeko received our distributions. Machiyo, Yoshino, and I agreed to save our distributions to support Mama in the future.

Back home in Maryland, I reflected upon how Papa's passing had impacted both me and the rest of my family in Japan. Instantly afterward, I'd noticed big changes. At the airport before my departure to the States, my sisters and their spouses were more sincere, open, and wholehearted toward me than they ever had been before. There were no more lies and far fewer boundaries between us.

As for me, I could see the positive changes all the interactions I'd had with my family during this time in Japan had created in me. I'd become a catalyst to promote goodwill in our family dynamics; I'd finally reconciled my awkward position in our family.

The unconditional love and support I'd received from Patrick over the last few years had fundamentally transformed me into the person I was originally meant to be. Life with my husband was about continuously transforming ourselves—living a mindful life. As long as we stayed with our truth and sincerity, I knew we would be able to create deep meaning in our life together.

I was gradually learning that life is not about finding something elsewhere, outside of us, but rather something we build and accumulate within us through sincere effort. Life consists of many footsteps, and the path we take is dictated by how we place each step.

The year 1997 was a big turning point for Patrick and I. Patrick lost his father in March and completed the site visit for his scientific reviews at the NCI, NIH at the end of April. I completed the steps to become a pediatric dentist that spring. And Papa passed away and led me to the Buddhist teaching I would soon embrace toward the end of the same year.

Throughout that year, we found ourselves at various points of "breaks and pauses" in our life, each of which forced us to stop and reflect. Then I began to sense a sort of irresistible "force for change" in our lives; every event we experienced seemed to be collectively leading us to change to a new direction. It was almost like gravity—difficult to sense individually yet at the same time undeniably everywhere around us.

In March, Patrick was very busy preparing for an upcoming scientific review site visit. Almost simultaneously, his dad was hospitalized in England. Patrick traveled to see him on several occasions before his death—but when he did finally pass away, he was alone.

His death was concluded to be caused by a sudden cardiac arrest. Patrick regretted not being there.

About a month after his dad's funeral, Patrick underwent the scientific evaluation of each project in his department that he'd been preparing for over the course of months. He was disappointed with the review's decision: to reevaluate and possibly promote him for a tenured position at the next site visit, four years later.

"There's too much politics around here," he complained. "Even after another four years, who knows if I will get tenure?" He was worried.

I saw the situation with Patrick's site visit differently—as positive rather than negative. I encouraged Patrick to see it as the opportunity to revisit his career choices closely and decide what he'd really like to achieve going forward. This was his chance to drive himself forward instead of letting his environment and condition make his decisions for him.

As for my work, I'd been a faculty member only for three months, but I was already exhausted from juggling the long commute (almost a hundred miles each way). I felt it was inevitable that we'd eventually move closer to Baltimore—which, of course, would affect where Patrick might work. Changes were on the horizon.

Our fathers' deaths put Patrick and me both into deep grieving and left us face to face with the vacant spaces in our lives. When we were deep in the emotions of our grief, it was hard to see what it all meant; but when I was able to clear my mind in quiet stillness, I began to see and hear the littlest inklings of potential; a message from beyond us; something sacred.

Beyond the door in front of me was the unknown—and I was ready to open the door. In order to grow, we would need to leave some comfort behind us. When we hold something tight in our hands, we aren't able to grab something else new and interesting. We had to let go!

A month after Papa's passing, we'd been entertaining the idea of Patrick's career change for almost eight months. Finally, Patrick had begun to seriously reevaluate his career at the NCI, NIH and begun to consider moving to a more direct and applied approach to his cancer research: generating anti-cancer drugs.

As he opened up to the possibility of a career in the pharmaceutical industry, more and more companies began to offer him jobs. Finally, he decided to move out of his comfort zone, the NIH, and life in Maryland altogether. Soon, we'd narrowed our options down to two possible locations: San Diego and Boston.

After the New Year break in 1998, my boss at the clinic where I worked greeted me, "Happy New Year!" and asked me how I was feeling.

I replied cheerfully but mentioned that Patrick and I were still grieving our fathers.

Seemingly surprised by my response, almost laughing, my boss said, "Oh, really? But your dad was in Japan and you've been here for many years. And most of all, his death was anticipated, wasn't it?" He made it sound like I shouldn't feel the way I felt.

Obviously, this man had very little empathy and imagination. He didn't seem capable of relating to someone else's sorrow.

This realization took me to another: I couldn't recall his *ever* expressing any emotion or empathy toward anyone in our clinic, not even our pediatric patients. He was mechanical, disciplined, and well-mannered with patients—like a robot.

In that moment, I knew clearly what I wanted in my life—exactly how I'd want to lead and create my life with Patrick. I reflected, with much appreciation of my life, upon how lucky I'd been. I'd built my armor around me in my tender years to protect my vulnerability. But I didn't need that armor anymore. I could stay as vulnerable as I felt.

As I treated patients in my clinic, I always felt my patients' pulsating heartbeats, their lives and livelihoods, and their various backgrounds as parts of them. I sometimes felt overwhelmed with by how much empathy I felt for them.

Now more than ever, I wanted to live a life with my arms and heart wide open. My conversation with my boss that day filled me with recognition about how I wanted to lead my life. I wanted to treat my patients as whole beings. This was a call from *my* being.

I'd learned and achieved much in Maryland, but I was ready for the next challenges in my life. The door was about to open.

It was time to go west.

— 14 —
Living in the West

In the first week of 1998, Patrick and I attended a First Merit Transfer service at my teaching's New York temple in White Plains. This was the first time we'd attended a service in the States. Afterward, Patrick surprised me by saying, "I'd like to join you as a member of the teaching."

Patrick had been watching me devotedly chanting each day and reading about the teaching at home since Papa's passing. Since my only experience at the temple in Japan, however, I'd had nobody to guide me; my pursuit of the teaching had been a solitary one. Still, it was clear to me that this teaching was what I'd been looking for. I had the sense of having encountered the right path.

Since Day One of my practice, I'd offered a small glass of water and incense, and my sincere prayers, to the Buddhas every day. I'd then extended the practice to our parents and ancestors, mostly by offering their favorite foods, tea or coffee, and sweets. This had moved Patrick to also offer a cup of tea every morning to his parents and ancestors, and over the months it had become natural to both of us to express our love and prayers in this way to the people in the spiritual realm.

Right before our move to San Diego, my first formal training opportunity arrived. At the time, I was still commuting to the university in Baltimore every day. In the piercing cold, snowy winter, I attended my first Annual Training (held globally at the beginning of each year for practitioners to experience chanting, testimonials, dharma talks, teachings, and short meditations) in Washington DC. Every day, I drove to a fellow practitioner's home and soaked myself in the teachings.

Patrick didn't attend the training with me that year, but each day he checked in with me, asking, "How was training today?"

Each evening, I shared what I'd experienced—there was something new or special or moving each day.

Patrick listened.

Back in Japan in my twenties, when I'd attended the iWD seminars and another self-awareness spiritual group's meetings, both of which had Hindu gurus, I'd never been able to hide my reservation and sometimes frustration with these groups. I felt their belief systems and doctrines weren't thorough or deep enough—at least in the way they were being presented. They purported to help members in the ways of spirituality, but too often the leaders' own egos and business concerns were intertwined with the practice, which showed up in how they favored members who were more beneficial to their businesses. This had troubled me.

In this Buddhist teaching, in contrast, I'd not only found profoundness and connectivity to the source of liberation and awakening—clarity, cleanliness, and purity—but also unparalleled sincerity and humility. The founding members, as well as the present head of the teaching, Her Holiness, never positioned themselves as superior to anyone. Throughout their lives, they'd placed the Buddhas and their practitioners first, and themselves last. I felt I could trust them, and from the beginning I looked up to them.

—

On the final day, Patrick dropped me off and picked me up at the end. When he arrived to collect me, he was showered with greetings from practitioners. While exchanging a few words with the coordinator, he joked, "Kyomi was a truck driver in her past life."

She laughed and said, "Yes. I see that. We've been blessed every day by your wife's firm and steady participation!"

I felt the seed of my faith growing in me, which was further solidified through this Annual Training. I knew it would keep growing in both of us, transforming us for the better. I also sensed that it would help me sustain my trust and optimism for our new life in San Diego, and living in an unknown world.

When Patrick and I moved to San Diego at the end of February 1998, we had no friends, no family—nobody we knew in San Diego at all, other than a handful of Patrick's new coworkers. Neither of us had ever even visited San Diego.

From the moment we arrived, Patrick started working hard in his new role in the Research & Development division of a pharmaceutical company. In his new company, he was the latest and youngest addition to a group of executives, all of whom were original members of the company, who'd been there for the past decade.

Patrick had always been at the center of his group of friends, most of whom were foreigners to this country. Now he was experiencing culture shock as he experienced only Americans in a competitive environment for the first time—and it stressed him out. He always stayed genuine, considerate, and compassionate, but he expected other people to treat him the same way; in this new company, this wasn't always the case.

I'd been with Patrick long enough to know that he could be rather reactive—that his emotional impulse was to act like a warrior who fights against injustice and maltreatment. His impulses and his vulnerability seemed totally opposite in nature, but they must have had the same origin, because I saw how they appeared in two ways: when others were victims, or when he was a victim. Whenever this vulnerability of his showed itself, I wanted to hold and protect him from the world, as if I were his mother.

At his new company, in this jungle of strong and critical personalities, Patrick maintained excellent performance and strong professional and collaborative relationships, but he didn't make friends. This seemed to be by choice, as Patrick often quoted his Dad's words: "The family are the only ones I can trust."

As for me, my concerns were more practical, at least for a while. Before our relocation, I knew there was no dental school in San Diego where I could continue my research. The nearest academic institutions or universities that had dental schools were in Los Angeles or Riverside County, which would require a brutal commute each day. I decided it wouldn't be realistic to pursue this avenue in California.

At the end of March, I made a decision to practice as a full-time pediatric dentist at a dental clinic, the Indian Health Commissure (IHC). It was located fifty-plus miles northeast from our home and partially funded by Indian Health Service.

From my first day on the job, I witnessed the socioeconomic and familial obstacles and challenges to dental care for our patients. It felt as if there were a huge iceberg in front of me.

Pediatric dentistry was my specialty, but people in the community didn't know me, and many distrusted me because of my ethnicity and because I was an immigrant.

In the beginning, I didn't know if I would be defeated by the challenges of my new role, or if I would be able to transform myself through and despite these difficulties, but I was determined to do my best. I hoped to turn these challenges into opportunities for me to grow, and also to help the community.

In mid-March, Patrick and I made our first visit to the Los Angeles temple in Anaheim, which turned out to be an important stepping-stone in our life. The LA temple was the closest of our teaching's temples to our home, though it took us an hour and a half to get there. At the time, it was just a small, wooden, single-story, ranch-style building, renovated from a residence with a huge orange orchard on the property around it.

In the warm, bright sun before the service started at eleven o'clock, Patrick and I were welcomed by the reverend and many practitioners—"Welcome back! Welcome back!" they all said.

I wondered aloud to Patrick about this; we'd never been there before, why were they saying, "Welcome back" instead of "Hello" or "Good morning"? But I didn't ask anyone to explain. I just followed quietly as they kindly showed us around and directed us where to leave our shoes. We were in the house of Buddha, and everyone showed each other much respect.

A month later, I would learn from a reverend at the temple why they said, "Welcome back." In the teaching, the sanctuary and temples are the places where our hearts, souls, and spirits truly belong, like our "home." Though we can physically visit the temple, the action of visiting is to fundamentally return our hearts to this home and sanctuary where the sacred and the divine powers will generate, heal, and nurture our hearts. Upon hearing this explanation, the essence of "welcome back" penetrated into my heart. I thought that even if we couldn't visit the temple, we would still be able to return our hearts to this true home by praying.

After that first service ended, we walked around the temple property. Oranges on the trees shone bright and happy under the warm sun, which enveloped us in its yellowish-orange light. The warmth in the atmosphere felt good through our long sleeves. We truly did feel at home.

Back at home that afternoon, over cups of tea, Patrick and I talked about our experiences at the temple that day. We'd been warmly welcomed and we both had a sense of spiritual restoration from the temple grounds; we'd both felt invited, comfortable, and relaxed.

"Let's go back within a month," Patrick said. "Let's visit regularly."

"Sure, we'll plan for it," I replied.

With a relaxed smile on his face, he asked, "Shall we do a barbecue tonight?"

"That's a great idea!" I said.

I was happy to hear Patrick's voice more vibrant. I hadn't seen him so relaxed in a while.

Despite our busy daily lives, the temple would become a cornerstone for us in the ensuing months. Patrick and I quickly realized the importance of the teaching in our very demanding, busy lifestyles in San Diego. Soon, it became an anchor for our lives.

Within a few months, Patrick and I began to receive meditative training after the temple services on the days we could attend. The idea of the training, unique to our teaching, was to touch one's heart with that of the Buddha's.

During the meditative training, a trainee reflects on his or her daily life and receives specific spiritual guidance with the help of a spiritual guide in accordance with the spiritual indication for the trainee. The spiritual guide is also a practitioner, but one who has cultivated spiritual faculty through years of spiritual training and undergone continued proper training to serve such a role. The goal of the training is for the trainee's intrinsic spiritual core, "Buddha nature," to meet with the ever-present *dharma body*, the essential, cosmic wisdom and loving compassion. This spiritual union is known as *interpenetration*.

After attending meditative training, both Patrick and I realized its direct positive spiritual effects on us.

"How do you feel?" I asked him after one.

"It's so good. I feel lighter." He did indeed look brighter.

"I know—I feel some hanging clouds were cleared away from my brain," I said, motioning with my hands over my head for emphasis.

Patrick smiled at me. "In such a short sitting, I feel like I've become a different person," he agreed.

Through this meditative training, the sense of purity, serenity, and cleanliness from the temple and its grounds seemed multiplied, and it penetrated into our souls. I would often shed tears, sometimes from a sense of repentance, sometimes gratitude, and other times awakening.

Patrick and I were also amazed by the accuracy and propriety of the spiritual guidance we received at these trainings. If our minds were open to listen and accept, the guidance we received was always right on target regarding what we needed to work on in our daily lives. We didn't know how it worked, but we trusted it.

Meditative training has two parts: the first is to sit and meditate to receive spiritual guidance at the temple, and the second is to put that guidance into practice. The second part is far more difficult, as it requires people to act on their spiritual guidance rather than simply receive and contemplate the guidance offered.

That's why, in our teaching, home, work, and greater society are referred to as our "actual training grounds." The efficiency and outcomes of our practices are dependent on our will, focus, and determination to carry through our practice and training every day. If we experience resistance or reluctance to practice, progress in our transformation won't happen.

At that time, I didn't know it would take me some time to fully understand this crucial concept of meditation, practice, and training. The teaching was at times esoteric and therefore hard to grasp until I'd gone through some trial and error of my own. The only way to learn was to practice. Unless we practiced wholeheartedly, we would never understand.

But once Patrick and I began to engage in active meditation—what our teaching calls "contemplative actions"—our whole lives changed. We were living the practice.

One of the ways I began to practice mindfulness, thoughtfulness, and compassion was in attending to how I spoke to Patrick, as well as to patients and their guardians at my practice.

As an English-as-a-second-language speaker, my intention when I spoke in English had always tended to be rather direct and straightforward: I focused on what was on *my* mind and what *I* would like to express. But as I reflected on the guidance I'd received in the teaching, I could see that I needed to pay more attention to how other people might hear my words. In other words, before I delivered my speech, I needed to be more mindful about how my audience might react to my words. When I did this, my words for others became kinder and more considerate, and I was able to better communicate with the people around me.

Little by little, I began to see the faces of the people I spoke with reflect more acceptance, smiles, and kindness. With the improvements I made on my side, overall communication and the degree of trust my patients had in me increased. I saw firsthand how more positive interactions with other people always started with trying harder in my own thoughts, speech, and actions.

I had attended our teaching's regional meeting in San Diego in March, but there hadn't been one since then. In August, I asked the reverend if there would be another one soon.

"Tomoko san has gone to Japan for her medical treatment and we don't know for sure when she'll be back," he told me.

"Oh, is there anyone who can host a meeting instead of her?" I asked.

"No, nobody seems to want to take on the role."

I was surprised by this, and began to think about a possibility. Might we be able to help?

On the way home in the car, I shared my idea with Patrick and asked him if he'd like to offer our home for monthly regional meetings while Tomoko was gone.

"But you'll be busy with your Board Exams," he said. "If we host the meeting, it will mostly fall to you to organize and host. It's going to be too much for you."

"Maybe," I said. "But if we held it in late September, it would be still possible . . ."

Patrick didn't take much convincing. He said if I was fine with it, there would be no objection from him.

I felt warmth expanding inside of me. I was grateful we were on the same wavelength.

The following day, I called the temple office and proposed my idea. The reverend accepted our offer, and we made a plan to hold the regional meeting at our house in late September.

I felt grateful for and humbled by this opportunity to help our local community.

Since my residency program in 1995, Patrick and I had been only working harder and harder, without any vacations or other fun outlets. As soon as we moved to California, the situation got worse. Patrick's new job required much higher productivity and more responsibilities. He left home every morning at 7:00 a.m. and returned after 7:30 p.m. Luckily his office was located just five minutes from our home, because he was almost stumbling with exhaustion by the time he walked into the house. Sometimes he walked in with the words, "What a day!" dropped his leather bag in the office, and couldn't even change out of his clothes. He would take his pants and socks off, unbutton a few buttons from his shirt, grab a can of Sapporo Reserve or Kirin Ichiban, and immediately gulp it down. Then he'd invariably turn on the TV—loud.

"Are you okay? Do you want to wash your face before dinner?" I'd ask.

"No. it's okay," he'd mumble. "I'll wash before bed."

When dinner was served, he would eat mechanically and keep watching TV, beer in hand. I didn't receive much appreciation or acknowledgment for cooking. I tried to remind myself that he was just too tired to thank me every day.

He also began to travel for work, both domestically and internationally, which involved red-eye flights on Thursday nights and weekends. Mostly he wouldn't sleep on the plane; instead, he'd work. He was working like a machine.

Whenever Patrick returned home from a trip, I was always there to greet him, even if he arrived after midnight. Soon I began to worry about his health and well-being. His eyes were red and swollen, his face and legs all puffed up with water retention from the flights.

When I asked if he was okay, he'd reply, "Just tired . . ." Those seemed to be the only words he could utter. He was always so exhausted when he returned from his trips that he'd pour himself whisky to help him sleep. Despite his exhaustion, he'd then spend his shortened weekends working to prepare for the following week's meetings. He felt he had to prepare and organize everything meticulously and well in advance. And through it all, he never missed a day of work; he acted as if all the work he'd done during the weekend was part of his regular duties.

Within a few months, the life we'd enjoyed in Maryland, full of love and taking day trips to the countryside, was long gone. Our lifestyle had changed completely, and I felt that Patrick was giving himself over to the machinery of his company. He sometimes complained about his colleagues or his company, and even expressed regrets about our move to San Diego, but it felt too late to change it back.

I listened to Patrick's complaints and encouraged him to keep his mindset positive. But I knew that his drive came, in part, from his personality—so detailed, so meticulously organized, so controlling, and always dedicated to excellence.

My role in our life became acting as Patrick's caregiver. He always said he couldn't relax at work at all. "Home is the only place I can relax, rest, and sleep," he'd say.

For the first six months in San Diego, I'd had to juggle a long commute for my job and study for the California Dental Board Exams, so I was busy as well. But I'd promised myself that once I'd sorted out the upcoming the state exams, I would shift my focus back to my most pressing issue: my husband, and his well-being.

As soon as I completed the Board Exams in early autumn, I shifted my focus back to Patrick and his extremely stressful and unbalanced life. I was starting to see his drinking habit as inching toward becoming a problem, and I began to contemplate what needed to change in our lives.

Around that time, I received spiritual guidance in a couple of consecutive meditative trainings to become a foundation for those closest to me—which, of course, meant Patrick.

This had been one of our wows and wonders of meditative training. When the guidance we received was properly applied in our daily practice, the spiritual guidance at the next training would be different from the last, aiming for other areas of practice or further deepening such practice. But if daily practice was still short, the spiritual world somehow knew it, and would often repeat the same or similar guidance from a different spiritual guide.

I saw my insufficient application and practice of the guidance I'd received and the impact that was having. The teaching had become the compass of my life by that point, and I'd trusted it through any turbulent times. Now I needed to help Patrick. By helping first him, then both of us, I could pull us out of this ongoing, worrisome situation. When we have a raging fire in the house, first we have to extinguish the fire, then we can think about other issues. I needed to extinguish this fire.

Both of us had professional careers and busy lives. But my immediate concern was how I could rescue Patrick and thereby contribute to our long-term happiness. As I analyzed our circumstances, I realized that part of the problem was that we were both equally powerful professionals with busy careers. I saw that the key to harmony in our house would come not from intensity but through a balance—like Yin and Yang, the sun and the moon, the earth and the sky.

I knew Patrick's stress wasn't only extrinsic (the work), but also intrinsic (his perception of the importance of the stressors affecting him). Transforming our minds, and how to perceive these stressors, would be the key to reduce our daily stress. But achieving this would take time and efforts—tenacious, everyday practice.

For now, I was the only person in our relationship who could see this picture clearly. I was therefore the only one who could take actions. I decided it was time to make some changes—starting with myself.

The primary goal for my intended practice was to make our home truly *home*. Since Patrick sometimes didn't have time to return to the temple, our home needed to become his temple. I wanted him to feel that our home was his sanctuary, somewhere safe and comforting where he could restore his body, soul, and spirit.

To achieve my goal, I broke it into several concrete objectives and approaches.

First, I placed Patrick as the center of my focus, meaning I took the initiative to lower my own expectations and achievement goals for my own professional life in order to prioritize him.

It may sound like my needs became secondary to Patrick's. That's true. But because I *decided* to do this with a sense of purpose and full conviction, it didn't bother me. I'd known San Diego had no dental school even before we moved. I'd known our new existence there would alter my role in our life together. Now that we were here, I wanted to give all my commitment and pure devotion to Patrick, our marriage, and the teaching.

Throughout my soul-searching experience, I'd known what mattered most to me. *Ikigai,* which in Japanese means to fulfill both the purpose and fulfillment in our life, could be achieved in many ways, not only rigid objectives. Our relationship and our sense of wholeness mattered most. Applying our teaching to everything in my life—my clinical practice, home, and relationships—would become my *ikigai.*

I also *consciously* decided to dedicate more time to homemaking by reducing my workload from full time to part time. In a dental practice, a dentist is usually the only provider, but the dental team makes its clinical practice. Everyone in the team is essential to making the practice run smoothly. And a home is the same. Someone has to take on the functions unique to each household in order for it to flourish.

So, I decided: I would be the caretaker of our home; I would be our foundation.

After receiving my California license, I searched for a pediatric practice near my house. In November, I got hired to work one day a week by a pediatric dentist whose office was only twenty minutes from our home. I did keep the IHC practice on a part-time basis—I'd committed myself deeply to the welfare of this indigenous community, and I was willing to walk away—but I scaled back the time I spent there significantly.

I continued to make our home as clean and tidy as possible, and began to arrange fresh flowers and frame artistic images from my photo collections, as I'd done in Maryland. I cultivated a more creative, serene, and peaceful atmosphere in the house.

As I dedicated myself to these pursuits, my desire to become Patrick's *home,* and his best friend, developed. Since Patrick had left all his friends behind in Maryland, I wanted to deepen our relationship and love him even more. I cooked every day, including my workdays.

Everything I did for Patrick became a work of love.

At first, Patrick didn't seem to notice any of the efforts and changes I was making. He was always too tired to contribute. Before, he'd always made our bed before work when we were both working, but now I was doing everything and instead of acknowledging it he seemed to take advantage of it, even to expect it.

Was all this effort simply making him lazier and sloppier? Was he using me as a convenient housekeeper? I'd told him I would be appreciative if he could do small tasks, like at least bringing dirty dishes to the sink. He heard me, but sometimes he still didn't do it. I tried not to get angry or emotional, but I cried secretly sometimes because I felt I was chiseling away at an iceberg, only to have it keep growing before my eyes. He didn't seem to appreciate what I was doing.

Did I want recognition and appreciation? Yes, I did.

But each time I received spiritual guidance at the temple, the message was the same: "Be a *true* foundation for others' happiness." A *true* foundation; that meant an egoless state of dedication. So I reflected and kept trying, until finally I became appreciative of my own tireless chiseling works. This helped me to solidify my conviction and transform myself to be a foundation for our happiness.

Toward the end of 1998, slowly but surely, my daily practice finally began to bear fruit.

"*Tadaima*! I'm home!" Patrick cheerfully announced when he walked from the garage into the kitchen one afternoon.

"*Okaeri nasai*! Welcome back home!" I greeted him.

Patrick kissed me on my lips and then went upstairs, a bounce in his steps, seemingly lighter than he'd been in a long time. He changed into pajamas, but when he came downstairs, he was all smiles. He'd clearly washed his face and combed his hair as well.

"You look nice, Patrick," I said appreciatively.

He kissed me again on my cheek, looking into pots and pans on the stovetop.

"*Oishi so desu ne*! Oh, they look so delicious!" he said, smiling. Patrick enjoyed employing his limited Japanese anywhere he could. I appreciated this cheerful side of him dearly.

He opened the refrigerator and cracked a can of Kirin Ichiban, his favorite lager. Though I'd worried about his drinking, it was only when he used it to numb his mind that it bothered me. Now, it seemed he was just enjoying it. It didn't carry a heavy energy. And when he sat down and turned on the TV, its volume was not too loud, its sounds not overpowering.

From that day forward, Patrick's joy seemingly returned. Once again, he enjoyed talking over dinner, laughing and smiling. This was all I wanted: his smile and comfort.

Finally, they had returned to our lives.

Patrick started to look forward to coming home every day. He also began to carve out time, however little, for us to share local activities during the weekend. Sometimes we walked on trails at the Torrey Pine State Reserves, or went to the Torrey Pine State Beach near our home. We always held hands as we walked.

For a while, I hadn't been able to feel Patrick's heartbeat through our joined palms. But now I felt it coming back. We were becoming more attuned to one another. I felt how he was feeling and where his soul was as soon as I saw his face each day.

I still understood that his job defined him, that he was an important professional working with anti-cancer drugs upon which many thousands of future, unknown patients would rely on in the courses of their treatments. In taking care of Patrick, I felt that I would be, in part, responsible for those patients too.

Patrick started to want to share more concerns with me around his work and his research. Sometimes I listened to his professional talks at home as he prepared for his presentations, giving him a chance to practice with me.

This experience showed me that our good wishes and diligent efforts can improve the outcomes in our life.

When our mind is in the right place, we can build love—we can build a home.

— 15 —
Living in Dharma – I

At the beginning of December, after meditative training, the reverend called us at the office.

"O'Connor san!" He explained that Tomoko had called the office to say that she wouldn't be back early enough to prepare for the following year's Annual Training. He asked if we'd be able to host the next one.

"Yes!" we said at the same time.

The actual preparations for the Annual Training would fall on me, however, as Patrick was in the midst of the final phase of his company's possible acquisition and was swamped.

The order of the teaching and the local temple office encouraged local practitioners to get involved in the organization and preparation for the Annual Training so they would get more motivated and build harmony before it took place. But when I asked for assistance, many people immediately declined, making various excuses, and others didn't respond to my calls. It seemed nobody was willing to help us.

I wondered why; soon enough, I found out.

The reverend told me that Tomoko had called from Japan to express her reservations and objections regarding us taking over the

Annual Training. Though she wouldn't be available to do it herself, she was now seeming to stand in our way.

As I listened to the reverend talk, a hot sensation rose in me.

"Oh, but we're not taking over," I said. "We just wanted to help."

I knew this feeling—it wasn't anger, but rather a sense of protest against an unreasonable claim. I realized I should tamp down this emotion, since it wouldn't help solve the issue. But it wasn't easy. Tomoko had clearly told our fellow practitioners about her feelings; that explained their attitudes. They must be feeling uncomfortable, or like if they got involved they would hurt her feelings.

"Knowing what I've just told you, please work well and carefully with people around you," the reverend said. "That said, it might not be an easy road for you."

As I said yes to the reverend, I began to digest what he'd just told me.

It was big. I felt as if I'd been thrown into the wilderness without any help. People around me had already shown that they were difficult to communicate with, and continuing on might only invite more problems. It would require more effort and commitment than I'd originally imagined. I felt I'd been asked to cultivate an oasis in the heart of a scorching hot desert.

I had a choice. Should I listen to my small ego, which was saying, "I'm just a beginner, I should step aside"? Or should I follow my instincts and let go of my fears?

When the reverend told me what was going on, part of me wondered why he hadn't told Tomoko that she was wrong to be behaving in the way she was. And yet at the same time I understood that this wasn't about who was right or wrong. He was leaving this matter for me to figure out myself.

What was in front of me was about our spiritual community. We all aimed to be liberated and happy. The goal was to not engage our own egos any longer. We weren't there yet, but over time we would get there. I had faith in the long game.

Right before the Annual Training, Patrick's original company announced its acquisition by Walgen Pharmaceutical Company. Now his job got even busier and more stressful. Still, he supported me in my desire to host our first Annual Training. Though he couldn't help, he attended as many trainings as possible. During the night trainings, he'd come in late, slipping in quietly.

Tomoko came back to San Diego a few days before the training started, but she missed the first five days of the morning sessions—because of her jetlag, she said.

When she arrived to her first night training, I said, "*Okaeri nasai!* Welcome back!" as I welcomed her at the door with a smile.

She looked at me suspiciously. "Thank you for hosting this year's training. But I am here back now, so I'll take care of my responsibility after this training as I used to." She noted that she didn't know how often she'd attend this one that I was hosting. "I'm not sure even if I can stay tonight until the end," she added. She was polite enough, but assertive.

"Oh . . . please don't worry about it," I said. "We are just helping. Whenever you are able, please come, even if for just a short time."

Though I tried to convey this casually, I felt nervous. I was worried my voice might sound high-pitched, betraying some of my underlying concerns with her behavior.

As if she knew exactly how I felt, she said, "Oh, no. I wouldn't bother you by coming for just a short time."

Every day during the Annual Training, I got up at 4:00 a.m. and filled a small, clean glass with water while I chanted some mantra in my heart. Then I offered the water to the Buddhas with sincere prayers for the day. As I took deep breaths in the chilly darkness, I felt the cold air flowing into my chest and vigor expanding inside of me. A sense of cleanliness and purity flooded me, and tears fell down on my cheeks. In these moments of silence, I felt centered in the world that I cherished.

Before people's arrival and after they left our home, I'd pray for their wellness and safety. Each night, I tidied up the rooms, prepared materials on the table, and mopped the floor for the next day. Sitting in front of the Buddhas, I was filled with gratitude. I was taken to the infinite space.

During the ten days of the Annual Training, I devoted myself wholeheartedly to every session, but it didn't feel like sacrifice, because I was getting so much from the experience. This made me even more grateful.

Right after we completed the Annual Training, a couple of practitioners came to thank me for hosting.

"Thank you for hosting," one practitioner said. "It's been wonderful; there was something fresh and sincere every day."

Others expressed their gratitude, and tears of appreciation filled my eyes. I noticed a sense of wanting to "win," that somehow the compliments meant I'd done better than Tomoko in this situation. But no. There would be no winner in a situation like this; either all of us would become winners or none of us would.

I blinked my tears away and said, "Thank you very much!"

I was grateful for what we'd all done to make the Annual Training happen, and that I'd persevered. In my heart, I promised the Buddhas that I would never again feel sorry for myself. I tried to align myself with this intention by accepting what was real. I would never be able to change others, but I could mindfully support them in their growth.

I must focus on being reflective, and know that the only thing I could control was my own mind.

Since the previous summer, after completing my first intensive practice in deepening my relationship with Patrick, I'd begun to feel like I was ready to have a child.

Patrick and I had long delayed having a family. I'd miscarried while I was at the residency program, but we hadn't been pursuing a family back then. Both of us being immigrants, we'd been too focused on establishing our professional lives—but now my biological clock was ticking.

When I was in Japan, I'd never thought about having a child. The experiences of my youth had affected me so negatively that I'd been afraid before—but now I really wanted it. Patrick was kind and supportive, and I was truer to myself. We would be good and mature parents, and I imagined a child adding to our dynamic; it would be wonderful to have someone in our lives we could both support and nurture.

I also knew Patrick was good with kids. He loved his niece, Katie, and Paul and Elli's two daughters, who'd been born after we left. I felt his ease around them, and saw how they loved him.

Now we'd been together for nine years, and I saw Patrick as someone who brilliantly radiated light from within. We had our life full of love and light. My belief was that if we had a baby, he would be able to completely embrace his emotions and all shadows from the past would go away. A child would be my gift for Patrick, and for us. These two originally desperately lonely souls who had been raised in the two separate countries would bear a fruit of who we were now.

In February 1999, I started experiencing severe breathing difficulty while I was seeing patients. I was scared, but didn't go to the doctor.

It became more and more labored throughout the next day, when I was off work. I didn't call Patrick at work because he'd had meetings all day and I didn't want to disturb him. But the problem was getting more critical . . . I couldn't breathe. I felt like fainting. I needed to go to the ER, but I didn't have the strength. I clung on to our bed.

As soon as Patrick came home after seven o'clock, he called out to me from downstairs. He knew that I'd been feeling very poorly since a few days earlier, when I'd had surgery to collect the eggs from my ovaries.

He continued to call out until he found me upstairs.

"There you are, Kyomi!" He sat next to me on the bed. "Are you okay?"

"No . . . I can't breathe . . . Can you take me to Emergency?" I still felt like I was going to faint.

When I tried to stand up, I was too weak to hold my body upright; I collapsed onto Patrick. He held me up, shouting, "Kyomi! Kyomi!"

My brain sensed I was about to lose consciousness, but I told my body to hang on tight.

Patrick had to literally drag me downstairs and to his car.

At the ER, I was too weak to sit alone on the edge of the bed. I leaned against Patrick, who was standing by me. Through blurred vision, I watched a young male technician sterilize my skin on the left lower corner of my abdomen. He held a long, thick needle attached to a few feet of a Teflon tube, the end of which was placed into a gallon-sized clear glass bottle on a small stool below my bed. As he poked the needle through my skin, a stream of chocolate-colored fluid rushed into the tube so fast that it splattered the sides of the jar.

As the jar filled, I became lightheaded.

"Wow!" the technician exclaimed. "Amazing . . . you've accumulated so much."

The dark, bloody fluid had now almost filled the jar. I felt nauseated watching it.

The technician quickly picked up the end of the tube from the bottle and asked me to hold its end, with gauze, stopping the flow for a moment. He replaced the jar with a smaller one and placed the tube end again in it.

The fluid was coming out much slower now. He picked up the gallon jar from the stool, put it on the bed, and showed it to us. In the dim emergency room, the bright white sheets on the ER bed contrasted with the chocolate-colored contents of the jar. I touched the glass bottle. *Warm.*

When the technician had extracted everything he could, he finally removed the needle and placed a band-aid over the puncture mark. My head became vacant. I laid on the ER bed and rested for a while, holding Patrick's hand.

"When I came home tonight," Patrick told me, his face pale, "I thought you might die there in my arms."

I saw his unspeakable fear in his face, and felt his love for me.

The next day, after my discharge from the hospital, I went to the fertility clinic for a follow-up exam.

The nurse who came to see me seemed stiff—perhaps from anxiety? Her body couldn't tell a lie. All her facial muscles were tight as I explained what had happened the previous night.

"Oh . . . that was anticipated," she told me.

The way she responded to me made me understand that she knew what had happened to me at the ER. She deliberately avoided using the word "sorry" or expressing any empathy.

I felt I was being blamed for what had happened.

I thought about what had happened. The hyper-stimulation of my ovaries preceding the egg extraction must have released not only a larger number of eggs but also fluids associated with these "hyper-ovulation" processes. My guess was that when the doctor harvested the eggs a few days earlier, bleeding must have started, and the blood as well as fluid from my ovaries must have continued to secrete.

If all these had been anticipated, they could've warned me and properly monitored me for the risk. But they'd failed to do so.

"I wasn't informed of any of these possibilities," I explained. "None of you took any measures to monitor this 'anticipated' condition."

The nurse gulped a breath and looked down, as if willing me away.

We couldn't change the past. I stayed quiet but inside me I felt a firm sense of opposition to what was happening. I didn't like the way she was trying to manipulate me by imposing their version of events. Overpowering a patient in this way was wrong.

"But the good news is," the nurse continued, now in an artificially high tone of voice, "we are still growing the embryos in the incubator. Dr. Miller wants to transfer them back to you tomorrow, or at latest the day after tomorrow. Is that okay with you?"

What? I'd just returned from the hospital, where I'd almost died. Surgery tomorrow? They wanted to put me back on their conveyer belt already?

I wanted to protest, but practically speaking, we'd already paid the entire three courses' payment in full—tens of thousands of dollars. And I knew that Patrick really wanted this. I would talk this over with him before making a decision.

—

That night, Patrick and I discussed our options. Ultimately, we decided to drop this first course and resume the next one in a couple of months.

After all the hormone therapies and surgeries, the second cycle did not result in pregnancy. But after our third cycle, I finally got pregnant. All the agonizing experiences I'd gone through seemed to finally have paid off. The news made us so happy. Patrick began to imagine whether we'd have a boy or a girl.

Patrick had gifted me a big brown teddy bear with sweet eyes years earlier, which he'd named John Taro, and a girl teddy bear a few years after that, which he'd named Omi.

Now he teased, "If it's a boy, John Taro, and if it's a girl, Omi!"

He was so happy with these names that it seemed one of these would in fact be the baby's name.

The news of my pregnancy had brought us something new and fresh. I felt as if it had opened curtains, bringing light into our lives— one that was connected with a light inside me. I remained cautious, since I'd miscarried before, but I also began to think about our future with a little baby we'd created together.

Three weeks after our good news, I was praying for our ancestors at the home altar during the period of *Ullambana*—a day when a type of Merit Transfer is held to console ancestors' spirits at the temple— when a small shock, like a jolt of noise, suddenly traveled through my lower abdomen. I felt as if someone had stabbed me, or cut a rope connected to my organs. It wasn't painful, exactly, but it felt like a bodily impact.

I became immediately anxious that something might have happened to the baby. But there was no pain, no bleeding, and no physical signs, so I didn't take any action. I decided I just needed to convince myself everything would be okay, so I said nothing about this incident to Patrick.

My feeling of anxiety persisted until our next visit to the clinic ten days later.

"The embryo has stopped growing," our doctor announced seconds after beginning the examination.

Ah . . .! I'd known the moment it happened.

Our baby was gone. After all the painful efforts, we'd lost our future light. I felt like a spineless, rubbery animal. Patrick became quiet. He put his hand on my shoulder. We left the clinic in a state of confusion, deeply immersed in loss and total defeat.

Patrick and I still had each other, but the incident prevented us from speaking to each other for days after that. We both felt as if we'd failed each other. Our baby had been only an imaginary creature at this point, but the idea of it had grown so important and powerful that losing it was devastating.

We began a period of grieving. I was hard on myself. The more sense of responsibility and effort I'd put into the trials, the heavier and larger my sense of guilt and failure had become.

Within a week, I underwent a D&C procedure to clean my uterine lining and remove the embryo. It was incredibly difficult to go through with it—I knew the embryo was dead and wasn't growing anymore, but I still had a strong instinct to hold on to it.

Patrick was in his own cocoon and wasn't communicating with me, leaving me to feel isolated and unbalanced. I felt upended by the loss of this possibility and my attachment to it.

As the anesthesia from the surgery wore off, I was floating atop of dim consciousness. In my cloudy brain, I was thinking about the baby. Tears fell from my eyes and trailed along my temples.

Reflecting on the last three attempts, I knew I'd failed. I saw a dead end—not just because of my age and biological challenges, but because of karma. I imagined all the outcomes if we were to try again—either the baby or I would die, I was sure of it.

What could we do? Could we ask someone to be a surrogate? Would we want to adopt a child? Could Patrick accept the idea? All of these thoughts dulled my brain. I was too tired, in too much pain and anguish. They gave me one small pain pill, which must've been an opioid, but it made me feel unsteady and nauseated.

A few hours later I got discharged from the hospital.

At home, I bled heavily and I was still in severe lower abdominal pain. I longed to feel Patrick. I followed him around the house—I wanted to be with him—but just being up made me lightheaded. Dizzy, I laid myself on the carpet in his office and cried.

Patrick came back inside from the garden and acted as if he was busy at his desk with some paperwork. Then he stood up and went to the kitchen. I knew he was trying to occupy himself, to distract himself, to remove himself from what had happened to me, to him, to us. He couldn't face it. Obviously, my presence was a painful reminder of what had happened.

When he returned to the desk, he almost tripped over me, at which point he lost his patience.

"Get off the floor! You're in my way!" he shouted.

"I've just had surgery and lost my baby," I cried. "How do you think I feel?"

"How do you think *I feel*?" he responded.

The veil of deep sadness quickly shut me off from this conversation.

I couldn't continue talking with him. I knew I was trembling, and I could see that Patrick was shaking from anger. We were each lost in our deep sorrow.

I must leave here, I told myself. I left his office silently, took another pill, and went upstairs, where I crawled into bed.

I don't know how long I was in a state of apathy—perhaps a couple of hours? I was in bed, sobbing, but I felt no feelings. I felt my body reacting to the impact of all that had transpired, but I couldn't integrate my body and emotions as one.

Then, as if my soul had just lifted itself up out of the rubble of my devastation, my lightheadedness got a little better and I was able to focus a little. I began to think over what had just happened in Patrick's office, and what he'd said to me.

Now I felt more aligned. I knew I needed to reframe my thoughts and behavior to restore our relationship. I didn't want to pity myself or be a victim. What was most important now was our relationship.

The fact was that I'd had a D&C and lost our baby. But I'd lost more than that too—all the efforts with invasive surgeries and stressful IVF treatments. I knew if I wanted to justify myself as a patient who needed to be taken care of, I could. If I wanted to be a victim of all the stressful treatments, I could. And if I wanted to criticize Patrick's harsh treatment of me, I could.

I was guiding myself through one of the mindful daily practices I'd learned from the teaching. I began to examine Patrick's behavior and his emotions. He seemed so stressed out, upset, and unable to control himself—unusual for Patrick. I knew he'd been under inordinate stress at work and at home throughout our IVF treatment.

I began to contemplate what emotions had triggered him to shout at me just now—and, suddenly, I had an insight. I *discovered* Patrick through this experience, saw him for the first time as a person who was also suffering. Suffering from all the stresses he'd undergone at work, and from the collapse of all his hopes and expectations for our baby, our relationship, and the future.

I could now see Patrick as a person who'd really wanted this baby too. He was in pain, too, he just couldn't express it.

My thoughts then traveled over a longer period of time—the entirety of our relationship. Even when Patrick lost his dad, I hadn't been able to be there as much as I wanted to be for his grieving because I'd had to stay in Baltimore to finish my program. There must have been many moments when Patrick had been sad, terrified, and helpless and I hadn't been able to fully understand and support his feelings.

As I knew already from my own experiences, Patrick was less tolerant of painful events than I was. At the beginning of our relationship, I was the person whom Patrick had always looked after. But now I could be that for him—the person who would look after him, whom he could truly rely on. I could be his best friend.

Later that night, I got out of bed and went downstairs. Patrick's face was gray. He couldn't speak, and he seemed to be frozen.

You must talk to him, I told myself.

"Patrick," I said, "I am very sorry for what happened, and for my shortcomings. I haven't been a good wife who truly understands you. But I promise I'll be a better person, and then we can become a better couple."

All of a sudden, Patrick's gray face softened and he smiled at me in relief. He'd clearly been under agonizing pressure, wanting to apologize to me but unable to.

He kissed me on my lips instead, showing me his happiness.

"Are you okay? Are you still in pain?" he asked me.

He'd just needed someone else to help him let go of his anxiety.

Through this painful time, I learned a lot about my Patrick. Nobody was perfect. No couple was without its struggles. I determined from that day forward who I truly wanted to become: the best partner and best friend Patrick could ever have.

— 16 —
Our Spiritual Foundations

Enlightenment, the essence of esoteric Buddhist teachings, was largely a kept secret of the monastic community until our founders reestablished the order and the teaching after the Dharma Crisis broke out in 1950.

Our founders rediscovered and adapted the Shakyamuni Buddha's last teachings, the Great Nirvana Sutra, into our teaching as the core canonical doctrine—and thus the essence of *enlightenment* became available for the first time to all people, including lay practitioners. Our founders also helped establish a path to connect this world with the spiritual world to help people out of suffering. Their transcendental workings also became the foundation for our teaching's spiritual meditative training.

In addition to regular meditative training after the services, we have another type of monthly meditative training in our teaching—one specifically aimed to cultivate practitioners' bodhi (an awakening heart) and to encourage practitioners to actively attain the essence of enlightenment: wisdom, loving kindness, and compassion. Once a month, overseas practitioners meditate at the training sitting, and once a year they can apply for "succession" meditative training sitting.

At "succession" meditative training sitting, practitioners can experience "succession" to the substance and essence of enlightenment. This process is very esoteric and invisible; in a nutshell, they can attain the essence of enlightenment in increments, step by step.

Elevation of *bodhi*, attainment of enlightenment—wisdom and compassion—is a continuous daily process and practice. However, in the case of "succession" meditative training sitting, within one and a half hours of meditation, a practitioner may experience actual "succession" through the surging forth of transcendental wonders. The practitioner's state of mind—cultivated through her diligent daily practice and reflection—is what determines whether or not she will advance to the next level of practice.

When Patrick and I began the bodhi-cultivating meditative training in 1999, we had no idea what "succession" meant, or what we would succeed to. We didn't know how the spiritual world could tell who should be chosen for each level of such succession. All we knew was that succession happened to only a few out of many. At the time, I'd been a member for a year, but everything around succession felt particularly obscure to me.

That July, I was pregnant, with no clue in the world that I would soon miscarry. I sat at a monthly meditative training sitting and received spiritual guidance. The spiritual guidance, which was actually a question, was posed by the reverend from Japan: "There is a vase in front of you, and you don't know what's inside. There could be a snake, or something else. But if the Buddhas ask you to place your hand into it, what are you going to do? Are you going to place your hand into the vase?"

As I listened, I had an image of a snake with its large mouth wide open. I could see its long, red, forked tongue flicking. Would I put my hand inside the vase regardless?

Yes, I thought, *I would*. But still I wondered what else could be inside.

I knew this was the Buddhas asking me if I was ready for this journey.

After my painful experience with the miscarriage later that month, I sat another monthly training in mid-August. Tears fell down my cheeks during the sitting. I was still suffering from the loss I'd just experienced. But that day, I also decided to renew and realign myself by focusing more on supporting Patrick and our local spiritual community.

In September, I had an opportunity to sit for succession training at the LA temple. Patrick didn't join me because he hadn't fulfilled his prerequisite for the sitting yet; he'd been swamped at work and too busy to even come to the temple lately.

During my sitting I shed tears like a waterfall, though I wasn't moved by any emotions and had no attachment to the phenomenon; it was almost like I was staring at it from outside my body. Then it was if I had just become solid ground: I experienced egolessness, perhaps for the first time. I didn't know how that happened, but I felt my true Self leave my body and observe from above the physical existence of me, sitting there. An indescribable warmth began inside me then expanded outward to the world. I didn't care at all for any outcomes, even for "succession," to come out of the sitting; I just wanted to remain in that state forever.

At that moment the spiritual guide came over and delivered the solemn words to encourage me to bring forth my courage and determination for the sake of others—for the sake of the world. As I heard those words, I experienced total surrender, as if I was floating in a pool of light. Below me was the vast, infinite ocean and above was the glaring sun and the universe. I felt totally contained.

At the end of the training, we trainees chanted the mantra, "Nomaku sammanda . . ." in gratitude. When I opened my eyes, I found a small note on the carpet in front of me. The note said, "Succession." I had succeeded to the first spiritual level of *Mahayana*. I was officially walking on a path toward Buddhahood.

There would be several more steps to complete before I could become a spiritual guide, but taking this first step had been humbling and unforgettable. I looked forward to the next challenge.

Since the sitting, I'd noticed some changes in my senses, as if I were now seeing people and the world through a pair of invisible glasses. Seeing, feeling, and putting my thoughts together felt different than before. I'd developed a pathway inside of me that allowed me to take others into consideration before accessing my own need. Though I'd tended toward altruism throughout my life, I felt a distinct difference in my experience of the world after my *Mahayana* succession.

A couple of days after the succession, while I was taking a shower in the morning, I saw a clear image of my own answer to the question that had been raised at my July meditative training sitting—whether I should place my own hand into a vase if the Buddhas asked me to do so. Before, I'd wondered about the contents of the vase; now, in the shower, I saw them clearly.

As I experienced this supreme clarity, my face was soaking wet, as much from my tears of awakening as it was from the shower. The vision put me into further awakening. I felt I was staring at the image; perhaps it was only in my imagination, but it didn't matter whether it was or not. The *message* was what mattered, and it was the most important and profound message I'd ever received from the Buddhas.

What I saw in the vase was the infinite space where the concept of time and space means nothing. It didn't matter when and where it started or ended. There were uncountable stars, planets, and shooting stars, galaxies and milky ways, and zillions of sparkling lights. The space was in the clearest, cleanest, coolest, and darkest black, with a bluish tint in its depths. When I looked carefully, I saw zillions of translucent biological capsules made of soft membranes suspended in this infinite space. Then I realized all these capsules were actually the stars, looked upon from afar. They were radiating their own light, some brighter and crystal clear like diamonds, others with tints of various colors. And they were alive; I could hear their breathing and heartbeats in my ears. Within each capsule dwelled a Buddha, Bodhisattva, deity, or other creature. Each capsule was an incubator, nurturing its dweller until he or she was born.

In one of the capsules, I saw the baby that was *me*, and I heard her breathing.

Most important of all was that all these capsules were interconnected. They were "unconsciously" conscious, awakened. They knew the truths of the universe.

In this vision, I sensed three beings: "me" in a physical form; my Self, the essence of my being; and the essence of the universe—the whole. This, I thought, must be the Dharma body. All three versions of *me* knew this vision was "truth." All three shared the same knowningness.

The reverend had asked me at my sitting if I had the courage to place my hand into the vase. In reality, though, it wasn't really a question; rather, it was an invitation for me to take the journey to the absolutely unknown.

Whatever journey I took, it would be filled with unknown wonders. The spiritual image that came to me in the shower depicted the Buddhas' wisdom, loving kindness, and compassion—the Buddhas' world. This was the very message of my vision: *Don't be afraid.* I felt sure that I would find the Buddhas in every person and event I encountered in my spiritual journey. They were all connected in the truth.

Now I felt no fear of the unknown. I wouldn't be afraid of anything in this timeless space, now or ever. As long as I held the Buddhas in my thoughts, speech, and actions, I would always find the knowning-ness in me. The answers were right here inside me. All I could do now was to continue practicing.

This knowledge wouldn't change me immediately, of course, or make me sit, all of a sudden, on the throne of the awakening. I was still a baby in the biological capsule in the image of the universe. But it did encourage me to keep making efforts as a trainee in the world of the Bodhisattvas.

Later I would realize I was lucky to experience this vision while I was still a beginner on the Buddhist path. With my awakened heart, I would be strong enough to face the forthcoming difficulties with Patrick.

By early 2000, Patrick was having a difficult time at work. His company had gone through a chain of acquisitions, and each one had involved a major restructuring of the company and the fate of their workers' lives. This takeover world was brutal, and it meant drastic shifts in Patrick's focus at work.

"I am not sure if I like this," he told me one day.

"I know," I said, "but things may be different soon . . ."

We'd been in San Diego for less than two years. I had to encourage him to give it a little time.

But by that summer, we'd had this conversation many times. Patrick was living under tremendous stress, and despite his wish to continue his spiritual pursuits, he had almost no time to visit the temple or receive regular meditative training. He'd signed up for special bodhi-cultivating spiritual meditative training over a year earlier, but he'd only attended for a couple of months, and now his spiritual pursuits seemed to have come to a full stop.

I felt a monstrous force was about to swallow Patrick and our life, and we needed to grow as quickly as possible to overcome anticipated hardships. I worried that he hadn't established his faith and practice strongly enough to get through what was coming. How would we be able to face the upcoming challenges? I was anxious.

At the end of that summer, Patrick got a special invitation and opportunity to assist Her Holiness during the outdoor fire ritual, *Homa*, that would take place near Mt. Fuji and Lake Kawaguchi at the beginning of October.

Patrick and I were shocked and extremely humbled by the invitation. We were still beginners, only two and a half years into this teaching, and Patrick had barely been practicing or going to temple, but they wanted him.

Near the end of September, Patrick and I flew to Japan. From the Narita airport, Patrick took a limousine bus directly to Tokyo, where all the ceremonial assistants and temple staff would meet in the following morning. They would then be transferred to Yamanashi to begin their training for the ritual before the event in October. Until then, I'd stay with Yoshino and her husband.

On October 4, the second day of the fire ritual, I arrived in Yamanashi by bus. Right after I'd paid respects to the deities in the courtyard, the reverend from the LA temple found me and took me to Patrick in the restricted area behind the building on the site so I could see him just before the ceremony began. All ceremonial assistants were there awaiting their procession to the *Homa* dais.

As I approached Patrick—looking much different than his usual self in the ascetic orange monk's attire—I paused and gulped, feeling my heart stop beating for a moment. He was relaxed, and radiating a light from his being. I blinked and looked at him again. He looked much bigger than his usual size. I couldn't take him in all the way; he was too precious and too bright. I was too humbled to say a word, so in silence I stepped back and bowed my head deeply.

I would never forget this day and how I saw his true being—dignified, yet serene and humble. This was who he was.

I got back to my seat and the procession began, first with the sounds of big conch shells, and then with the beats of huge Taiko drums that roared high into the clear sky and penetrated deep into my soul. Like thunder, they shook me with sensations—something very sacred and also unyielding.

The ceremonial assistants entered, one by one, followed by Her Holiness in a refined bright vermillion robe. I watched her make her way to the *Homa* dais, deep in my own prayers. Translucent, strong yet silky light radiated from her to the surrounding atmosphere, merging high into the sky.

A big pile of fresh brushwood, edged in dark green, had been placed in front of the *Homa* dais. The ceremonial assistants, in their colorful robes, were all neatly aligned in their assigned positions. Her Holiness sat under a large umbrella in the line of the brushwood and the *Achala,* still radiating the silky light. I felt like I was witnessing and experiencing the most impressive, serene, and sacred pictures of the secret Mandala world imaginable.

As soon as the *Homa* ground was purified by the ceremonial assistants, our collective chanting echoed in the mountains. The large bonfires at the center of the *Homa* dais burned strong and high, and now the prayers by the officiant priest led us in the rituals. I felt so cleansed and sacred that tears began to fall down my cheeks. The whole experience somehow reminded me of my very first Independence Day with Patrick in the summer of 1990, just ten years earlier. Here again I saw our future and our shared mission: to bring peace and happiness to the world.

When I met up with Patrick the following morning, I hugged him gently, still feeling humbled from the experience the day before. I shared my impressions of the *Homa*.

"It was so sacred," I told him. "I was very moved by it. And you looked too precious for me to even get close to you." I smiled at him. "How was it for you?"

Patrick told me about his experience, and it was clear that he, too, had experienced an awakening moment.

"In the first few days of practice, I couldn't give an arrow exactly in the way the archer, Eric, wanted it," he told me. "Without knowing how difficult it really was, I'd taken it for granted that I could do it, because it seemed so simple. But to serve the way Eric really wanted wasn't easy at all."

All other ceremonial assistants except for Patrick had specific and direct performances by themselves to purify the *Homa* dais during the ritual. But Patrick's role was indirect to the ritual: assisting the other ceremonial assistant, the archer, by passing an arrow to him from a kneeling position. Patrick's job was to follow Eric to every corner of the large *Homa* dais, kneel near him, and deliver an arrow in each spot in as easy a way as possible for Eric to receive it. Patrick's role was, therefore, not only physically strenuous but also one that required him to egolessly attend to the archer's needs during his performance.

"At one point, because of so much kneeling, my knees were hurting and my back was killing me," Patrick admitted. "I got so frustrated because I couldn't do the damn thing!" He smiled at me. "Then I had a moment of realization. I realized that the Buddha wanted me to learn from the very act of kneeling and serving others. The way I passed the arrow in the beginning was insisting on my own way. I didn't care what Eric wanted. To understand people's true needs, regardless of what I was accustomed to and what I took for granted, I needed to stop my own way and turn things around for the sake of others." His voice was calm and gentle, and light radiated from his face as he shared this with me.

"Wow!" was all I could say.

"Kneeling and assisting others were good for me," Patrick told me. "These were all the indications for what I should do and keep in mind throughout my daily life."

My thoughts drifted to what was going on for him back home. Many hundreds of people were now working for him. Though he'd always been a humble and kind boss, his reflection and learning from this precious event represented how pure and genuine his heart was.

Considering what he'd gone through in the past two years and what might be happening soon at work, I was grateful for the sacred spiritual support he'd just experienced. I knew it would help strengthen him in every area of his life. His beautiful Buddha nature would shine as the seed that had been planted during this experience grew and bore fruits; he would become a better leader at work and in the community.

Patrick believed what he'd graciously received at the outdoor *Homa* was a precious gift from Her Holiness and the Buddhas. The experience had brought him to a big turning point in his practice and his life.

After this, Patrick became more confident, independent, and determined in his practice, like a chick that had hatched with help from Her Holiness. It wouldn't be a straight road for him, but now he became willing to apply the teaching principles to his challenges at work with more unyielding commitment.

He also, despite a more demanding work situation, made even greater efforts to attend monthly spiritual meditative trainings, and he even signed up for studies at dharma school programs to become a dharma teacher.

In early February, Patrick went to Japan for a business trip. During his stay, he had an opportunity to sit a succession training at the Grand Holy Temple in Tokyo.

Immediately after he'd finished, he called me.

"*Moshi moshi, Kyomi chan, ogenki desuka?*" he began in Japanese— "Hello, hello, and how are you doing?"

He sounded happy and relaxed and it brought a smile to my face. "Oh, Patrick! How are you? Did you do your succession sitting?"

"Yes . . . I've succeeded to *Mahayana*!"

I gulped. "Oh my God! Congratulations! I am so very happy for you, Patrick!" Tears welled up in my eyes. I lost my words.

Then Patrick told me how wonderful and humble he'd felt at the sitting. He began to describe how it was: During the sitting, he was walking in a sea of abundant golden wheat crops that stretched as far as his eyes could see. Heat and the glare of the autumn sun merged into the fields. Then he saw our beloved two cats, Bui and Toto, joyously jumping up and down in the fields. As he moved forward, the crops, the cats, and the sun all welcomed and embraced him.

His voice radiated warmth and energy. I could see every bit of what he described to me. As I listened, I was overcome with gratitude for his being, the spiritual support in the teaching, Her Holiness, Yoshino and Hisashi, and even our cats, Bui and Toto.

—

By the end of that summer, Patrick had gotten even busier with work.

I knew Patrick's inner world had become more harmonized since his spiritual elevation. His succession had accelerated his commitment to embody the teaching in his daily life. But he'd been living at full speed for a while now, trying so hard to be a perfect person both at work and at the temple.

I stayed by his side, offering him a helping hand and a foundation, supporting him to find a way of steadily walking the path no matter how difficult daily life became.

But I had a gut feeling. The anxiety I'd held inside me since before the *Homa* ritual in October 2000 still hadn't gone away. I'd always been so protective of Patrick, and now my concern for him kept me on high alert.

Since we'd moved to San Diego, Rivera Inc., which violently took over Walgen Parma., had driven him hard. He had driven himself, too, with his desire to both develop excellent anti-cancer drugs for patients and to help people who were being impacted by the company's ongoing restructuring.

Knowing how little time Patrick was spending at home, I wanted him to be able to relax fully when he was there—have some leisure time for himself.

During the weekends, we shared a lot of things: We watched football (soccer) together. We spent time sun-bathing. We went to the beach and went fishing at every lake in San Diego. Making our home warm and peaceful and cooking his favorite meals were my ways of sharing a good time with him—and through these activities, I learned to love him even more than I had before. We became inseparable, like twins.

Was I a football fan? No. I wasn't. Did I really like fishing or bathing on the beach? No, I didn't. But I wasn't there to impose what I wanted to do. What I loved was doing these things *with* Patrick and *for* him. That was how I cultivated my love for him.

One evening, we were eating fish and chips that I'd cooked for him. Patrick poured lots of malt vinegar on the beer-battered fresh cod and golden-brown potatoes. He was very happy eating and watching the Manchester United game.

"You are my best friend, Patrick!" I told him lovingly.

"Kyomi," he said, "you are my *only* friend!" Then, with a huge, happy smile on his face he declared, "You are my *bestest* friend in all the world!"

As long as we had this partnership and love, I knew, we would overcome whatever came our way.

In this deepening relationship, Patrick became more dependent on me than he had been in the past. One of our fellow practitioners repeatedly teased me, "Kyomi san, you've spoiled Patrick. You shouldn't look after him so much." But that was alright for me. All that mattered was balance. He had much to accomplish for the sake of people and the world, and my role was to be the foundation that helped him do it. I enjoyed watching him shine from his own being, even in the midst of difficulties.

That same year, on September 11, one of the most dreadful events in human history occurred. Just ten minutes after rushing out the door for work that morning, Patrick called me, telling me to turn the TV on.

I turned it on to see funnels of dark black smoke pouring into the sky, and orange and red fires raging madly from skyscrapers I recognized as part of New York City's skyline. Was this real? Patrick was still with me on the phone, telling me that these were the Twin Towers of the World Trade Center.

Ah! The pandemonium of the tragedy was unfolding live. I watched the images and felt the impact penetrate through me—but smoothly, like a large knife sliding into a spongy cake. Watching the collapsing buildings was like experiencing my own body collapsing in slow motion. Nailed to the ground before the TV, I was frozen. Perhaps it was only for a few minutes, but it felt like an eternity. I barely even noticed the tears falling down my cheeks.

I sensed the chaos, agonizing cries, shouts, fires, falling rubble, and rushes of people inside the building as if I were there. The countless cries of family members who had just lost or were about to lose a loved one would linger forever in my ears. How could we endure this?

A few minutes later, I got into the shower to calm myself and I was reminded of the story of the Buddha before he attained enlightenment.

The story quickly unfolded in my mind: Before attaining enlightenment and becoming the Shakyamuni Buddha, Prince Gautam Siddhartha left his palace and went into rigorous ascetic training deep in the mountains for six years to find a way to end people's suffering.

In the middle of his training, he began to feel discouraged from seeking the path. One day, he sat on the bank of a lake, his shoulders dropped low. Suddenly, he heard splish-splash noises and noticed small ripples of water nearby. He got closer to take a look.

A small squirrel was busy scooping the water with his bushy tail out of the lake and onto the bank. He repeated this motion over and over again.

Siddhartha asked, "Why are you doing this?"

"I am emptying this entire lake," the squirrel answered.

"Oh, no," Siddhartha said. "Don't be silly. You can't do that."

"Never mind. I'll do it anyway." The squirrel went back to its task.

The squirrel's persistent effort inspired Siddhartha to stay the course, and eventually he attained enlightenment. It turned out that the squirrel was an incarnation of the guardian god Indra, who'd supported Siddhartha's attaining enlightenment all the way from the beginning of his quest.

With that reminder, I suddenly felt sure inside. No matter how small our efforts seem, no matter how far away and impossible our goals seem, we have to have the courage to stay the course toward hope and love and harmony, even in the face of tragedy and discord.

Within five minutes, I became a different person. I wasn't afraid any longer. I felt strength and profound gratitude. My sadness transformed into determination to carry through on my good wishes for humanity.

The things that had been tragically broken on this day wouldn't be erased. But these tragedies, agonizing pains, and outcries that we had witnessed would forge ways for humans to live in better and more harmonious lives going forward. No matter how long and how much collective effort it might take, we needed to courageously believe in ourselves and our unlimited potential.

Hope. We must believe.

— 17 —
Living in Dharma — II

By the end of the year 2001, what Patrick deemed to be "waves of brutality," similar to *tsunamis,* arrived one after another at Rivera, Inc. This started when John McDonald took over as CEO at the beginning of that year. The aggressions and pressures were everywhere—from the acquisitions of both domestic and international companies to the extreme downsizing of the existing research laboratories, limiting their R&D budgets.

These happenings would take over and almost swallow Patrick and our entire life in the years to come.

Patrick was still young, and still new to the company. At each decision junction, he faced a choice of whether to quit or to continue. But he felt he was one of few at his company who were willing to fight for the values and good science he believed in. He also felt a selfless responsibility to protect vulnerable people, both patients and employees, who would be impacted by the restructurings. He believed that he could still thrive in this increasingly competitive space, and as such he decided to stay with Rivera, Inc. a little longer.

Patrick took the processes of restructuring seriously, and was often heartbroken by the personal toll it took on people. He often talked about how many hundreds, or thousands, of people would be impacted as a result of the company's decisions.

"Can you imagine how these people feel who've been working at the company for so long? How betrayed they must feel?"

I heard the ache in Patrick's voice, but there was nothing he could do to change things.

His helplessness wounded us both.

In early 2005, Patrick's immediate boss, Robert, suddenly quit his job and joined another company. It was a big shock to Patrick and to me. By this time, almost none of the original company's founding members remained at Rivera. Robert had been the only one, and now he'd decided to leave it all behind. Patrick and I knew that he, too, had witnessed too much brutality and wanted to start anew.

Robert voiced that he would like Patrick to succeed his position, but instead Rivera gave the job to another scientist—a stranger to the oncology program, someone who specialized in animal toxicology at the New York site. Patrick was devastated and humiliated. He felt he'd been thrown into unknown territory, which left him full of anxiety and insecurity regarding the future of his job. He also found his new boss to be a bully.

By that fall, Patrick's frustrations had piled up to his limit. He began to contemplate resigning from the company.

Patrick's turbulent situation at work influenced our spiritual life in addition to everything else. Staying true to our practice and walking on the Buddhist path became harder for both of us.

The aim of living in Dharma is to live the life of the Bodhisattva. A Bodhisattva lives an ordinary life but seeks enlightenment. The Shakyamuni Buddha attained enlightenment in his life as he sat and meditated under the bodhi tree. But what made him enlightened wasn't just sitting in meditation; it was the culmination of all the good deeds he'd accumulated through his past lives.

Living in Dharma is a continuous and dynamic process of cultivating and appreciating our state of mind, moment by moment; in other words, living in the present moment with an awakened mind. People who live in such a mindset want enlightenment to be shared with others and with the world. That is to be a Bodhisattva.

Some people believe that living in Dharma is the final achievement—the "ultimate" state. But that's not the case. Living in Dharma can actually be attained by anyone at any moment, even by a beginner on the spiritual path. But it's not a fixed, "once achieved, forever achieved" state. In fact, if we cling to such an enlightened state, it won't come back easily, because then it will have become an attachment, when the real goal is to let go. As we let go of our attachment to outcome, we stay continuously open and curious, and are able to move forward.

In those turbulent years between 2001 and 2006, Patrick and I tried to keep our minds awakened. It was incredibly difficult to do, but with the support of our bodhi-cultivation meditative trainings, we held torches in one hand that became guides for ourselves and others in the darkness—and as we walked, we saw more lights, held by others, that when gathered together illuminated our path even more clearly. We were moving toward the world of the *Bodhisattvas*.

In our spiritual journeys, along with our daily practices, we'd made much progress. In October 2003, less than six years after becoming a follower of our teaching, I was appointed by Her Holiness to be a lineage parent, the head of a group of my own guiding people. By that time, I already had many guiding children whom I'd guided through the teaching and nurtured by helping them walk the path.

My lineage appointment resulted in the end of our hosting regional meetings, which we'd done for the past five years. Instead, I began organizing a couple of monthly meetings at our home. I also began to attend lineage parents' meetings in LA, and various leadership meetings at the temple. My responsibilities increased dramatically. This included making more information and activities available to the local community.

Practitioners in the region who wished to be under my extended fostering care began to gather at my home meetings, as well as the Annual Training. The former regional coordinator, Tomoko, and her guiding children, began to attend my meetings as well, though she seemed to hold some unresolved resentful feelings toward me and expressed them from time to time.

Since my first spiritual level of *Mahayana* in September 1999, little by little I'd cultivated the Bodhi, the essence of enlightenment— wisdom and loving-kindness and compassion—through daily challenges, trials, and spiritual efforts at meditative training. For me, the approach of judging two opposing ideas as either good or bad was long gone. I tried instead to apply Buddha-centered compassion and find truth and something to learn from in every situation, even from Tomoko's criticism.

Facing trials such as these gave me an opportunity to practice "Buddha moments," when my heart was filled with gratitude for the sacred. In the midst of difficulties, instead of wondering or complaining about a situation, I humbly appreciated the experience, because I knew it would present the answer I needed to learn. When I reflected on a situation with no emotions, only fairness and clarity, I could see the answer. I knew the difficulties I faced were gifts that were directing me toward what the Buddhas wanted me to become. In this way, I brought out my courage to properly "reflect," "recharge," "redirect," and "reapply" my cycles of trials.

In December 2004, a month before succession meditative sitting, I underwent the ordination, which solidified my determination to stay on the path I was walking for the rest of my life.

Just after hosting the last of a series of morning sessions at Annual Training in 2005, I sped to San Diego International Airport. I arrived in Tokyo the following night.

The next morning, I sat a succession meditative training for the level of spiritual guide. It was the final stage of Bodhi-cultivation meditative training. During the sitting, I reflected upon my appreciation of so many people, particularly Patrick. The people closest to me had become my foundation and polishing stones for developing my Bodhi. My life and my and Patrick's life together had changed so much compared to before, when we didn't have this Buddhist path; my gratitude for Patrick and the teaching had deepened immensely.

That morning, during the moments of the succession, I felt that experience of the three parts of me—the physically sitting me, the me observing the physical me with an awakened mind, and the higher version of myself—becoming *one*, just like I'd experienced at the first level of Bodhi elevation in 1999. I succeeded to the spiritual faculty that day and started a specific training as a spiritual guide. The training would take another year for me to actually help other practitioners with their meditative training.

That afternoon, after completing an additional initial training, I stood at the courtyard of Grand Holy Temple. Inhaling the temple's clean, sacred air, I was filled with profound serenity in the still moment. *This is home*, I thought, but no words were needed in the crystallized yet eternally expanding stillness.

The following morning, I returned to San Diego to prepare for the closing period of Annual Training, which would start in a couple of days. My stay in Japan had totaled less than thirty hours. But in those thirty hours, I had been transformed. My spiritual conviction and devotion to our teaching was even greater than before.

Even though Patrick had had countless demands at work, he'd also been putting time into cultivating his spiritual faculty; all the difficulties and challenges he'd been facing professionally had become the foundation of his practice and Bodhi cultivation. He also succeeded to the spiritual faculty and began a specific training as a spiritual guide in June of 2006.

Months later, Patrick called me in the afternoon from his hotel room in New York City. He'd planned to attend multiple meetings at the Rivera headquarters that morning, but when we spoke he told me he'd missed all the morning meetings.

"I am not sure exactly what happened, but I had a blackout," he told me. "I must've had a sort of brain attack or something . . . it could be a stroke."

"What?" I asked, feeling as if cold water had just been poured over my head.

I'd already felt a lot of apprehension whenever he traveled. He'd already experienced irregular heartbeats in the past that required monitoring, and was taking medication for his frequent, severe headaches and insomnia.

"I just sort of woke up, but I wasn't sleeping . . . I must've blacked out. And now it's already the afternoon. I have no idea what happened." He told me he'd had nothing to drink the previous night.

"Oh, no," I said, overwhelmed with worry. "You should see a doctor!"

"No," he said quickly, "I'm okay now. I'm jumping into a shower and then I'll go to the rest of the meetings. I'll call you when I get back tonight."

Patrick had been working like a mouse on a wheel. A mouse gives up his freedom in exchange for food and safety. And while there are different kinds of cages—some are big and seem luxurious, even look like castles—they are still cages.

The stress of living inside that cage was now taking a toll on Patrick's health.

When Rivera officially announced the closure of their entire operation in Ann Arbor, Michigan in early 2007, that was the final straw.

One of the biggest reasons for Rivera's hostile takeover of Walgen in 2000 had been to monopolize the drug Vastor, a first-line cardiovascular drug developed and produced in Ann Arbor.

Vastor had been the most mega-blockbuster prescription drug in pharmaceutical history at the time, generating $13 billion dollars annually for Rivera. Rivera had been working to keep monopolizing the drug's sales before its patent's expiration in the end of 2010, but one of the combination drugs they came up with failed FDA approval, and meanwhile Rivera was having no luck with its ongoing request for tax abatement from the city of Ann Arbor. So, at the end of 2006, Rivera made a quick decision to close the site.

The closure came as a great shock to everyone. Rivera had housed 2,100 workers and their families, and been the city's largest taxpayer. The impact of the site closure was enormous—devastating to Rivera's workers, their families, and the city of Ann Arbor.

When Patrick got the news, he was anguished. He walked through the door and collapsed onto the couch.

"These people have been working for the company for so many years," he said. "I can't believe they've done it."

He'd been chasing the fate of Vastor and their operation site for the last few years. He'd visited the site many times and had gotten to know the people. The Ann Arbor closure highlighted the brutality and lack of loyalty demonstrated by his company, and the reality of the pharmaceutical industry in general. It made him question everything he'd devoted himself to for the last seven years.

Work had always been Patrick's means of self-expression. He was driven to create goodness through his science. At work, he'd maintained himself as a good and compassionate leader. His daily act was to build something sacred. But the pressures he faced—not only from his immediate work environment, full of bureaucracy and politics, but also from the devastating restructuring of his company at large—had pushed him to his limit. They were denying and destroying his values. Rivera had and would continue to wash away tens of thousands of people's lives like a tsunami.

I had been asking Patrick to leave the job for a while. I didn't want him to carry on this neverendingly destructive lifestyle, along with the bad karma that work was generating.

Finally, he began to contemplate leaving more seriously.

— 18 —
The Indication

In spring 2007, Her Holiness conducted an outdoor *Homa* fire ritual at the LA temple, and Patrick was given the opportunity to assist her for the second time.

The first day of the two consecutive scheduled days for *Homa* ritual started with cold, rainy weather and gushes of stormy winds. It was highly unusual weather for Southern California; in fact, I'd never experienced such bad weather there. It put in me a sense of unease and made me nearly suffer from hypothermia while I helped set up the chairs.

As the sounds of conch shells and dignified, solemn music started, the ceremonial assistants, all in ascetic monk attire, began proceeding, in a line, toward the *Homa* dais. I bowed deeply, with utmost respect, until the last person in the procession, Her Holiness in her vermillion red robe, passed in front of me.

Though I was bowing deeply, from the corner of my eye I saw Patrick passing just before Her Holiness. He was in purple attire, carrying the *Achala*—the principal image for this *Homa*— from the temple altar room. He was wet, his glasses covered with rain droplets. He looked so sincere and serious. But then I recognized in him an agonizing pain that I could not shake. Chills ran from the bottom of my back and up my spine. It wasn't from his facial expression or body language; the sense of it came in the form of a spiritual message, and I knew immediately that it had to do with the future. As a spiritual guide, my senses had lately become very sharp. I knew in that moment that this was the message from the *Achala*.

Then came my response: *No!* I didn't want it. I heard my ego voice inside me. I quickly tried to erase these thoughts.

My eyes found Patrick again, and what immediately drew my attention was the heaviness of the *Achala*. It wasn't physical, but spiritual. I saw in him such weight—a heaviness that was almost crushing him. I saw him as if he were a prisoner in chains.

I allowed for the fact that my vision could be wrong. But in my mind I knew this was a spiritual image, a message from the Buddhas. The Buddhas wanted to let me know what might happen to Patrick, and to us. Now I understood what I'd experienced before the service, and what I now saw in Patrick. A picture—a premonition—was forming. Patrick would face something very heavy and difficult in the future . . . something bad was coming.

Could these messages I was receiving be related to Patrick's job? I sensed a deep fear inside me.

By this time, as a senior practitioner of the path, I'd gone through this cycle of indication, reflection, and determination while facing other hardships. I knew I couldn't let myself speculate; I must simply try to experience whatever unknown might unfold in our life.

On the second day of the *Homa*, Patrick and I attended as part of the audience. After the ceremony, one of the executive office staff from Japan called us for a conversation. I was asked to be there for translation.

On the call, the temple staff revealed the order's plan to bring a then-ongoing exhibition from Japan to the US and other countries. The order needed help from a devout senior international leader like Patrick, who had business skills and knowledge, to organize things on the US side.

A couple of days later, Patrick said to me over dinner, "I'd like to quit Rivera and help the exhibition tour for a while."

"Oh, that's wonderful!" I replied, delighted. "Are you sure of your decision? No regret?" I wanted him to be sure.

"No regrets," he said confidently. "I've done whatever I could do for Rivera. Now, it's time to leave."

In July 2007, just before his forty-seventh birthday, Patrick resigned from Rivera and began working on the planning of our teaching's US exhibition tour, set to debut the following year, 2008, in part to celebrate the Founder's centennial birthday. During his lifetime, the Founder had created numerous Buddhist images, portraits, photography, wood engravings, and calligraphies as expressions of the Dharma world. The exhibition was designed to share his faith, prayers, and sincere wishes for all sentient beings to find the inner light, the Buddha nature, in them through his art.

In late 2007 and early 2008, Patrick traveled at least once or twice a month to Japan, as well as biweekly to New York City, and soon to Chicago and Los Angeles. He did it all out of his soulful dedication to the teaching.

Finally, at the end of February, the first exhibition opened in Chelsea in New York City. It was a serene and sophisticated event. Elegantly designed, narrow banners were on the streets in Chelsea; large posters depicting the Founder's sculptures were posted in the subways. It was wonderful to see his art everywhere in New York City. The main attraction was a sixteen-foot-high golden reclining

Buddha, a replica of the image in the altar at the sacred site in Tokyo.

While the exhibition was there, Patrick traveled weekly to New York City and stayed there for a few days at a time. I visited twice, and the second time I was there, I was able to fully witness him in his role. From a distance, I saw him standing in the dimness of the early evening. A light radiated from him as he guided and explained the art exhibits to people. I'd never seen him so happy and content with overflowing his *bodhi*. I was happy because he was happy.

One of the other highlights of the exhibition, besides the reclining Buddha, was the Dharma Meditation, a type of meditative training specifically designed by Her Holiness for non-members. During the very first meditative session, Her Holiness guided the attendees with her words. Patrick—clothed in black robes, the attire of serving monk, a true disciple of the Buddhas—served Her Holiness closely. Afterward, he also took her role and humbly guided people as the master of ceremony at meditation. As I watched him in that deeply humble yet radiant state, I knew he was living his destiny.

Since the beginning of 2008, Patrick had been so busy that I'd rarely seen him. I consoled myself, however, knowing he was dedicating himself to our teaching, and to people all over the world. In April 2008, he was appointed to be a dharma teacher, and was ordained that same year. I was so grateful that he had humbly succeeded to the dharma lineage and become a true disciple of the Buddhas, the Founders, and Her Holiness.

Later that year, Patrick wore his brand-new orange priestly robe for the first time at the service, radiating his contentment and happiness as a true Buddhist trainee. Tears streamed down my cheeks and warmth expanded from the center of my chest. I'd never felt so proud, and I was enveloped by a profound relief for Patrick.

My thoughts hovered around the memories of the stormy roads we'd walked together, but I felt a deep happiness nonetheless. Whatever might come next, this was not only his destiny but *our* destiny. Profound gratitude for him, the Buddhas, and the teaching filled me like spring water.

Patrick became one of the most favorite international leaders in the teaching. When he was at the temple, everyone wanted to see him, yet he was always so humble and kind as he said hi and bowed to everyone—never showing any pretention or arrogance. As it always had, his presence exuded compassion and kindness.

In early 2010, just after Patrick finally completed outlining the plans for the Dharma Center, envisioned as a hub for the general public in New York City to gather and explore their spiritual pursuits, I brought a cup of coffee to his desk late one morning.

He was standing by his desk—seemingly busy, or pretending to be busy, tidying up the papers on his desk—and as I set his coffee down in front of him, he said, "I won't renew my contract with the order this year."

What? Did I miss something?

He wouldn't look at me in the eye. "I am going to quit working for the order," he said. Somehow, I'd known this was coming. Still, I utterly lost my voice.

"I just wanted to let you know that I've already decided. Please don't try to stop me, or ask me anything about it." Then, as if he'd sensed my apprehension, he said, "I'll continue my faith with the teaching."

I felt great relief upon hearing those words.

"But I tell you, I wish I hadn't done it to begin with," Patrick added.

This hurt my feelings for some reason. I think it was the hardness in his voice; it was as if he'd said it to hurt me. The way he talked about it bothered me.

I wondered what had happened. I imagined something must have occurred within the organization that he wasn't telling me about. But since he refused to tell me any details, I didn't push it. I knew he was a man of honor and integrity; I left it at that. But internally, I was thrown deep into a wilderness of confusion—*Why?* What had happened to him?

I would wonder about this for years to come.

While I knew Patrick to be a person of pure pursuit, I also saw that he was struggling to locate the true meaning of the Middle Way.

The Middle Way is one of the fundamental concepts in Buddhism. It doesn't mean to seek something in between, but rather to master Buddha's wisdom and perceive the truth beyond the two opposing concepts, such as good or bad, sacred or mundane, or pure or impure.

At Rivera, Patrick had encountered some ego-centered individuals. He'd also tested his own limits through the painful restructuring. I was sure he'd been traumatized by those turbulent storms and their aftermaths.

Then he'd begun working selflessly and tirelessly for the order, where he'd expected the people to always be purer—to value something more sacred. But it was of course possible to come across imperfect, ego-driven situations and people who were still trainees in the Buddhahood but the opposite of what he'd expected in the monastic world. I can only imagine that mundane and worldly attached mindsets and actions that he sometimes came across in the Sangha had not only made it more difficult for him to complete the project but had also disappointed him far more than they would have in the everyday world. His expectation that our fellow practitioners would be purer, more perfect, than the average person, might've created further torment for him.

What Patrick couldn't see then was that lotus flowers can bloom out of muddy water—what is sacred can flower out of the mundane. While we humans live in the world, we cannot separate ourselves from that world. We all are interconnected. Here is where the true Middle Way lies.

Although I made peace with Patrick quitting his advisor position in the order, I couldn't deny my fear regarding the unknown future. I hadn't forgotten the indication by the *Achala* in April 2007.

I'd thrown myself into the unknown so many times in the past, but this time I felt as if I were being pushed to be alone. I sensed something big on the horizon, something unfolding that we'd never experienced before.

— 19 —

The Creeping Force

By late 2010, though Patrick and I still enjoyed living as Bodhisattvas, I sensed a small yet undeniable change in him—a few thinning spots that were threatening our original tightly knit and beautifully interwoven fabric.

It started with the fact that Patrick still hadn't communicated with me about why he'd quit his advisor position. While the choice in and of itself didn't bother me, the fact that he was hiding something from me, and keeping distance from me in doing so, hurt me deeply. This was *our* faith, something we'd built together. My reaction was to cling tight to the beautiful fabric we'd created over the years.

Patrick had held a series of short-lived positions at various organizations between 2008 and 2010, but he couldn't seem to find a job he liked. During this time, he told me assertively, more than once, to keep the details of our life private, separate from other people. I felt a wedge had been inserted deep inside me. It was as if he didn't trust me any longer. I didn't feel a need to tell anyone about our lives, but his desire to keep me isolated from the world made me feel like he'd placed me in an emotional prison. His hard words echoed in my mind, slowly changing my perspective and eventually creating an empty pocket in my heart. I'd lived my life filled with concerns for others. Patrick had always been my number one. But in prioritizing him, I'd unwittingly put the armor of my upbringing back on.

Much later, I'd be able to look back at that critical time and think that I should have asked for help, but at the time I assumed that the liberating powers of the teaching and our practices would be enough; I believed we could overcome any hardships we might encounter.

I was wrong.

At the end of May 2011, when we returned to San Diego from a trip to England, we found our beloved cat Toto, who was fourteen and a half years old, gravely ill. We took her to the veterinarian, who tried to help, but she'd already lost significant weight and didn't get any better despite our efforts. It was devastating for us.

On Independence Day that year, while Patrick and I were gardening outside, Toto attempted to escape, likely to go die in isolation. Patrick eventually found her stuck in front of the dividing fence in the community, crying helplessly. She didn't have the strength to go beyond the wall. We immediately took her to the ER, where she underwent esophageal surgery. We were able to take her home a few days later, but they told us she'd have to be fed through a feeding tube.

For the rest of Toto's life, which was just a couple of months, we devoted everything to her peace and comfort. It was the only thing we could do for her.

Since I was working most days, feeding Toto became Patrick's task. For a month that summer, he also worked hard on our garden to make it prettier for Toto. She had her favorite spot on the living room sofa, overlooking the garden through the window. Patrick placed hundreds of heavy, rounded, stone-like bricks on all the grass edges, and he also placed a tall wrought-iron bird hanger and a matching wooden feeder in the shade right outside the window so she could see the birds—goldfinches, blue jays, and warblers—picking at seeds from the bird feeder. These were tender moments, when Patrick showed how much he cared for her.

Every day he sat on the raised patio stones near pear trees, holding Toto on his lap and feeding her through the syringe the vet had given us. He sometimes cried while feeding her. The sadness that radiated from the pair of them sent me reeling into my own deep thoughts, proliferating pain.

During this time, I began to understand Patrick's tender yet strong attachments—how he had unrealistic wishes for things that are changeable to be unchangeable. The world keeps moving forward regardless of our wish to stop it; the things around him—us, our life together, Toto—couldn't stay as they were forever. But he couldn't seem to accept that.

Since first meeting Patrick, I'd known this hidden part of him existed. It was a stubborn, raw, and ancient place where nobody could trespass . . . not even me. But now it stood high in front of me, more obvious and demanding, like a barn made of big stones. I began to feel lonely, isolated from him. His obsessiveness and private nature felt more pronounced than ever before, and this weighed heavily on my heart. I felt as if the thinning spots I'd sensed in our interconnected fabric were thinning even more, and the fabric was losing its light. I began to worry that what I was seeing and experiencing might not be fixable.

On September 11, 2011, on the tenth anniversary of the 9/11 terrorist attacks, Toto passed away. Patrick and I wept for her throughout the day while we dug a hole for her burial right next to the pear trees that he and Toto often sat by while he fed her. We buried her with lots of her favorite things and a dozen fresh red roses.

After Toto's death, Patrick and I both underwent a long grieving period. It was clear to me, though, that he was suffering too deeply for this grief to just be about Toto. I was more worried than ever about my husband.

Several weeks later, he was invited to Japan to attend the final panel planning discussion for the Dharma Center. Though he'd quit his advisor role, he'd promised to complete the center's planning. That trip would be among the last and final efforts he would make for the order.

On the way back from Japan, he stopped in New York for some business meetings.

As soon as he walked into the house after the trip, he nearly collapsed onto the couch from exhaustion. I served him a bowl of soup and a slice of French bread, and immediately noticed something was wrong with his face. The muscles were spontaneously twitching and at the same time losing their tone, as if they were loose. I gazed at him. Within thirty seconds, the left side of his face began to droop and a sip of soup spilled out of his mouth.

Aah! I wanted to stop it.

"What's happening, Patrick?" I asked him, putting my hand to the corner of my mouth to show him what I was seeing. But he didn't seem to notice and just swallowed another sip of soup.

This time, however, his tongue seemed unable to coordinate its movement enough to allow him to swallow.

"Is some . . . thing wrong with me?" He said, stuttering a little, and touched his left cheek.

He seemed to get worse right in front of me; suddenly, his left eye began to look less focused, as if it was floating on its socket. *Oh my God!* I thought. *He's having a stroke!*

"We need to go to the emergency room," I exclaimed. "You might be having a stroke!"

Within another minute, his face lost all its integrity and muscle tone, and his speech was slurred and heavy with stuttering.

I was terrified.

Thirty minutes later, we were in the ER waiting area, but it took another five hours before a CT scan and a few exams and other tests were performed. The ER doctor couldn't find anything remarkable, so he concluded that Patrick had idiopathic Bell's palsy—paralysis of the facial muscles from an unknown cause—prescribed some medicines, and discharged Patrick.

Perhaps, I thought, it wasn't as bad as I'd feared.

A week later, Patrick visited his primary doctor, Dr. Blum, who ordered an MRI. No significant results were found in that test either.

After a few weeks, however, Patrick's condition didn't improve. He'd been handsome his entire life, so this physical alteration was a challenge for him, and he was extremely sensitive about it. Between that and his ongoing depression from Toto's passing, he became even more introverted. I often tried to cheer him up with a picnic for just the two of us in the garden, but he was touchy with his mood—quick to snap at me. He tried to hide his face behind a napkin—which, besides being partially paralyzed, was becoming rounded due to prolonged steroid intake.

I pretended not to see any of these changes, though, because I wanted to prove to Patrick that his condition would do nothing to our relationship. Whenever we went out to Balboa Park or a show, I would bring my camera or iPhone with me and try to take a photo of the two of us, but he would only walk ahead of me, saying, "Hurry up! You're too slow!"—dodging the camera.

I don't have a single photo of the two of us from this time period.

Now Patrick seemed always to be hiding. He hid his face as well as his emotions, from me and from the world.

I wanted him to get help, but I was too afraid to suggest it. He was unreachable.

I decided to once again become a strong foundation for Patrick and our life together. What wouldn't I do to restore our relationship?

I committed myself to getting us back to a better place—to not let our beautiful, shiny fabric fall apart.

It wasn't lost on me that we *both* needed help.

In 2011, before Toto died, Patrick had been working on a few critical projects for several start-up biotech companies around Southern California.

In the spring of 2012, I saw our tax return and was shocked. Since we got married, we'd consolidated our individual accounts into one. We both had worked hard, so I'd never needed to worry about money before. However, this time I found all the work he'd done for these various companies hadn't created any substantial income; his entire income for the year amounted to just a few thousand dollars. How was it possible that he had spent all that time and effort and been compensated so little?

"How could you collect such a small amount of money for what you've done?" My voice was sharp; I couldn't contain my frustration.

"They paid me for the work I did," Patrick said, clearly a little hesitant to tell me what was going on.

"What? What do you mean?" I felt heat inside of me, quickly

rising up to the temple, pulsating in my head. I couldn't understand how tens of thousands of dollars had become only thousands. I felt as if I'd just been smacked in the face. How could he have hidden this from me for so long?

"I calculated all the work by the hour," he explained.

"Don't you think you should have been paid a salary?" I said. "What about the company you've been working for every day? You're working more than eight hours a day!" I had noticed that there was no income listed from that company on our return.

"They haven't paid me yet," he said uneasily. "But once they get funded, they'll pay me back in the millions!"

This revelation blew me away. All the tension held in my head suddenly exploded into small particles in the air. He was working for them for an uncertain promise of future payment? How could he do such a thing? Was he simply too kind—too naïve? Or worse, was something critically wrong with him?

Up to this point, I'd been very careful not to share my financial concerns with Patrick. I hadn't wanted him to develop any sense of guilt or shame about his failure to find another solid job, feeling that it would be detrimental to him, to us, and to our relationship. But now I saw a distinct crack here in front of me—more tears in our fabric.

"Patrick, don't you see they've been taking advantage of you?" I asked, suddenly feeling as if my whole body had been drained of all its energy.

"No," he said, "it's just one of those situations with start-ups, a common practice."

"I understand that," I said. "But how long have you been doing this . . . over a year? For nothing? At least they should've given you *some* compensation." I now felt my body was disintegrating, falling into pieces.

I couldn't see my way through this predicament. I feared that this small crack, this tear in our fabric, might be the end of us. I had a creeping feeling, like an insect crawling up my abdomen, that terrified me.

I was imprisoned in a ventless cage—another form of my armor—and I was the one who had let it happen.

In January 2013, fifteen months after the Bell's palsy started, Patrick still hadn't recovered; in fact, it sometimes got even worse for short periods of time. When that happened, Patrick was afraid to go out in public at all.

He'd also been suffering from persistent headaches for about a year. I was constantly concerned about him.

I told both Patrick and Dr. Blum to check his condition more carefully. I also shared my specific concerns about Patrick with Dr. Blum, telling him about his cognition issues, sleeping habits, headaches, and what seemed to be decreased lung function—he was no longer able to jog as he once had. Dr. Blum listened to me but he did very little for him, from what I could see. Meanwhile, he and Patrick were exchanging emails frequently and seemed to be withholding information from me. I felt frustrated and alone.

In April, I visited Japan on my own to attend a leadership meeting for the teaching in Tokyo. While I was there, I saw a friend, a retired leading practitioner in the country.

After our lunch, we sat down at a quiet coffee shop and she asked, "How's Patrick these days?"

"Well . . . I've been concerned about him . . . a lot," I admitted. "His health, his ways of handling things, finance, his personality . . . nothing seems right." I whispered these words, feeling as if there was a pressure on my throat.

"What do you mean?" she asked.

I began to explain about Patrick, his doctor, all of my worries—and as I spoke, I was trembling. I already felt guilty and in need of punishing myself for disclosing these things. I knew Patrick wanted me to stay quiet.

"I've even begun to contemplate a possible divorce," I admitted impulsively. Hearing my own word "divorce" out loud was a huge shock.

"Oh," my friend said. "Wow." She was a woman of perseverance and the last person to encourage divorce. But she didn't seem surprised, and she didn't try to discourage me.

That day, I recognized clearly for the first time that I'd been blind to how much the difficulties I'd been facing with Patrick had hurt and tormented me. Patrick had indeed prohibited me from disclosing anything regarding him and our home to other people—but now I began to recognize that it was me, not Patrick, who had truly prohibited me from being honest. I'd chosen not to be truthful due to my own pain and internally imposed restrictions.

I wasn't sure if I had the power to fix or reverse the tears in our fabric and the relationship, but I needed to try. I wasn't ready for a divorce—not yet.

In May of that year, I nearly died.

I was driving in the mountains in a heavy rain shower on my way to the IHC when my tires slipped and I lost control of my car. While buckets of water hit my windshield, my car spun around into the opposite lane, swimming in a pool of rain. I struggled to return the car to the original lane, and a few seconds later, my car stopped—no more than an inch from the edge of a cliff. It was a miracle I hadn't collided head-on with another car in the opposite lane, or careened down into the deep valley.

I drove the rest of the way to the IHC with great care, feeling that my life had been spared somehow.

The showers stopped by lunchtime, so I went to the clinic parking lot to take photos of my tires. They looked like black, smoothly rounded tubes; there were no grooves on their surfaces. I was totally shocked by the fact that I'd had no time to even take care of my car for such a long time, and that Patrick hadn't bothered to look at it either.

After work, I drove carefully to the nearest tire shop, where I bought four new tires on the spot.

"So what happened?" Patrick asked me after I got home. He already knew the short version of the story, because I'd called him from work after the accident. But now, as soon as I began to explain in more detail how dreadful the situation was, he stopped listening. He seemed to be floating away somewhere.

"Are you listening, Patrick?" I asked him, trying to get his attention.

"Oh, yeah . . . oh, terrible!" he said quickly. "But I'm glad you're safe."

He wasn't there. But I wasn't upset. I just knew he couldn't concentrate for some reason.

Something must be wrong with him. This wasn't the Patrick I knew.

I reflected on this incident, and on another incident that had happened in Japan a month earlier: chipping a bone in my foot after tripping on some stairs.

Feet. A common feature of these incidents—my foot, my car's tires. Something that occurs with our feet is usually an indication of matters around family and those closest to us.

Now I knew the indication by the *Achala* back in 2007 was real.

I began to contemplate what I'd told my friend a month earlier in Japan. The lying and the hiding had been bothering me a lot. I knew the situation I was in was not okay. I'd imposed myself into voicelessness and helplessness, and I didn't see that changing for the better. I needed to think this matter through more clearly before it became too late.

— 20 —
Patrick's Illness

By 2012, Patrick and I had been together for twenty-two years. I knew the man I'd fallen in love with, my bestest friend, and now I saw that the changes in him were *not* normal.

Patrick's tendency to keep hurtful events inside of him was only getting worse, but he denied what was going on and refused to seek medical assistance. That only made things worse, leading to depression and other mental difficulties. Still, I reproached myself for my negative thoughts, full guilt, and self-doubt. Was I selfish to be contemplating this? Was I just seeking something idealistic and unattainable in our marriage?

It was hard not to look back at our younger selves and see how happy we'd been. That was why the wedge that now divided us made me throb so badly. We had been happy. We'd been so in sync. The loss of that beauty was devastating.

I tried to maintain our life and my love for Patrick as well as possible. I punished myself for the doubt I felt and pushed myself to try even harder to believe in us, to cultivate more through my love, devotion, and faith practice every day. I was desperate. Often I'd felt his absence during these years together, but we'd always managed to hang on to a sense of togetherness, even if I was the one doing all the work.

Now, I wasn't sure how many threads connected us.

In the beginning of 2012, Patrick started developing severe head-aches and obsessive behaviors, and completely lost the ability to jog. We had been growing increasingly isolated from one another for months, and I began to think more and more about divorce. I felt my efforts to constantly look after him had been wasted; I was losing my own purpose and direction. I was tired of worrying about Patrick and our life instead of building something positive and good for us and others.

In the autumn of 2012, every evening after we came home, we would take a walk at the community park near our home, despite the emotional distance between us.

With fingers interlaced, we talked as we walked.

"I'm thinking about quitting the consulting job," Patrick said. He began to explain how difficult it would be for the company to get funded.

He'd said these same things and I'd given my same advice for three days. I didn't know if he was repeating himself because he didn't remember it, or if he was just still undecided about quitting.

I started talking about my job, and Patrick couldn't focus on the subject. Eventually, I just stopped talking. Terrified, I felt a weird impulse to scream, "This is our new normal!" Even as we still held our hands tight, I began to weep.

It took another year before Patrick finally decided to leave the company. They'd still never paid him, but I was happy that he was finally walking away from the dismal situation.

At the beginning of 2013, he began to work as a scientific con-sultant for Tygon, a local biotech company that had a few medical and oncology diagnostic products. Michael, the CEO of Tygon, and

Patrick had known each other since Patrick had joined Michael's previous company, Areozyme, in 2008 for a short time. They came up with some ideas for a new R&D oncology division within Michael's company.

Patrick was excited for this new beginning. I hoped it would be the positive change we both needed.

At the beginning of May, Patrick and Michael completed the acquisition of Axegen, a company Patrick had founded, by Tygon. Upon this acquisition, all the chemical compounds and designs of the drugs that Patrick had developed for the past few years were transferred to Tygon. He began to work as a CSO for Tygon, receiving a salary.

Among Patrick's early accomplishments in his new role was developing a new compound for clinical trials.

By that point, his headaches were a daily occurrence. Within a few weeks of starting his new job, it'd gotten to the level of "excruciating." On June 2, while he was attending the American Society of Clinical Oncology's annual meeting in Chicago, he called me during a break.

"Ah . . . hi . . . Kyomi . . ." His voice was unusual, troubled.

"Are you okay? Patrick, what's happening? How are your headaches? Are you in pain?" I rushed to express my worries, one after another.

"They're pretty bad," he confessed. "I've been taking maximum-strength Tylenol all the time and it's not working. And . . . something else . . . I'll tell you . . ."

"What is it, Patrick?" I knew somehow that the very piece of information he was about to disclose held the key to all the mysteries that had been plaguing me about our relationship. I felt afraid.

He lowered his voice. "I've had *double vision* . . ."

I knew it. I felt chills. His excruciating headaches and now double vision were all connected. These were all neurological symptoms from whatever was happening in his brain that Dr. Blum had been ignoring for over a year and a half. And yet my mind rejected this idea, as if an electric current had shorted out my neural circuits and my own brain was unable to run any longer. I started shaking.

"Are you safe to walk?" I asked. "Can you walk?" I tried to maintain as normal a tone as possible, but my jaw was trembling and I could hear the clacking of my own teeth. I took deep breaths, trying to soften my reactions to what he was telling me. Otherwise I knew Patrick would sense I was scared and that would be devastating for him. For his sake, I needed to stay calm and subdued.

"Can you come back home?" I asked.

"Not yet," he said. "I need to stay at least one more day to present my poster session tomorrow. But I'll try to come home earlier than planned."

"Okay, and then let's visit Dr. Blum ASAP," I said. "I will make an appointment with him. But if it gets any worse, go to the hospital . . . okay?"

I made him promise me he'd be safe and come back home as soon as possible. Then we said goodbye.

After hanging up the phone, fears spread from my mind into my body. *What happens now?* I knew this was the culmination of what had been happening for some time and we couldn't turn back. I felt like I was nearing a cliff.

And beyond that?

Patrick visited Dr. Blum the day after he returned from the trip, and Dr. Blum prescribed steroids again. He also scheduled an MRI exam for two weeks later and referred Patrick to an ophthalmologist.

The ophthalmologist performed various exams that went on for several hours, but was unable to diagnose Patrick's condition.

—

A week later, we had no information about what might be going on or anything besides steroids to help treat Patrick's condition. In the meantime, he'd developed more symptoms. Every evening as soon as he returned from work, he'd collapse deep into the couch. Within half a minute, he'd fall not to sleep but into an "unconscious state," then begin loudly snoring. The extreme loud, rather mechanical, and almost acoustic percussions spooked me. They made the whole house shake. And the persistence and depth of his unconsciousness scared me even more, because he couldn't or wouldn't wake up out of it. It was like he was drowning in a deep mud that just kept pulling him down deeper and deeper.

I was so terrified that I sent an email to Dr. Blum, telling him about my fears and requesting that he expedite the MRI exam.

That night, Patrick was laboring so much that soon he began gasping for air. I put my hands over my ears and closed my eyes, trying not to hear the noises and not to see what I saw every day and night. I wanted to run away from our situation, but there was nowhere to go.

I was in the middle of an abyss, trapped but still hoping this whole thing would go away and our normal life might return.

But it was too late for that. This thing, whatever it was, was here to stay.

On Friday morning, June 14, 2013, Patrick's condition rapidly worsened. It took at least thirty minutes that morning for him to come out of his ghostly, muddy sleep. I thought he'd fallen into a coma.

"Patrick . . . Patrick! Wake up! Patrick!" I was desperate, shouting at him over and over and shaking his body vigorously.

He might die today, I thought to myself, chilled to the bone.

"Patrick! Wake up!" I shook him, shouting and shouting. Tears ran down my face.

Finally, his eyes rolled open, but I could see that he wasn't fixing his vision on anything. He looked tired, and I wondered if he'd woken up to an excruciating headache. But he didn't acknowledge any pain, or even the fact that I'd shouted him awake.

"Oh, I gotta go," was all he said when he realized he was late to work.

"Are you kidding me, Patrick? You are ill! You need to go to the ER, not to work!" I was angry at him because I'd been so afraid.

"No. I have to go to work. We have three investor meetings today. Michael is expecting me." He dashed upstairs to take a shower before I could protest further, and then he was out the door.

Patrick called me after the meetings. As expected, he'd had an "unbearable" headache throughout the day. Because of the headache, he hadn't answered a couple of the investors' questions, he said. He still seemed more worried about work than his health.

I had already gotten him a 3:30 p.m. appointment for an MRI that day; we agreed to meet each other in the radiation department waiting room at Hope Memorial Hospital in La Jolla.

I arrived at three o'clock, my anxiety building. It felt as if the center and bottom of my stomach were pushing up into my throat. I worried that if it kept going I'd lose the contents of my stomach. It took everything I had to steady myself while I waited.

When Patrick got there, we moved to the small waiting area outside the MRI room. It was freezing cold.

"Mr. Patrick O'Connor?"

A radiation tech emerged and introduced himself. Patrick followed him through the heavy metal door, looking back at me, both of us exchanging silent words. Then he vanished inside, and soon the loud mechanical noises began. The machine's sounds echoed, assaulting my head and making my heart beat even faster. Though I was trying to stay calm, I was terrified. I sent Dr. Blum a text and then waited. I couldn't bear this—the time, the noise from the MRI room, everything clicking, my heart pounding so fast. *Be quiet!* I wanted to shout. The rhythms from inside seemed to grow even louder, as if they were trying to aggravate my feelings.

The heavy door next to me opened. I stood up to see Patrick. As the tech released his arm, Patrick—suddenly unable to hold his body up or take a step forward—threw his body over onto my right shoulder.

The sense of fight or flight hit me quickly. My mouth went dry, my eardrums were blocked. I became a mass of muscles, holding him as tight as I could with my whole body. The tech wasn't much help.

"Patrick!" I cried. "Are you okay?"

But he couldn't answer. He had no strength to hold his own body upright; he was dead weight. I had to drag him onto a nearby bench.

Once I got Patrick seated, leaning against me, I sent another message to Dr. Blum: "Patrick can't walk!"

"Come and see me straight away in my office," Dr. Blum immediately replied. "Hurry!"

Chills traveled down my body. My muscles froze up. I was sure Dr. Blum had already seen Patrick's results, and whatever was wrong was big—as big as a tsunami. The thing I'd feared so long had finally hit us.

As the door opened, Dr. Blum moved his eyes from his computer, yet kept them at an angle from us. He couldn't meet our eyes. His face was frozen.

"Ahh . . . hi . . ." he said stiffly. With a hand gesture, he invited us to sit.

I braced myself.

"I've just gotten your MRI images, Patrick. Unfortunately, they don't look good."

I stopped breathing. Dr. Blum turned his computer to face us and it was a full-on assault that penetrated through my eyes, hit the back of my skull, and extended its hand straight down to grab my heart and stop it.

I looked at Patrick. He, too, was frozen.

A tumor. My eyes were drawn straight to this huge, rounded, white mass. It was so perfect, so shiny. Like a king seated on a throne, it rested at the center and bottom of Patrick's brain, a tyrant already ruling our destiny. *I knew it.* But at the same time I couldn't believe what I was seeing. I felt as if a heavy block of iron had struck my head. My consciousness had flown away to the farthest place in outer space, unable to find its way back.

Now my eyes slowly moved to look at the surroundings of the image. Huge black spaces. So much fluid—inflammation from the tumor must have led to the accumulation of fluid in his brain. That was what was causing the headaches. I couldn't believe we'd already been living with this monster for so many months, and perhaps even years—not seeing it, not acknowledging its presence. I wanted to run screaming from the room.

This whole process took only a few seconds before Dr. Blum broke the silence.

"You need to go to Urgent Care at Blue Ridge Hospital straight away. I've already called Dr. Martinez. He is a Harvard graduate and an excellent brain surgeon. He will be waiting for you there." He now seemed to find his own ground and stand a little more firmly.

His words brought me back to reality. Patrick had almost no strength left in him. I would have to be the one to carry on and do whatever was needed. I was the only one who could do this. I felt the pressure of that responsibility—responsibility I'd carried for so long. But now was when it counted most; Patrick needed me.

"Sorry, but good luck." He still couldn't look us in the eyes, and I imagined he bore some sense of guilt for having ignored my concerns for so long. He quietly passed me papers he'd printed: the map to Urgent Care and the website bio for Dr. Martinez.

We departed.

It was already dark when I parked my car at Urgent Care at Blue Ridge Hospital in La Jolla. I walked to reception and asked for someone to help bring Patrick inside in a wheelchair.

We met Dr. Martinez, who'd already reviewed the MRI results, and he redirected us to Neurosurgery. By that time, Patrick looked like he was about to lose consciousness. In the exam and consultation room, I helped him get through additional exams and provide further information to Dr. Martinez.

Within a few hours, Patrick underwent emergency surgery. The tumor and its associated inflammation had caused accumulation of his cerebral spinal fluid. Over time this excess fluid had caused hydrocephalus, which was what was causing persistent headaches.

The surgeon placed a drainage tube in the right side of Patrick's skull to release the excess pressure.

A few hours after the surgery, Patrick was already awake.

"I feel much better," he told me. He was happy to be relieved from the excruciating headache of the past few weeks or so.

We didn't talk about the tumor. I wanted him to have a good rest . . . at least for now. It had been a very long, exhausting day.

I left Patrick's room in the ICU at one thirty in the morning and got home at two. The first thing I did was search online for a possible surgeon for Patrick's tumor. I found one at the Skull Base Institute in Los Angeles. With a small amount of relief that I had at least identified a possible next step, I laid myself on the bed—but my brain was too exhausted to sleep.

Only after four did I finally manage to doze a bit.

I woke up just after six o'clock to a red dot on my voice messages indicating I had a voicemail.

I gulped. *Oh, no.* I rushed to open the message.

It was a nurse saying that something had happened to Patrick and I needed to come back to the hospital at my earliest convenience. He was okay, she assured me.

I listened to her message again and again. What did she mean by "something" had happened?

I hurried back to the hospital and rushed through the ICU toward Patrick's room. The nurse was standing just outside the door when I arrived.

"I'm sorry for what happened," she said emotionally, blinking her eyes.

"What *did* happen?" I asked rather sharply. I didn't want to spend too much time with her before actually seeing Patrick with my own eyes.

"We don't know why, but your husband had a seizure and we needed to intubate him."

Oh, no! I rushed into his room.

Patrick was lying in the same bed where I'd seen him a few hours before. But now he had a ventilator mechanically gushing air into his lungs.

Oh my God.

"He's fine and stable now," said the nurse, who'd followed me in.

But I was shocked at this turn of events. All of a sudden I was overcome by the feeling of being swallowed by fear and relief at the same time. Tears came down my cheeks. The nurse hugged me. I felt the heaviness of what had happened in the last twenty-four hours and thought of what might happen next. I felt like crying.

I held Patrick's hand tight as he lay there in his bed. In a matter of hours, he'd become incapacitated, a different person. They made a mistake, which caused a large hematoma on his skull, that was still bleeding. But there was nothing I could do.

While Patrick was sedated and still on the ventilator, I became extremely vigilant. Though he was sleeping, I stayed by his side and watched, always staring at the monitors closely.

As Patrick had wanted to keep the situation around his condition secret, I hadn't talked to anyone about it—not his family, nor anyone at his work, nor even our spiritual community. My younger sister, Yoshino, was the only one I'd shared with, telling her about his hospitalization and possible tumor.

Every night after I left the hospital around eight or nine o'clock, and every night at home I groaned in agonizing pain . . . but I couldn't cry. It was as if the tears had totally been dried up. I was holding my emotions too tight deep inside of me to release them naturally. And, most of all, ever since Patrick had called me from Chicago my fierce desire to protect him had been in overdrive, preventing me from sleep.

Most nights I went to my computer to do research on tumors, their treatments, and specific surgery options that might be available to Patrick. Since he had become a much more critical and complicated case now, his surgical options were limited. Now I couldn't take him to Los Angeles, as I'd originally expected to do, for the expert to remove the lesion from his midbrain.

I stayed at the computer until 2:00 a.m. every morning, searching, feeling all the while like I was going to vomit. The pineal region, the location of this brain tumor, was one of the most difficult areas even for the most skillful professional neurosurgeons to operate on. The success rate for resection of a tumor in this area was low, and its associated risk was huge by contrast. And now, with this additional issue of Patrick's accidental hematoma, my top choice of surgeon was no longer an option.

The sense of being trapped, pushed into a very small corner with no exit, sickened me day by day, moment by moment. Was this my destiny—Patrick's destiny?

— 21 —
Our Destiny

It had been three days since Patrick had gotten intubated. Early that third morning, Dr. Martinez came by and said that Patrick would be off the ventilator soon, most likely the next day.

After sitting in Patrick's room for hours, I stepped out for a break. A doctor who'd been glued to the computer in the hallway saw me and practically ran over to me, as if he'd been waiting for that moment.

"Good morning, Ms. O'Connor. I am Dr. Phan, a pulmonary surgeon." Without waiting for my response, he went on: "Patrick might have another lesion in his lung."

"What do you mean?" I asked, though I'd heard him. It was the worst thing he could have said to me. My whole body reacted to his words—my heart felt like it stopped, my ears seemed blocked. It was as if my system was shutting down. If he'd found another lesion, that would indicate that Patrick's brain tumor was metastatic and malignant. This conclusion left no room for me to breathe.

"I'll show you the x-ray," he said, and took me straight to the computer he'd been looking into before he approached me. The image was taken right after Patrick got intubated, he said. In the ten seconds it took me to follow him to the computer, I repeated my teaching's core chant in the hopes of centering myself.

A huge, white, rounded mass with a wide base pointing to the top, like a mountain, sat on top of the left side of Patrick's diaphragm. I felt as if my head was wobbling, no longer supported by my vertebra. I imagined my whole body crumbling into pieces and falling to the ground in the heap. But even as I lost control of my whole body in just a second, my mind kept working fast, killing me.

He was right. But I struggled to accept it. Using my medical knowledge, I tried to argue with him that it looked more benign in nature. But now that two lesions had been detected, that argument didn't hold; it was a waste of time.

Patrick's tumors were malignant.

The tsunami's waters crashed over me.

The next day, early in the morning, the anesthesiologist came to Patrick's ICU room and removed the intratracheal tube. Patrick was about to come out of his prolonged sedation; from now on, he could be monitored with fewer wires.

As the tube was removed from his mouth, Patrick's eyes were still closed, and he coughed several times during the extraction. A nurse suctioned the phlegm from his mouth until he began to breathe normally by himself as an anesthesiologist closely monitored him. Then the anesthesiologist began stimulating him.

Patrick took one very deep breath, gushing the air out all at once.

Then he opened his beautiful blue eyes.

"Patrick!" I called to him. He had a sweet smile on his face—the smile I'd been longing for. I felt like crying; it was as if my baby had just come into this world after a difficult birth.

"Ah, I just woke up." He stretched his body like a little boy.

"Good morning, Patrick." I squeezed his hand. This was all I'd been yearning for—the simplest expression of love and trust. I wanted to hold on to this feeling. But inside me hovered the knowledge of the dark spot I'd tried to erase: the image of his lung tumor.

Another fear then emerged. How long would this next phase of our journey last? And what would come after?

In the early afternoon, Dr. Martinez visited us in Patrick's ICU room.

"Good afternoon, Patrick," he said. "Good news—your surgery will be in a couple of days."

"Is it safe for Patrick to undergo surgery now, with that big hematoma in his brain?" I asked uncomfortably.

Patrick still had a bleeding wound in his head; could he really handle a surgery?

"Yes," Dr. Martinez assured us. "It's become more stable."

He showed us the CT scan images of Patrick's head—one taken right after the accident, one that morning. There was no difference in the hematoma in terms of its size, which was still more than two and a half inches in diameter.

"Throughout the surgery, we'll monitor Patrick's brain activity closely," he said.

Patrick looked at the pictures, but he said nothing. He'd become more and more subdued and introverted with each disclosure of the challenges facing him and us. He now left everything up to me and Dr. Martinez.

Dr. Martinez then showed us one of the lung x-ray images I'd seen earlier.

"I believe this is just an independent, benign lesion," he said brusquely, as if no argument or questions would be permitted. Then he swiftly moved on, focusing on explaining the procedure he would perform.

Though I'd requested the approach be minimally invasive, he recommended otherwise.

"I prefer an open-skull surgery . . . by removing the occipital bone." Dr. Martinez touched his hand to the back of his head to illustrate what he was saying.

I was shocked. "What about something less invasive?" I asked. The Skull Base Institute in Los Angeles, where I'd originally wanted Patrick to be operated on, flickered in my mind and then vanished.

"I believe Patrick's tumor is most likely benign, not cancerous," Dr. Martinez said again.

Of course I wanted to believe it was true, but intellectually it seemed unreasonable to believe two independent benign tumors would grow in two separate organs at the same time. And the pulmonary surgeon had implied malignancy; why was Dr. Martinez insisting otherwise?

Right now, Dr. Martinez seemed to want to leave everything up to the surgery and the pathology tests, and Patrick agreed with his decision. My fears soared, but for now I decided to close the small box at the center of my mind where the image of his lung was stored.

"I'd like to go back to work within two weeks," Patrick told Dr. Martinez as we wrapped up the conversation. It was the same drive and obsession he'd always shown.

Dr. Martinez promised to do what he could. "I will try to make the incision as small as possible," he said.

Did he really think this was possible? Even in the best scenario, returning two weeks after brain surgery sounded incredible. But for now, I couldn't think about even two weeks from now. I could only focus on what was ahead of us.

All of a sudden, Patrick requested, "Can you ask the pathologists to further examine the resected tumor with specific cancer markers?"

"Uh . . . oh, sure . . . what markers would you like?" Dr. Martinez responded, stuttering a little.

He took notes as Patrick directed. These pathological studies would determine the most effective targeted chemotherapies in case he did in fact have cancer.

He knows—that struck me hard. Perhaps from the beginning, Patrick had known his tumor was malignant. He'd never said the word "cancer" to me, but he must have been prepared for its possibility all along.

More than anything, the fact that he'd hidden his true feelings and preparations completely from me threw me into a place where I felt much lonelier and more vulnerable than before.

At home, I wept silently for a long time.

Right before his first emergency surgery, Patrick had sent an email message to Michael, the CEO of Tygon, explaining that he'd need to take a few days off for health reasons.

Patrick now sent Michael another email saying that he had a "small" lesion in his brain, which was most likely benign, and that he had to undergo surgery, so he'd need to take time off work for a while. With no more detail, he said he'd send an update after the surgery.

Clearly, he'd kept this whole thing secret from Michael, too.

I understood that Patrick didn't want to disclose what was happening to his family, but I'd recommended that he at least call his sister Brenda to let her know what was going on.

Finally, one day before the surgery, he called her from his ICU room to let her know what was happening.

On June 20, Patrick underwent a sixteen-hour surgery. Since before he was taken to the operating room, I'd been chanting one of our teaching's core chants—the *Achala*'s Benevolence and Liberation, "Nomaku Sanmanda Basarada Sendan"—repeatedly in my heart. I continued for the entirety of his surgery. Occasionally, I'd check the clock to see how long he'd been in the operating room.

As we needed good prayers and spiritual support, I'd shared a summary of what was happening with Patrick with the head of International Relations Department (IRD) in Japan, as well as one of the local LA temple staff, and requested special prayers for Patrick's safety during the surgery and a speedy recovery from his illness. But I'd had to ask them to keep the information confidential, at least for now. I'd also asked my sisters in Japan to directly request prayers from the Grand Holy Temple in Tokyo.

"Hi Kyomi." I was brought back to the present moment by a man's voice. I'd been in a deep, quiet state of prayer for about two hours. He was a local temple staff.

"I am so sorry for what's happening . . ." He hugged me and said the head of the IRD had contacted him and asked him to come, and share their good wishes.

I wanted to cry, but I couldn't.

This was the first person in our local spiritual community I'd spoken to about Patrick's illness. I wanted to tell him everything—to tell him how long I'd worried about Patrick's condition, and how fearful I was now, but instead I mechanically told him my "official" statement—that it was a great surprise and shock and we'd never imagined this happening. It wasn't a lie, exactly, but of course it was not the entire truth. I was so conditioned by Patrick not to share, to keep everything out of reach—I'd been prohibited from connecting with the world for so long—that I couldn't bring myself to share the depth of my fears and sadness even though I desperately needed the support.

The decision I made became my own sentence. In hiding the truth in this moment, I agreed to continue living in the cage as a dweller of the prison—once again, my armor.

—

After twelve hours, Dr. Martinez sent a nurse to let me know that the surgery had been successful and he would be wrapping up soon.

Tick . . . tock . . . tick . . . tock . . . Why was it taking so long to finish?

Hours more passed.

Finally, the automatic sliding door opened at the back of the waiting room and Dr. Martinez stepped inside, smiling. He put his right hand forward, offering me a handshake, then said, "The operation went very well—it was successful."

He explained, with the confidence of a man who'd predicted this would be so, that the tumor looked to be benign.

Benign. I'd been so worried. Tears flowed immediately. It was as if the clouds were cleared away and a beam of the sun was shining through. Perhaps there was a possibility Patrick and I might return to our regular life soon after all.

"The area where the tumor was located was vascular and complicated," Dr. Martinez said. "It was close to the optic nerve and difficult to remove. I didn't want to damage the nerve, which might affect his vision, so I left some tissues behind. But I did my best to remove as much as possible—about 95 percent."

All I could think about now was the tissue left behind, and how it might cause metastasis.

I felt even more nervous when Dr. Martinez seemed to falter as he passed me a piece of paper: the report from the pathology department on the mass that had been removed.

Dr. Martinez explained a few more surgical details, including the fact that he'd had to make a hole in Patrick's skull to drain the CSF to the spinal cavity, and then he left. When he was gone, I dropped my eyes for the first time to the pathology report and read a few lines:

"high grade and enlarged nucleus ratio," "pleomorphic," "various stages of undifferentiated cells" . . .

I knew these words were typical descriptions of cancer cells, not benign tumors. Why was Dr. Martinez telling us the opposite of what the pathology suggested?

And if the tumor was malignant, what would happen with the portion he'd left behind, and the big opening in Patrick's skull?

I shivered, the terms from the pathology report spinning violently around in my mind. This was anything but a happy report.

Since day one of his hospitalization, Patrick had been unable to go to the bathroom or eat by himself. At the hospital, I was there every day to assist him with eating, going to the bathroom, whatever he needed.

Several days after the surgery, Dr. Martinez organized a biopsy of Patrick's lung.

While we were still waiting for the final pathology report, they decided to discharge him to begin rehabilitation at Cradle Rehabilitation Center.

Before he left Blue Ridge Hospital, Patrick had directed me to send part of his specimen, the pathology block from his tumor, to Functional Genesis Inc. in Cambridge, MA. The company, which had recently been founded by Harvard medical school graduates, would provide genetic profiles for his tumor. Patrick was an oncology expert, after all, and he felt this company would do the job properly. It was clear that he, too, doubted his tumors were benign. I began all the paperwork, and did as he'd asked.

The head of the rehabilitation center, Dr. Hasan, gave Patrick an initial interview when we arrived there.

"How long will my rehabilitation take?" Patrick asked bluntly.

"Most likely a little longer than a couple of weeks," the doctor said.

"No. Ten days," Patrick said. "I want to go back to work as soon as possible."

The doctor looked surprised, but didn't say anything.

During the next ten days, there were some improvements in Patrick's physical strength and coordination. But because of the extremely high dose of steroids and opioids he was on to control the ongoing inflammation and the associated pain in his brain, he was often exhausted and rehabilitation wasn't as effective as anyone wished. Soon, he began to realize his limitations.

Every day I stayed at the center all day, helping him change clothes and eat and assisting him with showers and visits to the bathroom. I sometimes commuted back and forth to and from the center three times in one twenty-four hour period. In between these visits, I contacted a social worker for help identifying and purchasing all the equipment and home improvements I'd need to have in place when Patrick came home: a medical bed in his office downstairs, regular and transporting wheelchairs, and more.

At the end of his stay at the rehabilitation center, Patrick was able to walk about eighty feet using a walker. He was totally compromised. From the beginning of the rehabilitation, I'd known that his returning to work wouldn't be an option after the massive brain surgery; Patrick, however, still wasn't ready to admit defeat.

"You may not be able to work for a while," I said.

Patrick was quiet and kept his lips pressed tight together.

"You may need to explain to Michael," I pressed gently.

He was staring at the air in front of his wheelchair. My heart clenched. I could feel how unbearable this was to him.

During this time I began to think about how our lifestyle would likely change going forward. It was a heavy reality. I alone would need to handle all the tremendous challenges and disabilities he was now exhibiting, and however many more developed. How would I be able to face his dismal illness, all these challenges, and, worst, his possible death?

I heard the marching of heavy boots—the ominous sound of all that was coming.

In the second week in July, after the ten days of rehabilitation, Patrick was discharged from the rehabilitation center. That day, he had a series of appointments for a follow-up CT scan, blood testing, and an office visit to Dr. Martinez. After the therapists' and nurses' cheerful goodbyes, I drove him from the curbside of the rehabilitation center back to Blue Ridge Hospital.

After pushing him around in his brand-new wheelchair to various departments, we at last arrived at an examination room in the neurosurgery section. We waited for Dr. Martinez for a long time; finally, he appeared.

"Here's the CT scan, Patrick," he said, showing us the image on the screen.

To our shock, the tumor was there, already almost double its original size *before* surgery.

Compared to the original, rounded shape, it now looked wilder and angrier, as if the tyrant wanted revenge for the surgical assault that had been launched against it.

Clearly, Dr. Martinez hadn't reduced it by 95 percent as he'd claimed! I looked at Patrick, who was staring at the image but keeping his mouth shut tight. I was blown away and couldn't utter a word either.

"Yes, I know," Dr. Martinez said. "It's already grown so much.

Also, we've received the pathology report. It took a long time to finalize it. From the brain tumor sample alone, they couldn't make a conclusion either way, but the biopsy sample from the lung was independently determined as melanoma. With that information, the pathology department has finalized Patrick's brain lesion diagnosis as Stage IV metastatic melanoma in the brain."

I looked at Patrick. He was frozen, yet the corner of his mouth was twitching. He otherwise didn't move. I felt the ground we'd been standing on all of a sudden crack open. We were both falling into the darkness below—to the center of gravity.

"Both our team and the outsourced university pathology team believe that is the final diagnosis for you, Patrick. Unfortunately, none of the cancer oncogenes you chose to analyze for possible targeting chemotherapies matched with your cancer." He said all these words remarkably straightforwardly—a total shift from what I'd seen in his attitude before.

I couldn't believe the depth and severity of this diagnosis. One after another—accident, trauma, failed surgery—and now Patrick had no chemotherapies available for his cancer, one of the deadliest imaginable.

Patrick remained silent. I, too, said nothing.

I was already exhausted from all that had happened so far. But for Patrick's sake, I would carry on. Did I have any other choice?

That afternoon, three and a half weeks after the onset of his illness, I took Patrick home. It was mid-July.

Home, sweet home. The very thought of it made me weep.

Once home, our cats watched us cautiously from a distance, staring at us as if they, too, were afraid.

"Hey, Tommy and Omi—Papa is back," Patrick called them from the wheelchair.

They reacted with subtle bodily movement—frozen, turning their ears backward, raising their fur so they looked puffed up. Both of them peered at Patrick, absolutely spooked by this "stranger." Patrick's face was totally rounded by the side effects of prolonged steroids and he had no eye movement or facial expression whatsoever. He looked like a spiritless ghost or a zombie from the grave, as if he'd been lobotomized.

I tried to call to Tommy and Omi, but they didn't move. Instead they ran away to the foot of the stairs, still staring, ready to escape.

Tommy had always been more attached to me than to Patrick. But Omi had been Patrick's girl and always demanded to be on his lap before his hospitalization. Now, she wouldn't even get close to him. It was devastating. I'd hoped that they would be a source of hope and comfort in the middle of the abyss he now found himself in; I begged them in my heart to be kind to him. But I couldn't change how they reacted to him.

"Do you want a cup of tea and some of the bread pudding I baked last night?" I asked, trying to distract Patrick from the pain of the cats' rejection.

"Yes, please," he said.

Though we had many things on our minds, we couldn't say anything, particularly not about the results. We held the heaviness of what we knew but didn't have the courage to speak.

"It's good to be *home*," he said quietly with a deep breath.

I held back my tears, willing myself not to weep. This was not the end; it was just the mouth of the tunnel we were hurtling into.

— 22 —
In the Darkest Tunnel

In mid-July, Patrick received a series of radiation therapies. I prayed hard for his safety and the effectiveness of the radiation. I cried helplessly every day after I put him in bed.

Only one month after the onset of his illness, he'd changed so much. Along with the ongoing high dose of steroids he was taking for inflammation, the radiation therapies had wasted his energy. The exhaustion would waste him even more before we were done.

While he was undergoing the radiation therapies, Patrick used a medical bed downstairs to rest during the day. I'd gotten it set up in his office before his discharge a week earlier from the rehabilitation center. I'd also brought a mattress down from one of the guestrooms upstairs to the living room next to his office so I could stay downstairs and be closer to him.

But Patrick preferred sleeping with me in our bedroom upstairs—so, each night, with the little remaining strength he had, he'd trudge upstairs with me almost carrying him, all the way to our bed. After helping him lie down, I'd then lay myself next to him for a while, until he settled into sleep. While in bed, we'd clasp our hands together and he'd tell me, "Kyomi, you're my only friend, my bestest friend. You've been an angel."

Each time, holding tears back, I'd respond, "I hope you get better soon, Patrick."

Once he was asleep, I'd slip my hand gently out from his and let my tears fall quietly. I sensed his life was fading away. I loved him so much, more than anything. I couldn't let go of my suffering. *May these throbbing pains and aches, created by my own attachments, be accepted and transcended for the wholeness,* I prayed many nights. How many more nights could I undergo this—and once he passed on, would I really be able to let go? I was desperate, and seeking a light.

One day, after Patrick had finished radiation therapy for the day and was lying in his medical bed downstairs, I saw the name "Functional Genesis" pop up in his email on his laptop.

It was what we'd both been waiting for.

Leaping out of bed, I screamed with delight, "Patrick! It came . . . Functional Genesis!"

"Really? Let me see." He leaned forward.

I opened the email and passed him the computer. At the same time, I hopped on his desktop computer to open the email and print it out. But before the task was even complete, Patrick's "moon" face got paler and even more spiritless.

"Shit!" he said.

My heart dropped. *Oh no.* I looked through all the pages of analysis; there were no matches with any known mutations for cancers. That meant that Dr. Martinez was right: no treatments were available for Patrick.

He was mute, though the corner of his mouth was twitching, holding back either words or tears. My heart bled for him.

He'd saved so many thousands of people over the years, and now, in a sad twist of irony, he was sick and there was no hope for him. Patrick remained still, taking in what this surely meant.

His long silence spoke more than words. I wanted to scream, to shout in the air, at anyone who might be responsible for what we were going through.

"I must have had this for a much longer time than I realized," Patrick said. "I didn't listen to you, did I? I should have listened to you more carefully."

Regret? Or repentance? I didn't know exactly. Perhaps both. But it was too late to think about all the ways I'd expressed concern over the years.

"I've been thinking about . . . when I quit the advisory role," he said quietly. "I didn't tell you anything about it . . . I wasn't a good guiding child for you."

I waited for more, but that's all he could say.

Not wanting him to feel guilty, I tried to assuage his feelings. "No, you've been a beautiful guiding child to me. You've transformed yourself and others through the merits you've accumulated through your practice. You've become a person you couldn't have imagined being before. And you've done so much for patients and people in our spiritual community through your tireless efforts."

"Thanks, Kyomi." A gentle light lit up his face.

I held him warmly yet firmly. *My Patrick.* I wanted to cling to him, to hold him forever in my arms. This vulnerable person, my husband. I didn't want to let him go.

This was one of the most honest conversations we'd had in the past several years. I still didn't know why he'd quit the advisory position, but it didn't matter anymore, because Patrick had revealed his raw feelings. It was so rare for him to express anything emotional to me. His words sank deeply into my heart. Every small expression he made was precious.

I wanted to cry out aloud. I remembered the words he'd spoken to me after our first argument right after his thirtieth birthday party in 1990: "I did everything for you. I thought you liked it." Remembering that conversation, and hearing his words now, I knew he was devoted to me and had been all these years.

Looking back at our life together—almost twenty-four years by this point—my attachment to Patrick was beyond what I could have ever imagined. I loved him more than anything, even more than myself or my own life. What he'd said about me was also true of how I felt for him. I did everything for Patrick. It was, and always had been, about my love for him.

The recent radiation therapies had declined Patrick's health; he could no longer hold a spoon or folk by himself. In late July, I took him to Hematology and Oncology department at one of the university hospitals in Los Angeles, hoping to sign him up for the anti-PD-1 immunotherapy clinical trials. He wanted it desperately.

Dr. Kowalski, one of Dr. Lima's trial team physicians, saw Patrick at the clinic. He was too weak to keep his body straight: his neck was bent forward and his left arm was dangling from his wheelchair. I could read from Dr. Kowalski's expression that Patrick didn't have much time left.

"I'm very sorry, Patrick, for what you're going through. I understand your wishes. But you have limited strength, and this treatment requires testing, evaluation, and actual treatments, even if you qualify."

"But I need this therapy," Patrick insisted.

Dr. Kowalski shook his head. "I'm so sorry."

"Can you recommend someone in San Diego?" Patrick pressed. He was desperate. This clinical trial had been his last hope.

Seeing Patrick drooping in the wheelchair, lacking any of his former strength, I was reminded of the days when he'd been the light for others. This rapid fall felt like he'd been thrown from the top of a high mountain. I was overwhelmed by the bottomless helplessness I felt.

Dr. Kowalski offered us a referral to Dr. Jones of Panorama Hospital in San Diego and sent us home.

I called Dr. Jones's office that same day and we got an appointment for a week later. Even this short wait time made me anxious. I sensed our time left together becoming shorter and shorter by the day. I felt the pressure of the clock . . . tick . . . tock . . . tick . . .

When Patrick met Dr. Jones, he was again too weak to sit properly in his wheelchair.

"Hi Patrick," the doctor said. "I'm Dr. Jones . . . it must've been a tough couple of months."

"I'd like anti PD-1 immunotherapy," Patrick said straightforwardly.

"Well, Patrick, let me explain some treatment options," Dr. Jones began. He was calm and logical, albeit a little cynical. He allocated most of our appointment time to looking into all possible treatment options. While they talked, Patrick, though weak, still had the wherewithal to suggest some specific drugs for his own cancer.

But Dr. Jones seemed particularly keen to the option of "no treatment."

"No. I want the immunotherapy, the anti PD-1 trial." Patrick insisted again.

Finally, Dr. Jones agreed to order various tests.

I understood Dr. Jones' preference, and his prognosis for Patrick's case. But since Patrick didn't want to give up yet, I also wanted the treatment.

Though Patrick had shown lots of cognitive strain in recent weeks, I knew he understood his choices, and he wanted to live. He was as practical and responsible as he'd always been. His determination came from his strong beliefs as a scientist. In his career, he'd built confidence and trust in the advancement and future of modern medicine and science. It had been his desire and drive to progress science and medicine his whole life. He'd seen firsthand the future of cancer treatment. Of course he hoped he could be saved by these treatments he'd invested his whole career toward discovering and improving upon.

In the last week of August, Patrick and I visited Dr. Jones for a follow-up evaluation for the anti PD-1 immunotherapy trials.

"I'm sorry, Patrick," he said. "You were rejected from the clinical trials. We have only five cases in the trials out of so many."

Suddenly, I lost my sight. Dr. Jones's face looked as if it was behind silk curtain. The word "denial" sat emphatically in my mind.

"There were two new lesions about one millimeter in size. If it was only one I could have still recommended you, but two made it too difficult," he said regretfully.

Only one millimeter! No mercy! I thought. I wanted to scream, and I imagined either shaking him or begging him. I was sure the new lesions must have resulted from his recent surgery.

"Sorry, Patrick," he said again. "We cannot accept you with these active brain lesions."

After we left the exam room, the fact that no hope remained for Patrick pressed us both hard to the ground. I didn't know any longer what to say, how to smile, or how to live. What would we do now?

—

After this rejection, I didn't know practically where we should go or what options we had left for Patrick's *next* step. "No treatment" wasn't our choice but it became our destiny.

Two days after that rejection, Patrick got a severe headache, then incontinence and the dreadful, muddy sleeping habits he'd suffered from prior to surgery. I knew what was coming. He was developing hydrocephalus.

Who could I ask for help? Dr. Jones? Or should I take Patrick to the emergency room? Anger and resentment at the entire medical system and our doctors was rising in me, but I tried to control myself. Finally, I decided to take him to emergency.

At Panorama emergency, they admitted Patrick and ushered him into an emergency surgery to reestablish his drainage. But this was just a temporary measure to control the pressure in his brain and ease his symptoms. As expected, they recommended an additional surgery—ventriculostomy—to put in a proper intracranial drain for the CSF.

Patrick underwent his ventriculostomy a few days later. I was grateful for the intervention to reduce the risk of hydrocephalus, at least for a while. But knowing all these surgeries were only to reduce the symptoms—that nothing was being done to actually cure Patrick—left me feeling despondent. So much pain and effort for Patrick, and we were only prolonging the inevitable.

When this second hydrocephalus episode began, I'd gotten in touch with Yoshino.

"It's been just awful," I'd confided to her. "Patrick has no cure or treatment available . . . and now he's hospitalized again."

"Are you sleeping well, Kyom chan?" Yoshino asked me. "How about eating?"

"No, only for a few hours every night."

"If you become ill, who's going to look after him? You have to help yourself, Kyom chan . . ." Yoshino had been deeply concerned about my well-being since the beginning of Patrick's illness.

"Shall I come visit and help you?" she offered.

"Thank you, Yocchan," I said. "That would be so wonderful . . . but Patrick has been so private, he wouldn't allow anyone to be here . . . at least for now."

"Hmmmm, that'd be challenging," she said. "But how about this? I could help out around the house, and whenever he's awake I could hide in the guestroom."

"Wow," I said. "That might work . . . but maybe it would be too difficult." I was reluctant; if Patrick found out, how would he feel?

"It'll be fine," she insisted. "I'll stay out of his sight. If he's sleeping or at the hospital, I can help you any way I can . . . like cleaning or cooking."

I thought about it for a minute.

"Okay, Yocchan," I finally said. "You're very kind to offer. I really appreciate your help." I was so relieved; in fact, I felt like part of me was already leaning on her.

One day before Patrick got discharged from the hospital, Yoshino and her daughter Sae flew to San Diego. They would stay in our guestroom upstairs and out of sight for a while—at least until I could tell Patrick they were staying with us.

Soon, they would become the anchors of my sanity.

— 23 —
Septic Shock

Ten days after his ventriculostomy, Patrick was finally discharged from Panorama Hospital. Within a few days of returning home, he developed serious night sweats, ending up in soaking wet pajamas every night that I had to change. His fever fluctuated between 103° F and 104° F, with an occasional loss of consciousness. This was *abnormal*. What was going on?

I wasn't sure if Dr. Jones was still Patrick's doctor now that he'd rejected him for the anti-PD-1 clinical trial, but I had no other doctors to call. I decided to call his office and make an appointment.

For the following couple of days, I took Patrick to two specialty follow-up visits that had been scheduled before his return home, then to Dr. Jones. All the doctors concluded that his fever and other symptoms were caused by his ongoing brain condition; there wasn't much we could do. Dr. Jones gave me his cell number in case they continued to worsen.

Around nine o'clock that night, Patrick's temperature elevated to 105.2° F. He'd been in our bedroom upstairs all evening, repeating cycles of moaning, tremors, and losing consciousness. But this time he didn't wake up. I knew he was *not* sleeping. I feared he might develop seizures, or worse.

I sent a text to Dr. Jones, my mind spinning. *I knew it—I knew something was wrong. Why didn't I trust my own judgment?*

Regrets rose in me, my heart pumping fast.

No more delay. I called 911.

Within minutes of my call to 911, multiple sirens from different sources mingled on top of others. Yoshino and Sae—frozen in the upstairs hallway, holding their breath—watched me dash downstairs to open the front door.

As I opened the door, moving orange and red beams from multiple vehicles crisscrossed the front fence and part of the driveway. Noises of heavy boots and voices approached. Several tall men, some in yellow coats and helmets, poured through the door. They carried all kinds of equipment with them, prepared for anything they might encounter.

"Are you Patrick O'Connor's wife?" a middle-aged man holding a thick black binder asked me. "Where is he?"

"Yes. He's upstairs." I pointed. Then I moved quickly, leading them to our bedroom.

When we reached our bedroom, a short, muscular Asian guy in his mid-thirties, who seemed in charge of the team, began asking me questions—who I was, how Patrick was, what his symptoms were. The guy with the black binder took notes beside him. Four tall young men hovered in and outside our bedroom. One of them held a yellow stretcher at his side.

In front of our eyes, Patrick suddenly regained consciousness, now screaming with urgency, "I wanna go baathroom . . . I wanna go . . . Aaah! . . . I wanna go . . . baaathroom!"

I rushed to his side and looked at the Asian guy in charge who'd been directing the questions at me. "He's had a fever greater than

105 ° F for the last couple of hours," I said loudly. "He's just started tremors. His consciousness has been on and off, fluctuating." I held Patrick's shoulders.

"Mr. O'Connor has sepsis," the man in charge said.

I gulped and a small electric current surged from my lower abdomen, running through my spine and hitting my brain with a galvanizing shock. As fast as that happened, the electrical activity in my brain leaked out to total depletion. I had no current left in my brain to even think. Of course: sepsis.

I couldn't even begin to swallow the guilt springing out of my conscience. It all made sense. How could I have missed the simplest explanation for Patrick's symptoms?

His desperate screams continued: "I wanna go bathroom! . . . I wanna go! . . . I need . . .! Aaaah! . . . I wanna go baaathroom!"

Now I grabbed Patrick tight in my arms. "He's going to shut down! He's going to have diarrhea—and he's going into *shock*!" I was desperate, shouting. "I need help! Please do something!" I yelled at the young guys, who were standing there and watching but doing nothing. Tears ran down my cheeks.

"Patrick! My Patrick!" I didn't care about anything but my husband.

Finally, one of the medics sprang into action. "Mr. O'Connor! Can you walk to the bathroom? Mr. O'Connor?" he repeated.

"Are you kidding me! He is *not* going to walk! Can't you see? He is *failing*!" I knew I was shouting but I was irate. The young guy looked helpless. I must've frightened him with the severity of my reaction.

"He is about to shut down!" I snapped, still clinging to Patrick. *I won't let him go*, I thought fiercely. I looked at the paramedic. "You've got to *help* him!" I demanded.

He attempted to help, but the moment Patrick touched his toes to the floor as he came out of the bed, he moaned like a wild animal, and the watery contents of his GI tract burst out all over the blanket, sheets, and carpet.

And then he fainted.

Out of the corners of my eyes, I saw Yoshino and Sae standing outside the room, terrified, crying at the tragedy that was unfolding. I felt sorry for them to have to experience all of this just after arriving—but they'd come to help me, and I couldn't think of a time when I'd needed more support.

I was in tears. Guilt, resentment, and anger toward Patrick's doctors and myself welled up in me, alongside the fear of losing Patrick altogether. Finally, it seemed that all of the paramedics realized the seriousness of what was happening, because they hastily wrapped him up in the blanket, put him on the gurney, and placed an oxygen mask over his face, then removed him from our bedroom and took off in an ambulance.

Patrick was expedited through the routine ER process and immediately transported to an ER room. They took different sets of vials and small bottles of blood from him, and within a couple of hours he was admitted to the hospital ICU room for septic shock.

For the next several days, until the blood testing results were obtained, the medical team at Panorama Hospital tried one antibiotic after another. It would take more than two weeks for the bacteria to clear from both Patrick's urine and blood cultures. Every day and night I visited him at the hospital. Yoshino and Sae stayed home, always there to help me with tidying and other household chores.

Every night I came home and ate a simple dinner, kindly cooked by Yoshino. I felt some modicum of relief that Patrick had stabilized and my sister was there to help me, but still, I never allowed myself to totally let go of my fears. I felt that I was walking along the slimmest edge of a cliff, and that this all might soon end with a fall to the bottomless valley below.

Three weeks after the 911 call, Patrick's discharge was near. I realized I'd better tell him about Yoshino and Sae.

"Patrick, Yoshino has been so worried about us since day one of your illness," I told him. "She's been offering to help ever since. I wasn't sure if it was a good idea at first, but now she's here at our house to help us." I decided not to tell him that she'd been here since before the emergency call.

"Oh, that's very kind of her," Patrick said.

Internally, I sagged with relief: he wasn't angry.

"Was she okay to come here alone?" Patrick asked. He knew Yoshino struggled with speaking English.

"Actually, Hisashi and Sae were worried about that too," I said carefully, "so—I'm sorry for this inconvenience, but Sae decided to accompany her. So, Sae is also at our house." I offered an apologetic look.

"Oh, that's great," he said easily. "That's no problem. I'm glad you have Yoshino here."

Thank goodness. Now I wouldn't have to hide my family from him. Everything would be so much less complicated this way.

Tygon's CEO, Michael, was always on Patrick's mind, even during this difficult time. Michael was keen to finish acquisition of a compound from a European biotech company that Patrick had recommended and begun the purchase process shortly before becoming ill. Patrick was always alert for any communication from Michael, even when he should have been too sick to care.

Whenever I saw Michael's name on Patrick's caller ID, I brought the phone to Patrick and held it up for him, angled in an upright position—and Patrick always took the call, no matter his condition. Many of Michael's calls were answered while he was critical and in the ICU. Every time I held his phone, I wept for him. He was still trying to keep his job—for his sake, for our sake. Everything around his illness was a source of excruciating sadness.

One day in mid-September, while Patrick was still in the hospital for septic shock, Michael called. As soon as I saw his name pop up on the iPhone, I immediately passed the phone to Patrick.

After hanging up, Patrick went mute. I wondered what Michael had said to him. Various possible scenarios circled around my mind, but I sensed one of them was the most likely.

"Michael wants me to take a medical leave, starting from September 1. No more salary," Patrick said emotionlessly.

"Ah, okay . . . they finally decided," I said, waiting to find out how Patrick felt about this.

"His assistant will send me papers to sign," he said in a matter-of-fact manner.

"Okay, I can take a look at it when they bring it," I said.

That was the end of our conversation.

Tygon had paid Patrick's salary up to now despite Patrick's limited participation from his ICU bed in meetings or conversations with Michael, but the game was over now. In the blink of an eye, they'd ask him to resign.

One day in mid-October, Patrick was at home talking with me, lying on his right side on our bed with his head resting on his palm. Patrick didn't like something I'd just said to him, and his response was to scream, curl up his body like a shrimp, and hold his arm tight.

"It hurts! It hurts!" he wailed.

I stared at him blankly; I didn't understand what was happening with him.

"You hurt me! My shoulder. You hit me!" he screamed, still clutching his left arm.

"No, Patrick, I didn't do anything to you," I told him.

"You did!" he insisted. He didn't believe me.

The way he criticized me so sharply hurt me. It reminded me of the ways he'd kept secrets from me for years, holding seeds of negativity in the darkness. Still, he was in pain. So, not knowing what else to do, I put him in the car and drove him to the ER immediately.

After taking an X-ray, they found Patrick had a fracture on his left shoulder. Patrick still believed I'd caused the fracture; he seemed convinced that I had somehow abused him and couldn't let go of this stubborn, dark belief. I tried to believe he loved me, but his suspicion stirred up the sediment of insecurity I had accumulated before his diagnosis.

Within a couple of days, they concluded that the fracture had been caused not by Patrick's cancer but by bacterium from the sepsis. At this point I was going back and forth between the hospital every day because Patrick had developed severe anxiety. All the nurses were overstretched, so it was difficult for them to always be there when he needed them. On some occasions, I knew, they even deliberately ignored Patrick because they didn't like his obsessive attitude. So I made sure to be there to help Patrick whenever possible. But during the nights I had to come home.

When I was at the hospital caring for Patrick, Yoshino and Sae filled in for me at home. They supported the other parts of my life so I could devote myself to Patrick. I was unendingly grateful for their help.

At night, I talked with the two of them a little over dinner. Then I would go to my office upstairs to juggle the insurance claims, co-payments, extended tax returns, and other practical matters that were piling up. I got less and less sleep, and resorted to taking Ambien before bedtime.

One night, after I'd taken a half an Ambien, Yoshino and Sae stood next to me in the bathroom talking. I began to feel the effects of the Ambien, losing the wholeness of myself, my physical steadiness, and my focus. The world seemed to swirl together.

I was lightheaded and feeling a little silly, and I started to dance. I was trying to change into my pajamas, stripping my long knit shirt up and over my head, but it got stuck. Instead of correcting it, I wore it like a hairband, with the long sleeves dangling down on either side of my head like a clown's funny hat. I spun and danced, laughing hard.

"I just took half a sleeping tablet. I feel so silly . . ." I was laughing hard, hysterically, like a crazy person.

I am losing it, I thought. I hadn't laughed like this for so long.

"Kyom-chan, are you okay?" Yoshino asked, concern painted all over her face. "Did you take a pill? You're acting strange. Do you feel okay?"

My sister was acting like I'd been abusing drugs, but no. I was just taking a half a pill each night to help me sleep.

Sae, in contrast, was giggling and excited, taking photos of me, this crazy auntie of hers. I felt like a circus clown. Yes, I *wanted* to be a clown. I didn't ever want to stop dancing and laughing. I was so tired of being sad.

Then my toes caught on the rug and I fell to the floor. As I landed, a gush of sadness overwhelmed me and I flung myself onto the ground, weeping, suddenly totally sober.

Yoshino and Sae let me cry for a while, then quietly took care of me for the night. They took my clothes off, put my pajamas on, and laid me gently in my bed for sleep.

I was still sobbing like a little girl when they left me, but eventually I fell asleep.

A few days after that incident, as we all finished dinner—Yoshino and I sitting side by side on bar chairs sipping cups of tea at the island table, Sae standing on the opposite side of the table, leaning forward against it—I brought up Patrick's latest hospitalization.

"To be honest, this time has felt more difficult than the last septic shock episode," I said.

"Why?" Yoshino asked. "This time was much easier and less critical."

Sae nodded her agreement.

"True," I said. "But in a fight or flight situation that requires immediate action, you can act brainlessly. When you've had something stuck in your mind for a long time, on the other hand, it can be difficult to simply act." I looked down. "When he accused me of being responsible for his shoulder injury, it hurt me so much . . ."

"But Kyom chan, Patrick is ill," Yoshino said, trying to soothe me. "He must have just misunderstood."

"I know . . . you can say that . . . But it reminded me how long I'd been haunted and suffering from the situation even before all this illness stuff started." I began to choke up.

"What do you mean, 'suffering'?" Yoshino asked.

Of course she didn't know. Nobody knew.

"I haven't told you or anyone, except for Mrs. Hirota back in April when I was in Japan . . . but I'd been considering the possibility of divorcing Patrick for a while," I finally admitted.

Yoshino gulped but stayed calm, her eyes cast downward. Sae's eyes opened big with surprise, and she grew pale.

"I'm sorry . . . you only knew the best picture of us," I said. "But it's been challenging for several years. I've been trapped in this situation for so long." I shook my head. "I don't know exactly what's causing it . . . it could be part of his illness. But now that he's ill, it's impossible to know. If I was trapped before . . ."

I could say no more. My sister and niece were just as quiet as I was. Even though I'd started the conversation, I saw no end to it.

One day in early November, Patrick was again hospitalized after another crisis related to his recurrent septic aftereffects. Since the onset of his illness, he'd been in and out of hospitals.

While he was in the ICU yet again, I went to my ob-gyn clinic at Patrick's former hospital, Hope Memorial—still my primary health-care provider—because I felt like I might be developing a urinary tract infection.

The doctor performed a regular exam and ordered a urine test. A few days later, a triage nurse called me to tell me they'd detected a urinary infection, but she asked me to come back to the office instead of simply prescribing the antibiotics over the phone.

At the ob-gyn clinic, the nurse guided me to a counseling room. As I walked in, she passed me a paper: my urology test results. I was stunned. There in front of me was a list of countless bacteria, each described as resistant to multiple antibiotics.

My body muscles froze, then suddenly lost their tone. I felt like I was being disintegrated or liquidated. The bacteria that had caused my UTI were a combination of multidrug-resistant (MDR) strains of bacteria; none of the available antibiotics would kill them.

What's going to happen to me? Was I going to die from this UTI?

How could I be infected like this? I was sure I must have acquired the bacteria at the hospital. I couldn't think straight.

"Just to let you know, you need a *special* antibiotic and a *special* procedure for this," the triage nurse told me.

I nodded numbly. "Yes," I said. "I'll go to the ER at Panorama Hospital; my husband was recently hospitalized at the ICU there, I'm sure they'll know what to do."

I thanked her and left my spirit right there in her office. Then, like a zombie, I headed to the ER at Panorama.

At the ER, I showed my urine test results to a doctor and requested that they administer whatever antibiotics were available to treat the infection.

"Unfortunately, you'll have to be hospitalized for this treatment for at least five days," the ER doctor said assertively.

"No, no. I can't do that! I can't be hospitalized!" I explained Patrick's situation and begged him for other options.

"The only antibiotic available for your infection needs to be administered through an IV," he said apologetically. "You need to be an inpatient at the hospital."

"What if I came to the ER every day to receive the antibiotic?" I pressed, desperate for alternatives.

"Hmmm, theoretically that's possible, yes," he said. "But the procedure at the ER will cost a lot of time and money."

"Yes, yes!" I nearly shouted. I was so relieved. It was worth the money and the time, as long as I wouldn't be out of commission for a full five days.

The doctor gave me the first dose of the antibiotic that day. As soon as the IV infusion was complete, I went straight to see Patrick in the ICU.

—

Patrick's "septic" condition refused to clear up. He also suffered from a moderate persistent fever at the end of his most recent hospital stay. Eventually, the doctors decided to change his treatment plan from hospital to home care. We were on our own.

The positive side of this was that my own health crisis with the MDR bacterial infection turned out to be a wake-up call. Standing at the edge of that cliff, forced to reckon with an immediate threat to my own health, I suddenly recognized the reality of my life and the weight of my Self.

This traumatic event made me see, for the first time, that I was separate from Patrick—and that I was equally as precious and vulnerable as he was. While I tried to become a foundation for him, I had at some point erased the boundaries between us. Now those boundaries returned, and I could see them clearly—and as I acknowledged their presence, the thought of divorcing Patrick, this idea that had haunted me for so long, became no longer important. Without awareness of these boundaries, I'd felt constantly threatened and trapped within Patrick's power. Now, however, I understood it wasn't him but *me* who was causing the feeling. I understood I had a choice in every situation; my power had to come from within, not from someone or something else.

As all this became clear to me, I made my own conscious choice to continue and complete my journey with Patrick to the end, no matter where that might bring us.

Divorce would never again cross my mind.

— 24 —
The Devotion

One morning in mid-November, after eating his breakfast with my help, Patrick went to try to pick up his medicine from one of his plastic pill organizers. I noticed him struggling to pick up the pills from the container, and then—

Bang!

The loud noise was followed by the sound of pills scattering everywhere.

"Oh my God!" he uttered.

"Are you okay?" I asked. "Did you hurt anything?" I rushed to him and saw blue, purple, red, and white capsules scattered all over the table and the floor.

"Are you okay?" I asked again, pulling the medical table out of his way.

"I don't know . . ." he answered. He was clearly embarrassed, yet also seemed to be frozen and scared.

As I crouched down to pick up all the pills from the floor, I examined him closely and noticed his left arm was dangling in a funny way—twisted a little. But obviously he didn't notice it.

"Patrick, what's happening with your arm?" I held his left arm gently, showing it to him, as if I'd brought it from elsewhere and it wasn't a part of his body.

"I don't know." He was grabbing his left arm with his right hand. He appeared not to have any sensation in the arm.

"Can you move your arm?" I asked him as I held it.

"My arm . . . Something must've happened . . ." He held it tight, as if he didn't want to let it go. Then he hit it a few times in an effort to feel it.

Now I examined his left arm more intently. There was a scratch below the elbow, and redness around the skin there. I guessed it had somehow lost control, hit the corner of the table, then gone limp.

I touched it. Cold. And it appeared fatter, too—plump, with no wrinkles. My guess was that its peripheral circulation had slowed down, so it was retaining more fluid than it should.

I had to take Patrick to the ER. Again.

When we finally made it into an exam room, the technician took a few radiographs of Patrick's left arm, then brought him to the radiation department for a CT scan of his brain.

Waiting alone in the empty emergency room, I felt scared. *The cancer must have spread*, I thought, and I couldn't help repeating this "mantra" instead of *Goreiju* in my thoughts. I could hear the sounds of ghostly steps approaching.

When the technician brought Patrick back to the room, I sat on his left side, rubbing his fat, cold arm as if I could revive it. He didn't speak at all about how he felt, but that wasn't necessary; I just stroked his arm softly and we sat there in silence.

The weight of our silence was precious. I knew how we were feeling. We were in this together.

When the ER doctor finally came in, he didn't mince words:

"Bad news is you have a lesion in your brain. But the good news is it seems to be a benign cyst!"

He showed us the image of the CT scan: a nicely rounded white wall with a dark space on the inside, most likely fluid. "I think it's a reactive lesion to your recent radiation therapies," he told Patrick.

Oh my goodness! I felt like jumping out of my chair. I looked at Patrick, still holding his arm, and he offered a little smile. I was practically ecstatic. Though the doctor would have to remove the cyst, doing so could reverse this issue with Patrick's arm. The fact that the lesion was just a cyst and not cancerous was a huge relief.

For once, some good news.

Two days later, they operated.

When I returned to the surgical recovery area where Patrick had been kept all night after his procedure, I saw Dr. Kim, the attending doctor for Patrick's first surgery. It turned out he had been the attending this time as well.

Dr. Kim asked me to accompany him to Patrick's bed.

"Good morning, Patrick," the doctor greeted him.

He was still lightly sedated, but he was able to respond and cooperate with Dr. Kim's requests.

After brief physical and neurological exams, Dr. Kim asked Patrick to raise his left arm. I gulped in fear; could he do it? But to our delight and surprise, his left arm lifted—a little shaky, but he was undeniably doing it.

"Oh, wow!" Patrick's apprehensive face quickly changed into a smile.

"Fantastic, Patrick!"

We were both overjoyed. This rapid reversal and recovery was so encouraging.

—

A couple of hours later, Patrick was about to be transferred to a Level 2 unit, less intensive than the ICU but with more specialized care than a regular ward.

Before Dr. Kim left us, he whispered into my ear, "Patrick's brain isn't in good condition. When I was operating, I could see that its entire surface is covered with small, pigmented nodules."

The visual image of the cancer in Patrick's brain assaulted me violently. I felt as if I'd been stabbed in the stomach; the knowledge tormented me. But I kept these sensations and feelings to myself.

After we returned home, it was as if we had both agreed to enjoy every moment together, even though his tumor was only getting worse.

Patrick held his left arm like it was a precious child. Every morning after breakfast, he meticulously performed his physical therapy exercises. His earnestness made it a ritual.

"How's your arm, Patrick?" I asked one morning. I was happy to see him holding a small one-pound dumbbell. I put a warm wet towel down near him.

"Great!" he said, beaming. "It's getting stronger." He stopped his movement, picked up the towel, and wiped his face and arm with it. Then he looked me in the eyes. "Thank you, Kyomi. You're my only friend . . . You're my bestest friend in all the world!"

"You're *my* bestest friend, Patrick," I responded, tears falling down my cheek. I wanted this moment to last a long while.

These days offered up many of the first happy moments Patrick and I had shared in the last five months, which had been filled with rapid "downs and further downs."

But Dr. Kim's words lingered like poison, buried deep inside of me. I couldn't tell Patrick, and never would. I had to try not to let what I knew overtake me, either. *One step at a time.* I knew that was the only way Patrick and I could get through this.

A couple of weeks after Patrick's return home, as I was giving him an arm massage in the morning, I noticed it had become a rod again, heavier than before. Unless I held it up in the air myself, he couldn't lift it. It was once again puffed up and cold.

I took Patrick to the emergency room again and they took another CT, which showed that the previously vacant space Dr. Kim had taken the cyst from three weeks earlier was now filled with some sort of tissue. Patrick was admitted back to the hospital for further examination.

The next day, they performed a CT-guided biopsy. A couple of days later, they concluded that the vacant space was now filled with cancer.

Upon hearing this news, Dr. Kim's haunting remarks resurged, defeating me.

One step at a time, I reminded myself—but this time, it seemed, the step was not to fix a problem but to face a much bigger reality: the inevitability of Patrick's end.

I wanted to vomit the blood that I felt had been filling up in my stomach since Dr. Kim first told me how dire Patrick's condition was.

From that moment forward, Patrick's left arm was unusable; it just dangled at his left side. He was no longer able to pick up his medicine from the plastic pill boxes by himself, so I helped him with his meds.

Though I knew his loss of function came from the loss of central control, I continued to perform passive exercises twice daily on his compromised arm, bending and stretching it to maintain circulation and prevent complete atrophy of his muscles.

Psychologically, this routine helped both of us. I was at least doing *something*.

During this very difficult time, Patrick also tried to help when he could. One night, as I struggled to open a jar of cucumber relish for hamburgers I'd just made for our dinner, he intervened.

"I can help you with my better hand," he said.

I held the jar with both hands and he used his right hand to open the lid, his other arm dangling. I thanked him but in my heart, I was weeping.

Not being able to use his arm wasn't the end of Patrick's life, but the cause of the disability might take his life soon. Until then, I would help him maintain his integrity of Self—his wholeness—through small acts like massaging his arm. It was all I could think to do to show him my love and respect.

Since the onset of Patrick's illness, I hadn't been able to visit the temple, and Patrick and I hadn't been able to attend any services or leadership training to maintain our roles as spiritual guides. Patrick did, however, spend a lot of time deep in meditation in his medical bed. Even during the worst moments of his illness, he'd never given up his faith. I, too, had continued my daily chanting and prayers.

Our spiritual practices helped to sustain us as Patrick's condition worsened. Over the course of months, we got all the equipment he needed—medical tables, walkers, transporters, commodes, and urinals—set up throughout our house for his use. But by early December his body had become too stiff and unstable to walk, particularly on stairs. Increasingly, rather than climb the stairs to our bedroom, he slept in the medical bed in his office and I on the adjacent living room mattress, until finally it became clear that he would never again ascend to our home's second floor. His living quarters now were limited to downstairs.

In mid-December, Patrick had his first massive seizure. It started with total stiffness, then twitching of the left side of his body, and soon he lost consciousness. As his body spasmed violently, I called 911.

From the ER, he was immediately admitted to the hospital, where he was sedated. His doctors monitored his brain activity for a week and ultimately finalized a new set of medicines for him—a combination of both long- and mid-acting anti-epileptic medicine.

On Christmas Eve, they sent him home.

Christmas had always been Patrick's favorite holiday. My sister and niece were still with us, so I'd gotten presents for everyone and arranged them under our seven-foot-tall tree; I was hoping to make the holiday special for everyone.

Looking at each of the ornaments on the tree, all the memories of our twenty-five years together flooded into my mind. Grief flooded my body. But I tried to center myself—to bring out my courage. To help him enjoy this Christmas with me, for *the last time* . . . I was determined to do that for him.

On Christmas Day, our home was warm and cozy, full of sun. Patrick opened his gifts one by one with much difficulty, using his right hand as I supported the boxes. He didn't speak much or even seem to be totally coherent. I figured it was due to both the cancer itself and the effects of the anti-epileptics he was taking.

Sae took photos. Until this moment, I'd never wanted photos since Patrick had fallen ill. I didn't want to document this time; I hadn't even journaled about what we were going through.

Expressing my feelings felt too painful. But today, Patrick posed for Sae's photo-taking. My husband, who'd been so secretive about his illness and so self-conscious about how his appearance had changed, finally let go.

That night, I served Patrick an early dinner of his favorite: roast beef with lots of au jus and side dishes. I cut the roast beef into small cubes so that he could eat it with just one hand.

When he was done with his dinner, I ignited the blue flame on the dark traditional Christmas pudding with golden caramel–colored brandy I'd made and brought it from the kitchen counter to the table. The aroma of the brandy burning over the sweet plum filled my nostrils.

Seeing the pudding, Patrick's eyes brightened a little. But as he tried a small bite, he began to seize. His spoon flew into the air, scattering heavy cream everywhere.

The spoon bounced and then settled to rest on the floor, but Patrick's seizure didn't stop; his body was stiff and kept jerking for over two minutes.

His favorite holiday, I thought, despairing inside.

I remained calm, but I sensed a deep sorrow seeping into the cracks of my heart, reaching the center. I feared this might be his end of journey.

He was now unconscious. I called 911.

In order to stop Patrick's seizure activities, the doctors needed to sedate and intubate him. An ER doctor urged me to sign the document for his advance health directive and the consent not to resuscitate in case he stopped breathing.

By that time I'd signed this same document several times before.

But this time, the ER doctor, who had obviously reviewed Patrick's CT scans, acted like this might truly be the last time.

"We'll try our best . . . but it's unlikely he'll survive this," he said nervously yet assertively.

I was mute. My heart was closed and resisting. *He can't be dying.*

What the doctor said, along with Patrick's current state, pressed me into feeling like we were at the edge of a cliff. I could even look down to the bottom.

However, deep in my gut, I for some reason disagreed with the ER doctor. I could feel that we weren't quite there yet because I knew that Patrick hadn't agreed to go yet. He and I hadn't found a quiet moment to say our goodbyes. He wouldn't leave me like this.

At the ER, I texted Patrick's oncologist, Dr. Jones. He called back and told me the words I dreaded hearing: "Patrick won't survive into the new year. I am very sorry, Kyomi, but he will be gone by the end of this year."

"Only a week?" I said tearfully. "What else can we do to help him?"

"Nothing." There was a brief silence. "Kyomi, he's dying."

There was nothing else to say.

But miraculously, Patrick stabilized, and a few days later, he came off of the ventilator.

"Patrick doesn't want to give it up yet," Dr. Jones told me.

He began chemotherapy to control Patrick's brain inflammation that night. He used Avastin®—the exact drug Patrick had suggested to Dr. Jones on his very first visit, knowing that it would reduce the inflammation in his own brain.

Now we could see the light of the year 2014 before us. Though we were still on a steep downward roller coaster, I was grateful for Dr. Jones's merciful hands, and the spiritual wonders that kept helping us all along at the most critical times.

Several days after this near-death episode, Patrick was transferred from the ICU to a regular ward for rehabilitation. Only an improved medical condition and a recommendation by a physical therapist would make it possible for him to be discharged from the hospital.

The physical assistants who came to work with Patrick, a middle-aged man named Mike and two younger men, couldn't even lift him to a standing position. After the three of them tried (half-heartedly) and failed, Mike gave up.

"Mr. Patrick, if we can't lift you, we can't do any physical therapy. We need to order a Hoyer lift."

Thirty minutes later, Mike and another tall young man came with a huge machine, almost double Mike's height, that reached to the ceiling. It looked like a gigantic metal dinosaur with a harness hanging from it.

The men started to put the thick harness on Patrick so they could use the lift to stand him up. The young man climbed onto the dinosaur and took a seat. I looked up at him, then watched as Patrick's body slowly lifted into the air—then tilted rapidly, so he nearly fell over.

"Aaaah! Painful, painful! Aaaahh! Aaah!" Patrick screamed.

"Stop! It's hurting him!" I shouted.

They stopped and removed the harness.

"Well, Mr. Patrick is too *apprehensive* to do anything," Mike concluded. "There's no way to provide physical therapy for him."

They removed the harness—without even checking Patrick's skin, which had welts on it where they'd attached the harness—took the dinosaur out of his room, and left.

As soon as they were gone, I inspected Patrick's skin more closely. Not only were there welts, there was a big, bleeding gash on his groin.

I called an internist, an MD in charge of the patient wards at the hospital. She arrived ten minutes later.

"How can I help you?" she asked.

She seemed cold to me, distant, but I explained what had happened and said I wanted a plan for Patrick's discharge.

She explained that there was no plan and that she wouldn't be able to provide one because of the assistants' evaluation.

"Look," I said, "Patrick has already been in this ward for a couple of days, but no therapy has started. Now, if there's no plan, he won't be able to go home, will he?"

The doctor was listening. I continued.

"As far as I saw, the assistants didn't try properly. Nobody can carry the weight of any man in the way they did. Most patients still have some physical strength remaining. My husband does; he is still strong. I'll show you. He can stand up if you just do it right. You just need to use his own strength and momentum to make the most of his ability. I can show you how . . ."

I pulled Patrick close to the edge of the chair.

"Patrick, ready? One . . . two . . . and three!"

On three, Patrick rocked forward and we got him up to standing without any difficulty.

Once he was up, I showed her the injury from the harness and continued my plea, begging her to give us a chance. "Let me administer his therapy," I said. "We can do it, I know we can."

Finally, she agreed. She gave me some instructions for safety measures and suggested I shower him every other day. Then she left the room.

"Did you hear that?" I asked Patrick, squeezing his hand. "We can practice physical therapy together!"

Patrick had a happy look on his face. His trust in my ability to help him made me feel stronger.

For the next four and a half days, I provided Patrick with intensive physical therapy two to three times a day. One session lasted thirty to forty minutes.

When we started, he was too weak to even keep his body in a standing position, but I knew we could get him to a better place.

Before each session, I moved his heavy medical bed to the side and tucked all furniture and obstacles in the space to the corners of the room. Then I folded a fresh pillowcase lengthwise and wrapped it around his left hand and his walker handle so that he could balance his body better on the walker.

For his walking exercise, I held him firmly and guided him forward as he walked one step at a time. Simultaneously, I dragged a huge, heavy wooden patient hospital chair behind him with my free hand so that he could sit back or collapse onto the chair if he needed to.

At the beginning, Patrick could hang on to the walker for only a second. He would lose his balance, often dropping into the chair behind him, when he tried to take a step forward. And every time he dropped into the chair, the walker flew almost upside-down in the air because he was connected to it by the pillowcase bandage. This happened many times. But we never gave up.

One step became two steps, then two steps became three. It was hard work, but by the end of day three, he could walk—with help of the walker and me—all the way across his big private hospital room. By day four, he was able to make a round-trip journey from the far corner of the room to his bedroom door and back.

On the morning of day five, a physical therapist and the assistant, Mike, came over to assess Patrick for possible discharge. Patrick and I were ready to show off the fruits of our "team effort."

"Are you ready, Patrick?" I pulled him forward, as I'd done since his illness, and counted, "One . . . two . . . and three!"

He showed off how beautifully he could stand up with my help. Then I swung a walker in front of him. He stood comfortably, his right hand secured onto one handle of the walker, while I wrapped his left hand onto the other. Then he started to walk, one step at a time, by himself toward the door, as I walked alongside him. He made it there smoothly, without any breaks.

Explosive clapping erupted in the room.

"Mr. Patrick, you've done so well!" Mike shouted, smiling wide.

"Well done . . . Congratulations! Well, Patrick, it looks like you're ready to go home now."

Patrick and I smiled at each other. We knew what we'd achieved. Once again, we'd proven that, together, we could face any uncertainty in this world.

That afternoon, Patrick left the hospital with a great sense of pride and achievement.

As soon as we got home, we sipped tea over my home-baked bread pudding.

"It's good to be home," Patrick said—a rare full sentence.

We both smiled, holding hands. As I contemplated everything we'd experienced together since the onset of his illness, I found myself filled with gratitude and a profound, serene peace.

"Thank you, Patrick, for being my husband," I said.

He smiled back at me. "Kyomi, you are my bestest friend. With your help, we can do anything . . . We can conquer the world." His words were not loud, but they were firm.

This was the first time in weeks that he'd spoken to me so freely. Hearing him speak, I realized that he must have been not only physically guarded but also nervous and intimidated while he was at the hospital. I was thrilled that he was able to express himself now.

It was clear to me now that my husband's condition would only decline from here—that he would not be reversing course and going back to his former self. But I was ready for the challenges ahead.

Since my personal awakening one month earlier, my commitment and determination to support him had become stronger and more resilient than before. I hadn't been able to work in the clinic since the onset of his illness with only worsening (and would never be able to return to work.) But I was standing on solid ground, and I would continue our journey through to the end.

By the beginning of March 2014, the doctors had exhausted all possible treatments. The cancer was widespread all over Patrick's brain and taking away much of his physical and mental strength. He was failing quickly; he was almost a zombie.

To prolong his life by a few months, Dr. Jones and the radiation oncologist suggested a series of radiation therapy to the whole brain. They made it clear that this was a "last resort" measure.

Patrick was cautious. The radiation oncologist didn't say exactly how massive the side effects would be. What did it mean to prolong his life by several months? Would there be any positive effects beyond keeping him alive? It would surely cause massive irreversible damage and associated inflammation in his brain.

But Patrick didn't have a choice. He was dying. We signed the consent for the therapy.

Once Patrick began radiation therapy, I felt that every day was a death march. I'm sure he knew he would die soon, but he continued

to demonstrate a strong wish and determination to continue his journey for survival.

His unyielding faith and belief in the advancement of the anti-cancer drugs was the backbone of his determination. But I came to see
that the other unbreakable resolve for his survival was his wish to be
with me as long as he could. After each of the most difficult setbacks
we encountered, he told me, "You are an angel, Kyomi. With your
help, we can do anything, we can conquer the world."

He truly seemed to believe it.

One day after radiation treatment, Patrick said he wanted to tell me something. He was talking more and more in full sentences, which surprised me.

"I am so grateful, Kyomi, for what you've done for me, even before
this illness," he said slowly. "I was born in a simple Irish immigrant
family, and we stayed poor. I went to a university and graduate school,
which brought me here to the United States."

I was crying, wanting him to stop. If he continued, it would end
his story. I didn't want him to end. But he continued.

"Then I met you. That's why I had a wonderful life—a rich life, a
life filled with flowers that I couldn't imagine at all before. Because
of you, I met the teaching, and grew together with you. We've had a
wonderful life together. I am so grateful. Thank you, Kyomi."

With that, he was done speaking.

But how could I end our story?

In late March, ten days after the brain radiation therapy, we got a
great surprise. "Compassionate use" of the drug anti-PD-1 had been
approved by the FDA for clinical application. The drug had been
proven to be effective in reducing and stabilizing melanoma and a
type of lung cancer.

This meant that patients who'd once been rejected for the drug's trials were now allowed to reenter their applications. But only clinics that had been approved to carry out the use of "compassionate" trials could administer anti-PD-1, and Panorama Hospital's clinic wasn't one of them. Dr. Jones couldn't help us with this; I had to take Patrick elsewhere.

Saints Clinic was located in Santa Monica, 125 miles northwest of our home. I wasn't sure if Patrick could even make the trip to get an interview. But I felt we had no choice but to try.

I left a message for Saints Clinic's principal investigator, Dr. Omar, about Patrick's wish to be on the trial. He called me back the same day and told me the office would call to set up an appointment for him.

Both Patrick and I were blown away. We'd been walking the darkest of tunnels, and suddenly we saw light.

Two weeks later, after a series of nerve-racking interviews and tests, Dr. Omar finally approved Patrick for the treatment. It was the best day we'd had since this journey began.

I scheduled Patrick's infusion appointments for 9:30 a.m. every other Friday. I began to plan and organize that biweekly trip as the sole priority in our life.

Patrick was too weak to make the 250-mile roundtrip to Saints Clinic from our home in San Diego in one day, so we'd stay overnight in a hotel. My preparation for our visit would therefore begin on Wednesday afternoon. We'd drive up Thursday and arrive at the hotel before Thursday afternoon traffic got too bad. We'd finish the infusion on Friday morning, then drive back home before Friday traffic started.

I organized and equipped every trip meticulously since there was so much we had to bring with us—medications, devices for the ongoing home Invanz® infusion since his septic shock seven months earlier, Patrick's walker, wheelchair, and a wooden stool. For every infusion trip, our car was piled up to the ceiling with Patrick's gear.

Every infusion exhausted Patrick. The first few times, he had to lie on a gurney. After that, he was able to hang on to a huge patient's chair with my support. During the first few visits, I was afraid he might die at any time. The side effects from the infusion were tremendous, causing him constant, watery diarrhea and joint aches. I was shocked by the fact that he could lower his baseline even deeper. But this treatment was the last resort for us, and I had to continue to be the anchor for his confidence. I kept my dismay to myself.

In late June, a couple of months after receiving the first infusion, Patrick began to regain some strength. But there was a new side effect in addition to the existing severe diarrhea and joint aches: he was now developing skin lesions throughout his torso.

That said, I could tell his mind seemed clearer than before. Thanks to all the efforts by Saints Clinic, Patrick was finally experiencing a remission of his tumors: some of the cancerous lesions in his brain and liver had started to disappear and/or decrease in size. As this happened Patrick's sense of balance became much better, and he began to walk in the house with a walker with my assistance.

In the last week of June, I helped Patrick get dressed in his favorite red T-shirt, shorts, and baseball cap, and then took him out on our backyard patio. I dragged big pots to the edge and made decent enough room for him to walk around the patio table and chairs.

"Wow . . . it's so nice out here," Patrick said. He stood in front of the walker so I could fix his left hand onto a special plastic mold, and then he began to walk around.

I had left the sliding door open, and now Tommy and Omi came out to the patio, coming near Patrick for the first time since his illness started. They didn't get too close to Patrick, but they were hanging around him in the distance.

"Tommy and Omi, Papa is back!" Patrick was at his best regardless of how little he had in his life.

"Wonderful Patrick! We're a happy family." I said this cheerfully, though my throat was tight with emotion. I wished that moment could last forever.

"You are an angel," Patrick proclaimed. "You are my bestest friend. You are *absolutely* the best thing that ever happened in my life."

Again I choked back tears. *Please . . . please do not stop this story of us . . .*

At the end of June, Merck & Co., Inc., which had developed the anti-PD-1 drug Keytruda®, announced the drug's approval by the FDA. From October onward, it would be available on the market and throughout the country. Dr. Omar, therefore, planned to complete Patrick's therapy at Saints Clinic by the end of September and transfer him back to Dr. Jones at Panorama Hospital.

In mid-September, as I pushed Patrick's wheelchair through Saints Clinic on his last day of treatment, the doctors, nurses, and staff all greeted him and showered him with cheers:

"Congratulations, Patrick!"

"You did it!"

"Fantastic!"

"Thank you . . . thank you . . ." Patrick said to each one, beaming.

"Thank you," I told them. "Thank you for saving Patrick's life."

A nurse led us into one of the exam rooms. The room looked almost empty—no bed, no computer desk. I pushed Patrick's

wheelchair deep into the room and stood next to him, waiting for
Dr. Omar.

"Hello Patrick!" Dr. Omar smiled when he walked into the room.

"Hello Dr. Omar," Patrick said.

"You look so great, Patrick," Dr. Omar said warmly. "It's been
almost five months . . . do you think you can stand up by yourself?"

Patrick had never done this by himself in all the months he'd been
treated at Saints. I was a little worried.

But Patrick lifted his feet from the footrests, and I swung them to
the side for him. Then he came forward in the wheelchair and—with
me helping him a little, just offering some guidance and an arm—
stood up straight from where he was sitting in the wheelchair.

"Good!" Dr. Omar said. "So, now can you walk a little bit?"

Again I was worried, because I couldn't remember the last time
he'd walked without any assistance. But Patrick walked several steps
by himself without a walker toward Dr. Omar.

"Oh my God!" I uttered with joy. Then I swooshed in with the
wheelchair behind him, which he plopped down into, his energy
spent.

"Patrick, you look totally different from how you did before," the
doctor said. "You look much healthier. I'm very happy for you and
your wife."

"Thank you Dr. Omar." Patrick smiled.

"Good luck with your treatment at Panorama in the future,"
Doctor Omar said, reaching out to shake Patrick's hand. Then he
turned to me.

"Thank you so much for all that you and your staff have done for
Patrick," I said, shaking his hand enthusiastically. Dr. Omar's kindness brought tears to my eyes.

That day, we left Saints Clinic filled with gratitude. The progress

Patrick had made during his time there was profoundly uplifting, and something we'd never before experienced since the onset of his illness. After all the downs and farther-downs, our future suddenly seemed a little brighter, at least for now.

— 25 —
The End of Our Journey

B y early November 2014, Patrick had received three infusions of Keytruda® at Panorama Hospital, and he had experienced significant severe headaches each time. Two additional chemotherapies were added to reduce the inflammation—but Patrick had life-threatening reactions to the new drugs.

"The inflammation in Patrick's brain is now excessive," Dr. Jones told us. "Perhaps it's caused by all the therapy itself."

His words splashed cold water on my heart.

"What do you mean? What do you suggest we do next?" I asked.

Patrick was quiet in his wheelchair beside me. We'd known the last few therapies seemed to have given more severe side effects without substantial improvement.

"The overall positive effects of the PD-1 are still working," Dr. Jones said. "Images from the MRI show no signs of cancer progression, only remission and stabilization of his cancer. But for now, it would be better to discontinue the therapy and observe the inflammation."

I blanched. Did he really expect the inflammation would stop? No more treatment meant letting Patrick's condition worsen again. It meant . . . death.

"And if pausing treatment doesn't stop the inflammation . . . then . . . what do we do next?" I asked this, but I knew the answer. I was protesting against Patrick's fate.

Intellectually, Patrick and I had always known these treatments wouldn't cure him. But by this time we had not only developed hope, we were clinging to it.

"Nothing," Dr. Jones said. "Just wait and see."

A cruel fact. We'd faced near-death situations many times. But now, it seemed, there were no more miracle treatments to be had. All roads would lead us directly to Patrick's death. This simple, excruciating fact was hard to swallow. Patrick and I absorbed Dr. Jones's words in silence, subdued and intimidated by the future we saw before us.

One day in mid-December, Patrick was resting on his couch and wiping his face with a warm towel after his daily exercise—he'd been meticulously doing physical therapy at home for the last half-year—when he suddenly cried out, "A noise!" and covered his left ear with his palm.

I gulped. "Are you okay, Patrick? Is it loud? What kind of noise is it?" I tried to stay calm, but I was hiding my fear.

"It's like swishing . . . swishing water . . . but I guess it's not too bad." He became quiet, listening, still pressing his palm to his ear.

"Don't worry, Patrick. Just try to relax." I hoped it would go away.

I went to the other room and sent a text to Dr. Jones. He said there was no need to come in yet, but to observe it closely.

My stomach clenched. I knew any negative additional symptoms to Patrick's existing baseline meant we were inching closer to his death. I needed to prepare myself. *One step at a time*, I reminded myself—the only way through.

—

A month into the new year, the subtle swishing noises in one ear had spread to both ears. The noises had rapidly worsened to sound like constant, metallic rubble crashing and banging in the construction site of Patrick's head.

"Noisy! It's noisy!" Patrick became furious with this constant assault.

The many trips to ENT, as well as audiology departments, didn't make his symptoms go away or improve at all.

I was anxious—no, terrified. Was the end as close as I feared?

Looking back, I can see that because I was so busy juggling everything during this time, I had no time to digest everything we'd been through. I had to hide my own vulnerability and emotions in order to be a functionally available *me*. I donned my protective shield, my armor, and continued to be a warrior to the outer world.

And now we were facing death—the point of no return which demands total surrender. I'd committed to being on this journey with Patrick knowing the eventual end point. But accepting this reality, the end of the tunnel, without any more fighting, was hard.

So, did I face reality? No—I couldn't. Seeing it there waiting there for us was too scary. I wasn't ready to end this journey.

In mid-May 2015, after taking care of Patrick's lunch, I left the house intent on finding some of the drugs I'd found online that I thought might help with Patrick's tinnitus.

When I came home, Patrick was unconscious in his bed, lightly yet continuously seizing. I froze for a moment in shock. *Oh my God! What's going on?*

"Patrick! Patrick!" I called.

He'd wetted the bed and was unresponsive. I didn't know how

long he'd been seizing. In front of my eyes, his breathing became weaker. I called 911.

A woman dispatcher asked what I needed. I explained quickly.

"Where is he? Is he breathing now?" she asked me.

"He's in the bed. . . Yes. But he's very weak."

"Check his pulse . . . do you know how to?" she continued.

"Yes, but I can't tell from his wrist. The pulse is there, but weak," I told her. Things were going downhill.

"Drag him onto the floor," she said calmly, "if it's safe to do so. Do you know how to perform CPR?"

"Yes," I told her with confidence. I quickly untucked the bedsheet from the bed, dragging them in a circular motion so Patrick's back was to me, and then pulled him carefully onto the carpet.

"Start CPR, beginning with chest compression," she directed me.

"Yes." I switched my phone to speaker mode, put it on the carpet, and began chest compressions.

"You should count aloud," she said. "I can count along if you like."

Together, we counted off the compressions, and then I gave Patrick two rescue breaths. Briefly, a thought flashed in my mind: *How surreal is this situation?* As a healthcare provider, I'd been trained for emergencies, but I'd never imagined this could happen in my life, or with Patrick.

I kept on going with CPR for several cycles. Then I heard the paramedics at the door. Thank goodness.

"They're here!" I told the dispatcher. I thanked her and ran to the entrance to let them in. They brought in a gurney and checked Patrick quickly.

"He's breathing now," the man told the dispatcher through his radio.

They lifted Patrick onto the gurney and attached an oxygen mask to his face. A man with a black binder took the lead. I confirmed with him that I wanted Patrick to be taken to Panorama Hospital, and then they were gone.

After Patrick had been sedated for four days, a CT scan showed that his condition had become more stable. But while he was still intubated, he began to develop a mild fever—and when they detected bacteria in his built-up phlegm, they began an antibiotic, which further prolonged his intubation period. It seemed he'd gotten yet another hospital-acquired infection, perhaps from the ventilator.

A few days later, just before the start of Memorial Day weekend, his temperature finally came down to normal and they took the intratracheal tube out of his chest, though they continued to administer the antibiotic.

During this hospital stay, Patrick's team of neurologists had repeatedly warned me that after this prolonged sedation, Patrick wouldn't be the same as before. He would likely be incoherent, his neurological problems more severe. Still, they said they would be discharging him the next day.

I was concerned because Patrick seemed over-sedated, and I wasn't sure if he was safe to be discharged. But they insisted that he was ready.

After breakfast the next day, I noticed a new symptom: Patrick was awake but dim, not communicative, and I could hear a high-pitched, windpipe-like noise in his upper chest when he inhaled.

I talked to one of the doctors, but his resistance to even examine Patrick was apparent. It was too inconvenient for them to prolong his hospital stay into the holiday weekend. I insisted, and another doctor reluctantly checked him. She agreed to treat him with a nebulizer for one more day, but said they'd have to discharge him after that.

I wept inside. I got it. His condition wouldn't improve in a day; it wouldn't ever improve. He would be discharged regardless of his weak condition. His time was nearing its end, and the pressures from the medical system were too great for us to continue to push up against. It was time to cease, or at least minimize, his treatment and care.

Patrick spent a week at the rehabilitation center, where they prescribed him an antifungal medicine for the windpipe noise, before we finally returned home together.

"It's good to be home," Patrick said, a relieved look on his face.

It had been weeks since he'd spoken in sentences. I didn't know how he had felt about anything we'd experienced lately.

As for me—I wasn't exactly hopeful that we ever could or would be out of the woods anymore, but at this point, I was no longer afraid. I'd made my own clear shift. I was ready for whatever might come.

As soon as I got Patrick home, I started preparing for the end. I began two projects: one to look for a company to modify the powder room downstairs to a walk-in shower room, and the other to hire a caregiver.

Patrick's condition was worsening, and with it his obsessive fear, confusion, and anxiety were increasing. His anxiety had become more pervasive and aggravated, sometimes too difficult to control. The more care he needed, the more new people I had to introduce to our home life, and I wasn't sure how he would react to that kind of intrusion. Nonetheless, I was determined to provide him the best care possible, and that meant hiring people.

For the remodeling project, I designed the changes carefully so as not to alter the appearance of his original office. The construction started in late summer and was completed in the beginning of October. I didn't yet imagine it clearly at the time, but somewhere deep down I must have determined that his original office would be his last resting place.

Throughout 2015, the doctors continued to evaluate Patrick's "end-of-life signs" and started to recommend "the next and last step": hospice care. Dr. Jones had also mentioned it a few times. Under hospice care, I would no longer be able to call 911 or take him to the ER—big adjustment.

Patrick's memory was declining, so I made a simple calendar board for him to easily grasp the day and month. Every day, after he repeatedly asked, "What day is it?" I showed him the board, simultaneously saying the date aloud. Then we repeated it together. Sometimes my voice trembled as I said the words. In fact, every small exchange we had made me feel like crying. Listening to the few words he could manage to get out made clear how much we had lost.

At the end of November, I had to make up my mind. I finally registered Patrick for hospice. He would remain at home but a hospice company, not his usual team of doctors, would now be in charge of his care.

Within twenty-four hours, a box called "the Comfort Kit"—a morphine bottle and a syringe, a new electric medical bed, and a huge Hoyer lift—were delivered to our home. I also received a new list of medications. All the "end" remedies had arrived within forty-eight hours of hospice registration.

I was in a shock, devastated by these aggressive and sudden changes. In my mind, hospice was supposed to provide terminal patients comfort and assist them to the very end. Until then, I thought all patients should have the right to live or die *naturally*, following the organic course of their illness. But now it seemed like we'd opted into a machinery that was aggressively pushing time forward, trying to legally kill Patrick in as short a time as possible. Upon signing the contract with them, I discovered they had planned to "finish" their tasks within a couple of months. I understood that some patients' families were probably already exhausted and vulnerable and the only thing they wanted might be a peaceful death—to let go—but this wasn't right for Patrick.

Or maybe I just wasn't ready.

Whatever the case, on the day I received the Hoyer lift, I called the hospice company to complain. I said that all patients had the right to live or die naturally—that it sounded like there was no room for Patrick to die on his own terms.

They seemed puzzled by my objections.

After I hung up the phone, I had a bitter taste in my mouth. I picked up the phone and again called the company. This time I directed a clear complaint to the program director.

Within one day, both the original management nurse and the social worker assigned to us had been replaced. The doctor agreed to change Patrick's medication plan back to what he'd been taking before, and I again became the major player in Patrick's daily care, working alongside the new managing nurse who visited us weekly, under the supervision of the medical doctor.

Within a few days, the Hoyer lift was removed.

At the beginning of December, as I was cutting chicken and vegetables in cream sauce into small pieces for Patrick—in the last few months, he'd begun to have more difficulty swallowing—he stopped eating and looked at me.

"Why . . . people are here . . . these days? Who . . . are they?" he asked in snatches.

"Your caregivers, and the people from hospice," I said gently. "Don't you remember? I've told you before."

"Hospice? . . . What . . . do you mean?" he asked.

Oh no . . . he'd forgotten about the hospice. My throat went dry and I coughed a little before saying, "Yes . . . do you remember the doctors recommended it? Dr. Jones said he'd finished all that the hospital could offer."

"When did you . . . register it?" he asked.

"At the end of November."

I watched as he went deep into his cave. Silence. Unbreakable silence. He didn't speak with me for the rest of night.

Looking back, I should have explained to Patrick more clearly what was going on. But knowing how he was, I didn't want to scare him. It seemed he didn't understand the extent of our "home-based" care—or perhaps he did but he was not yet ready to face the end.

Though I continued to care for him, Patrick seemed to feel a sense of abandonment—by all the hospitals and doctors, yes, but mostly by me. Nobody could cure or fix him; I knew this. Still, it was hard not to feel guilty.

In recent months, we'd started to have round-the-clock care. I scheduled caregivers from 7:00 a.m. up until 3:00 p.m., then for a night shift that started at 9:00 p.m. and continued until the next morning.

After the night shift caregiver came, I prepared Patrick various homemade foods: wilted power greens, spinach, asparagus, stews, meatloaf, meat sauces, cakes, bread pudding (his favorite), and muffins, divided into small portions and frozen. I usually shared the baked goods with all the caregivers as a treat as well. I slept very little.

At first I kept the middle six hours, from late afternoon to night-time, to look after Patrick by myself. Patrick had been the center of my life for so long; I didn't want to give up our alone time together. Patrick, too, appreciated those moments of togetherness.

However, later toward the end of year, our private time turned into Patrick's most difficult hours. His physical ailments, as well as his mental state, worsened quickly, and they were at their worst in the afternoon and evening.

This phenomenon had a name: "sundowning." I didn't know this at first, but I soon learned it was common for patients like Patrick to have a time when they became most agitated and confused. For Patrick, this time of day was often when his anxiety triggered panic attacks. He sometimes shouted for help or demanded to be taken to the hospital. Then he'd shout, "Where am I? Where am I? . . . Take me home! Take me home!"

In these moments, he was almost unrecognizable as the man I loved. It broke my heart every time.

By the end of January, Patrick was often confused about time and space and unable to differentiate between his past and present homes. He called me Kyomi at times, but other times he mixed everything up. He sometimes recited his siblings' names aloud in chronological order, trying to remember, but he couldn't.

Remarkably, the one thing he did always remember was the Founders and our teaching. Sometimes he talked about his admiration for the teaching out loud as if he was giving spiritual guidance to practitioners—perhaps to me.

One morning, he started the day in a good mood.

"Kyomi, it's good to see you," he said, stretching his body out comfortably.

"Oh, thank you, Patrick." I smiled at him. "How are you feeling?"

"I've been so lucky and happy," he said. "I've had a wonderful marriage and life with a successful career, a beautiful home, expensive cars, lots of travel . . ." Then the tone of his voice changed to sadness. "But my wife Kyomi fell ill," he said mournfully, "and since then I've had to look after her all the time."

"Patrick," I said gently. "You're the one who has been ill." The correction was automatic.

"*Ah*," he said with a gulp.

Oh, no . . . I immediately regretted my words. My instinct had been to tell him the truth, but now I saw that I should have said it differently.

"I have a bad headache," Patrick said quietly, and after that he stopped talking—got quiet and went down into his cocoon.

Inside, I let out a moan. Profound guilt tightened my throat. Why couldn't I leave his misunderstanding as it was? At this point of his illness, there weren't any rational thoughts. I needed to try to accept who he was now, not correct him . . .

Logically, I knew our time together was coming to a close. I should have recognized that his words were part of his nearing the end. But I didn't feel that way at all. It felt so personal.

The weight and the reality of what was happening, what he'd become, what I was losing, how my devotion mostly went unnoticed by him—I couldn't accept any of it. Worst of all, the many *whys* constantly circling through my mind precipitated a deep sense of shame and guilt inside me.

—

One evening, a few hours before the night shift's arrival, I was trying to help Patrick eat but he was resisting; he wouldn't even open his mouth. Though impaired, he was still physically strong.

"Where am I? Where am I?" he suddenly shouted in panic, moving violently. "Call the police! Call the police! Help! Help!"

I tried to calm him down, but he got even more violent and agitated. I grabbed his wrist and tried to distract him, but that just made him angrier. It was as if he was fighting against a murderer, and that murderer was *me*.

All of a sudden, I stopped and surrendered. I started to cry aloud, weeping in front of him.

"Patrick, Patrick, I understand that you want to live a little longer," I said between sobs. "Even that you want to live longer for me. But you've changed. You've changed . . . to become *a monster . . .*"

I said all of this as if he could understand, but in that moment he was beyond understanding.

I was still deeply in love with this man, and I needed support too. He was the only person I'd ever been able to speak to completely honestly in all my life.

A thought flashed through my mind: *We could die together. Right now, and right here . . .*

Then another thought hit me like a thunder: *Tell him how you feel.*

I wasn't sure if I could, but I had this sudden trust in *truth*, so I began to speak.

"Patrick," I said earnestly, "listen to me. Please listen to what I'm going to tell you now."

He stopped fighting me; he seemed to be listening.

"You used to be an intelligent, kind, and brilliant man," I said, looking into his eyes. "And I know you still are. But if you can hear me, please understand what I'm saying."

He was completely still, silent. Was he hearing me? I didn't want to hurt him. But for the sake of my love, his love, *our* love, I had to continue.

"Instead of acting like a monster, you can choose who you are, who you want to be. I know you, Patrick. It is up to you; you can choose your own path. I love you, Patrick. I really love you."

I stopped talking. I felt totally exhausted, my body depleted.

Patrick continued to sit there in silence.

I felt what I'd just said might separate him forever from me. But I'd meant every word, and it had all come from my sincere love and compassion for him.

I hoped he would see it that way.

At the end of February 2016, after a pleasant breakfast, I listened to a conversation between Patrick and his new caregiver.

"Hold my hands! Hold my hands! Can you look after me?" he asked her. "Can you look after me?"

When was the last time he said something like that to me? I thought in response. I knew it wasn't rational to long for words like those from Patrick at this point, but I was the one who'd been there, day and night, for years, and she was basically a stranger. What was going on in his mind?

I stepped into the conversation. "Who am I?" I asked him.

"Kyomi," he said.

"What am I?" I asked.

"You've been in charge of all the people . . . a manager," he said.

"Do you have a wife?" I asked.

"Yes," he said, nodding.

"What is your wife's name?"

"Kyomi," he said.

"Where is she, your wife?" I was becoming furious but doing my best to control it.

"Oh . . . well, she went somewhere . . . a while ago." He paused. He seemed hesitant to tell me this.

Oh my gosh. I was in shock!

"Where are you?" I pressed on.

Nothing could have prepared me for what he said next.

"I've been in a facility near home," he said. "My wife, Kyomi, used to visit me every day from our home, but lately, she hasn't." He stopped.

Upon hearing those words, I realized that he must have been dealing with this sense of abandonment for a while. After all the pain and tears, was this how it would end? Was he going to die with this belief—that I hadn't been there for him?

I fell to the bottom of a new abyss.

Finding out there were two Kyomis in Patrick's life was the worst experience of my life.

I knew Patrick's condition was worsening, but I couldn't have prepared for such an aggressive downturn. Though I'd been experiencing his "sundowning" every night, I still believed and expected something beautiful would transpire between us before the end. Now I regretted ever having taken our once-wonderful life together for granted.

The new caregiver had overheard my conversation with Patrick, and she clearly sensed my shock.

"It's just due to his illness," she reassured me.

It didn't make me feel any better.

Life was cruel. Patrick was ill and decaying, and though I was trying to be what he needed, I wasn't as perfect as I wanted to be.

My expectations for myself had always exceeded what I was capable of. My own insistence on excellence was a constant pressure that tormented and exhausted me. For all these years I'd protected my vulnerability from the outer world, but inside I was still my own worst enemy. I never once told myself I'd done my best or patted myself on the shoulder after advocating for Patrick. Instead, I continued to exhibit lack of trust in and compassion for myself, shut off my vulnerability, and retreat into my armor.

Toward the end of June, the irreversible nature of Patrick's condition became more evident. It felt too late to fix things between us. There would be no explanation for the many questions I'd held since long before his illness. I was trapped in the uncertainty of the unanswered, and felt I always would be.

On June 30th, I visited the LA temple for the first time in three and a half years. Immediately after that, Patrick's condition declined and became critical, as if dammed water had suddenly gushed out beyond its threshold. I knew instinctively that he'd been awaiting my return to the temple—that knowing that I had gone there had triggered him to surrender to death.

As he declined, his hospice caregivers discontinued his existing medicines and switched him to the "comfort kit." For some reason, we were left alone without a nurse—and later that day, Patrick began to suffer from withdrawal syndrome.

As I watched my dying husband moan, growl, and pant like a wild animal I became furious with the hospice company. It seemed we would both suffer to the very end. I wanted to cry.

Then, as if a light bulb had just been turned on, I experienced a sudden shift in perspective.

It was an awakening moment, an epiphany: Patrick would

complete his journey with dignity. He would face whatever came his way, no matter how hard it might become. He was walking straight toward death with sincere surrender. This was his last wish. And it set my resolve to support this surrender together to the very end.

Finding out about the "two Kyomis" a few months before had been a hard blow. I'd felt I was walking the last part of our path alone, that the abyss before me was bottomless. However, in this moment, I felt that Patrick had come back to me as a spiritual being, and I suddenly felt at peace.

My Patrick was here—he'd come back to me. And he was radiating a light as bright as he had under the infinitely blue sky at the *Homa* in 2000.

Epilogue
Finding the Truth

In my spiritual life, I've engaged in various practices over the years—chanting, disciplines, meditative trainings, reflections, and contemplative daily practices.

After Patrick's passing, though I had my own office upstairs, I turned his office into my writing room.

This is where I write now—at his desk. Behind me on the shelf spanning the length of the room are a couple of azure cloisonne urns, decorated with blue flowers in various shades, that contain his ashes; a large framed photo of Patrick; a small bowl of fresh flowers; and a cup of the milk tea I serve him every day.

I've often felt his presence nearby, supporting and encouraging me to continue. No matter how difficult writing becomes, he's always here for me.

Why do I have to continue? I've often asked myself. *Who will care about my story?* I've wanted to escape from writing, from being raw and vulnerable.

"Why can't I leave these secrets out of it?" I've moaned out loud, sometimes in conversation with Patrick. "Do you really want me to write this?" I've wondered this particularly at difficult times when I've encroached into the most private moments of our life together.

But I know my truth finding is not just freeing for me; it is also liberating Patrick from his past "curses," or karma, and allowing him to live in peace in the spiritual world. I know my courage has been for both of us, and possibly for our ancestors, and I've felt his strong approval as I've continued to write.

During the first fifteen months after Patrick's passing, often I cried helplessly, wailing, "I can't . . . I can't do this anymore." Writing itself became one of the most difficult spiritual practices I'd ever undertaken, and I didn't know where it would lead me.

But over time those cries turned into gratitude and joy as I discovered new truths about our situation—Patrick's, ours, mine, and even that of other people whose lives were and are intertwined with ours.

Over the course of our twenty-six and a half years together, Patrick— my late husband, bestest friend, and dearest partner—and I experienced many ups and downs.

It was important to me that he die with dignity. But the pain I felt at the end when I discovered that he'd come to believe there were two Kyomis took a very long time for me to resolve. That he believed I had abandoned him caused me unbearable, excruciating agony. Hearing that was the worst thing I experienced not only during my care for him but in our entire marriage. It caused me to go back to my old habits—to hide in my old armor once again.

Though I was a devout Buddhist practitioner and leader, it was too difficult for me to accept that the once beautiful fabric of our relationship had become so tattered, even destroyed. Ultimately, that fact became undeniable, and it shattered me.

The spiritual image that I had in the shower after my first *bodhi* elevation in 1999 showed me that our lives, whatever journeys we took, would be filled with unknown wonders. Since then, and particularly since Patrick's passing, I've learned that life brings whatever it brings—the unexpected, the unimagined. We cannot control anything, no matter how much we hope and wish we could. We constantly project our thoughts, expectations, and hopes because we want to love, to be loved, and to be happy. But just like Shakyamuni Buddha said, "Life is impermanent; everything is changeable and not permanent."

It's taken me many months to fully accept what happened and what didn't happen in my life with Patrick. I don't judge any longer whether what happened was good or bad. Through lots of daily practice and writing, I've made peace with what was, and what is.

When Patrick passed away, I thought I'd lost everything. I believed that my identity was deeply interconnected with his—that we were one. When he died all of the beauty of that interconnectedness was devastated, destroyed, wiped out. My dark thoughts and feelings nearly led to a loss of my faith.

But over the months, I found numerous twinkling stars and lights emerge here and there out of the rubble, like the fireflies we used to watch flit around the creeks and meadows we frequented during our earlier years in Maryland. What I came to understand is that each of those lights is a piece of my strong and shining Self.

In my reflections, I was reminded that the final struggles Patrick and I shared before his passing were proof that even in the end, we were connected through faith and trust. That beautiful fabric we'd woven together was not truly destroyed, only a little bent and altered here and there.

All the hardship I've experienced has ultimately brought me to a more grounded, truthful place. The difficulties I've faced have made my faith more immovable and resilient, and with that has come a better understanding of myself—of my past armor, and of the true *Self* within me.

As I found truth around me, it became my strength. I am still grieving, but I am open to my feelings now, no longer intent on hiding them away. I have learned to appreciate my scars and wounds, and to transform them into treasures.

This book, having emerged from my whole heart and being, holds all my truths. I am so very grateful for Patrick, who gave me the opportunity to experience all that we shared while he was alive and all that I've experienced since his passing. I feel peace in my own life, and I know he's at peace too. The love I now feel exists not only between me and him but also between me and you—between me and the entire world. May we all be so lucky to find such peace and love in the wake of loss.

Acknowledgments

The birth of this memoir is nothing but a miracle, while we've lived in the unprecedented COVID pandemic for over two years. But I know the special ingredients of this book— the love and the best wishes of many warmhearted people have made my book- our book- possible.

My sincere gratitude goes to Brooke Warner, coach, editor, and president of Warner Coaching Inc, and publisher of She Writes Press and SparkPress. I'd also like to thank Linda Joy Meyers, author and the president of NAMW, along with Brooke for giving me profound learning opportunities through their course, "Write Your Memoir in Six Months."

Special thanks to Editorial team managers, Lauren Wise, Samantha Strom, and Shannon Green for their supportive, diligent, and insightful works. Without them, this book wouldn't have existed. I'd also like to thank Krissa Lagos for her excellent editing.

Special thanks to Crystal Patriarche, CEO of Spark Point Studio and her publicist team, Tabitha Bailey and Grace Fell. The team has amazed me for their art, creativity, and practical power. I'd like to thank Maggie Ruf for her excellent Web construction. Special gratitude to Julie Metz for the serene beauty of the cover.

I would like to express my special gratitude to Mark Nepo and

Gail Warner for them to have provided path seekers including me hubs for many years with their art, authenticity, and grounding inspirational works.

My ever-lasting gratitude goes to my teaching founders and Her Holiness for their devotion to love, peace, and humanity. Patrick and I are eternally grateful for being practitioners of the teaching and their disciples.

Special thanks to my parents, two sisters, other family members, and our ancestors. They have generously offered me a true foundation for who I am today. Special thanks to Patrick's family and his ancestors for their unyielding support. I'd like to thank to my special friends, Cheri Hotalen and Junichi K, who first saw a writer in me and have supported all the way through, Greg Daniels, Maria Real, and Reiko H for their unyielding kindness and friendship, and many wonderful soulful friends in our Sangha community, who also loved Patrick. I would like to thank Ly Tran, Linda Joy Meyers, Lindsey Salatka, Cindy Rasicot, Leslie Johansen Nack, Gail Warner, Laura L Engel, Donna L Roberts, Mehmet Yildiz, Michael Burg, Gregory Daniels, Marian Young, Sally W. Buffington, Lori Shein, Bonnie Szumski, and Ed Robson for your friendship and insightful praises of my book.

I would like to thank you all, She Writes Press authors, and local SWP sisters, for your selfless kind support and love to each other. Each of you are a lighthouse for us to follow. Thank you!

My local writers groups from SDMWA, SDWI, SDWF, especially, founders, Marni Friedman, Tracy Jones, and Jennifer Thompson, a consultant, Caroline Gilman, Tricia Hedman, and other writers for allowing me to be part of the warm writers' circles and friendship.

My sincere thank you, all writers, MEDIUM writers, especially Donna L Roberts, Mehmet Yildiz, Lucy Dan, and Michael Burg, and kind readers, for your warm support and understanding of my book and me. I am so grateful for you to have found me in this place and my book. For this, I am eternally grateful- thank you.

Lastly, Patrick, where my deepest love and gratitude belong. You have been shining afar in the darkest and clearest night yet forever stays in my heart.

About the Author

Kyomi O'Connor moved to the States from Japan in February 1990 to work as a post-doctoral researcher at the NIH in Bethesda, Maryland. Soon, she fell in love with her husband-to-be, Patrick. Their journey together led them to change their careers, move to San Diego, and practice Buddhism. They grew spiritually together, and became leaders in their Buddhist community and inseparable partners through the many hardships they faced together. Patrick fell ill in the summer of 2013 with the diagnosis of stage IV metastatic melanoma in the brain, and passed away three years later on July 4, 2016. After his death, writing helped Kyomi rediscover light in her life. These days, she spends her time writing (she's an active writer online at Medium), practicing yoga and Qi Gong, cooking, traveling, and taking photographs. Kyomi lives in San Diego with her two cats, Tommy and Omi.

SELECTED TITLES FROM SHE WRITES PRESS

She Writes Press is an independent publishing company founded to
serve women writers everywhere. Visit us at www.shewritespress.com.

Indestructible: The Hidden Gifts of Trauma by Krista Nerestant
$16.95, 978-1-63152-799-9
Krista Nerestant endured multiple traumas as a child in the Philippines and
a young immigrant in the United States—yet she rose to face every obsta-
cle she encountered with courage and self-love. Along the way, she found
success and healing, discovered the hidden gifts of trauma, and eventually
became a spiritual medium and inspirational leader in her community.

Bless the Birds: Living with Love in a Time of Dying by Susan J. Tweit
$16.95, 978-1-64742-036-9
Writer Susan Tweit and her economist-turned-sculptor husband Richard
Cabe had just settled into their version of a "good life" when Richard saw
thousands of birds one day—harbingers of the brain cancer that would
kill him two years later. This intimate memoir chronicles their journey
into the end of his life, framed by their final trip together: a 4,000-mile,
long-delayed honeymoon road trip.

The Buddha at My Table: How I Found Peace in Betrayal and Divorce by
Tammy Letherer. $16.95, 978-1-63152-425-7
On a Tuesday night, just before Christmas, after he had put their three
children in bed, Tammy Letherer's husband shattered her world and
destroyed every assumption she'd ever made about love, friendship, and
faithfulness. In the aftermath of this betrayal, however, she finds unexpected blessings—and, ultimately, the path to freedom.

Bowing to Elephants: Tales of a Travel Junkie by Mag Dimond
$16.95, 978-1-63152-596-4
Mag Dimond, an unloved girl from San Francisco, becomes a travel
junkie to avoid the fate of her narcissistic, alcoholic mother—but everywhere she goes, she's haunted by memories of her mother's neglect, and
by a hunger to find out who she is, until she finds peace and her authen-
tic self in the refuge of Buddhist practice.